MW01196227

THE CHINATOWN WAR

Also by Scott Zesch

Alamo Heights
*The Captured: A True Story of Abduction by Indians
on the Texas Frontier*

The Chinatown War

———◆◆◆———

Chinese Los Angeles and
the Massacre of 1871

Scott Zesch

OXFORD
UNIVERSITY PRESS

OXFORD
UNIVERSITY PRESS

Oxford University Press, Inc., publishes works that further
Oxford University's objective of excellence
in research, scholarship, and education.

Oxford   New York
Auckland   Cape Town   Dar es Salaam   Hong Kong   Karachi
Kuala Lumpur   Madrid   Melbourne   Mexico City   Nairobi
New Delhi   Shanghai   Taipei   Toronto

With offices in
Argentina   Austria   Brazil   Chile   Czech Republic   France   Greece
Guatemala   Hungary   Italy   Japan   Poland   Portugal   Singapore
South Korea   Switzerland   Thailand   Turkey   Ukraine   Vietnam

Copyright © 2012 by Scott Zesch

Published by Oxford University Press, Inc.
198 Madison Avenue, New York, New York 10016

www.oup.com

Oxford is a registered trademark of Oxford University Press

Library of Congress Cataloging-in-Publication Data
Zesch, Scott.
The Chinatown war : Chinese Los Angeles and the massacre of 1871 / Scott Zesch.
p.   cm.
Includes bibliographical references and index.
ISBN 978-0-19-975876-0
1. Chinese Americans—California—Los Angeles—History—19th century. 2. Chinese Americans—Crimes
against—California—Los Angeles—History—19th century. 3. Race riots—California—Los Angeles—History—
19th century. 4. Lynching—California—Los Angeles—History—19th century. 5. Los Angeles (Calif.)—Ethnic
relations—History—19th century. 6. Los Angeles (Calif.)—History—19th century. I. Title.
F869.L86C459   2012
305.895′107949409034—dc23   2011039722

Sources for the maps on pages ix and x:

DOWNTOWN LOS ANGELES 1870
Sources: Map of the reservoir lands, 1870, Seaver Center for Western History
Research, GC 1310, 3-3-6; grading map, 1870, Seaver Center for Western History
Research, GC 1310, 3-3-6 (also GPF 4894); Ruth Saunders map, frontispiece,
The Historical Society of Southern California Quarterly 26 (June–September 1944).

CHINATOWN AND PLAZA 1870
Sources: Antonio Coronel's plan for adobe house, ca. 1840, Seaver Center for
Western History Research, No. 550; uncredited map in case file, Wing Chung Co.
v. Los Angeles City, Case No. 1941, June 22, 1872, 17th Judicial District Court,
Civil Cases, Los Angeles Area Court Records, Huntington Library; A. J. Stahlberg
map, 1876, Seaver Center for Western History Research, GPF 8119; Ruth Saunders
map, frontispiece, *The Historical Society of Southern California Quarterly*
26 (June– September 1944).

1   3   5   7   9   8   6   4   2

Printed in the United States of America
on acid-free paper

For the eighteen

CONTENTS

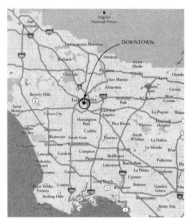

LOS ANGELES AND ENVIRONS TODAY

1. RAILROAD DEPOT
2. PICO HOUSE
3. CORONEL ADOBE
4. GOLLER'S WAGON SHOP
5. BELLA UNION HOTEL
6. TEMPLE BLOCK
7. COURT HOUSE
8. JAIL
9. TOMLINSON'S LUMBER YARD

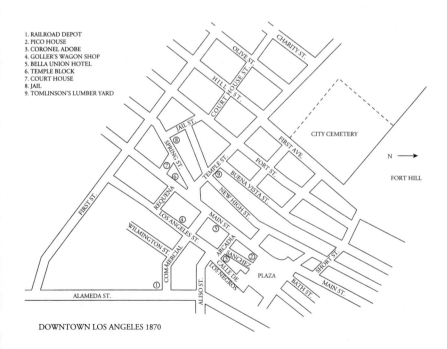

DOWNTOWN LOS ANGELES 1870

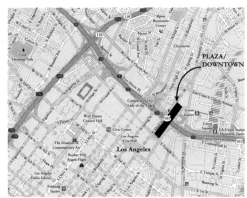

LOS ANGELES TODAY

1. BEAUDRY BUILDING
2. SAM YUEN'S HOUSE
3. GENE TONG'S OFFICE
4. WING CHUNG STORE
5. CORRAL
*6. MASONIC HALL
*7. MERCED THEATRE
*8. PICO HOUSE
*9. CHURCH OF THE ANGELS

*STILL STANDING

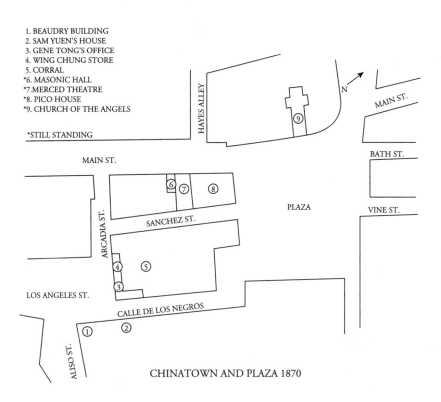

CHINATOWN AND PLAZA 1870

PROLOGUE

———❦———

ACCORDING TO CHINESE TRADITION, THE gates of the next world are thrown open every August, and the spirits of the dead are set free to visit their former haunts on earth. But, should that happen today, how could those immigrants who died in Los Angeles in 1871 locate the places they knew? The streets they walked—Aliso, Arcadia, Commercial—were rerouted long ago to make room for the Hollywood Freeway. The ghosts of these Chinese would need some time to get their bearings.

They might feel at home in their old neighborhood near the plaza. Our Lady Queen of Angels Church is still there, not so different from the way it looked on the evening of the massacre, October 24, 1871. To the south of the church stands the Pico House Hotel, now an exhibition space, where one ill-fated Chinese worker was catering to the needs of Los Angeles's affluent visitors just a few hours before his death. But what of their apartments, those cramped, threadbare adobe rooms where they joked and quarreled and told stories by the light of oil lamps? Those are all gone, not surprisingly in a city that is constantly tearing down and starting over. Even most of the ground on which the Chinese quarters once stood is missing, excavated for the freeway in the late 1940s. The returning spirits would be left hovering in exhaust fumes above the heavy traffic near the Los Angeles Street overpass.

To the south of the freeway, nothing would look familiar to them. Perhaps that is just as well. The section of Commercial Street where a parked wagon was used for grim purposes has disappeared entirely, covered in the early 1970s by the Los Angeles Mall. A blood-red pedestrian walkway in the middle of North Los Angeles Street's 300 block marks the area where it once ran. A little farther south, there is no trace of John Goller's wagon shop, another scene of the tragedy. In its place is the entrance to the mall's parking garage across from the Federal Building. Drifting northwest, some of the visiting souls might be gratified—or horrified—to discover that the site of Tomlinson's corral, where mob law governed that night, is now overshadowed by the United States Court House and the Hall of Justice.

The spirits, according to ancient beliefs, are at liberty to wander for a month. There would be no reason for them to linger that long in Los Angeles, as it would seem foreign to them now. Some Chinese ghosts are said to torment the living who have neglected their duty to remember and honor the departed, but who among today's four million residents would they begin to hold accountable for forgetting them? Most Angelenos do not even know what happened that night, for the city's fathers decided to put the incident behind them shortly after it occurred, and the victims were not people of consequence. They were ordinary immigrants whose American dream ended in a nightmare.

THE CHINATOWN WAR

PART I

GUM SAAN

I

Let Them Come and Settle with Us

ON A RAIN-SOAKED DAY late in the spring of 1861, while the people east of the Mississippi were still reeling from news of the bombardment of Fort Sumter, one of the newer residents of the West Coast—a world away—sat down with a correspondent from the *Portland Oregonian* and offered his impressions of America. The foreigner, who introduced himself as Ah Ning, had just written a letter to a friend back home. When the newspaperman asked for a translation, he patiently and candidly obliged.

"When left China land, said write you what should see." Though literate in Chinese characters, Ah Ning possessed only a halting command of spoken English, so he rendered his subtle observations in terse, simplified phrases: "Country here new found—wild—most trees. Portland on river—much wild—people just come—streets wide, bad, stumps, holes." Ah Ning had ventured to Oregon from San Francisco because he thought there were already too many Chinese looking for jobs there. "Ah" was not part of his proper name. It was a common endearment, sort of like referring to someone named Joe as "Old Joe."

Ah Ning reported that the Chinese newcomers minded their own business and lived peacefully. "No taxes," he continued. "No trouble [over] our religion. Chinaman worship [as] he please."

Most importantly, work was plentiful. The Chinese washed clothes for a "good price," he continued, "more than [in] China." Still, Ah Ning had doubts about how long the prosperity would last. He advised his friend not to come to the West Coast, which he believed was already overpopulated with Chinese hopefuls.

Of course, it was hard to dissuade ambitious young men in China from seeking their fortunes in America, where wages were much higher and good luck reportedly abounded. So Ah Ning offered his friend, Chin Hong, some alternative advice. If he did decide to make the long voyage from Hong Kong to San Francisco, he should "dig gold" in the mountains; the "print papers" said much could still be found. "Suppose he know more [than] I do," Ah Ning quipped to the newspaperman. He had learned from experience that the laundry business, though steady, was a slow, tedious way to accumulate wealth.

Portland seemed uncivilized by Ah Ning's standards, although it did provide his countrymen with a few of the comforts of home. Its sole "China shop" offered "good teas." But the adjustment to the New World was hard. He complained that he could not find enough of "what Chinaman loves [to] eat." Nor could he expect to marry and start a family during his stay there. Portland had only "two, three, four China women." To make his prospects bleaker, "One Chinaman [had] two."

He wasn't much interested in American ladies, although he did find them curiously amusing: "Dress spread out—much like balloon. Can't go [through] the door, crowd both sides. Dress cover all down feet. Can't see. Suppose feet very great," he joked. It was impossible for the homesick Ah Ning not to draw unfavorable comparisons. "No good like China woman," he tried to explain to the reporter from the *Oregonian*. "China woman smile good—show ankles—shoes turn up." No doubt he was frustrated by his inability to express his thoughts more articulately.

As for his dealings with the local merchants, Ah Ning found that the "barbarian shops" "trade well—beat Chinaman." He observed with disdain that American men "won't work—know not how." That was not all: "Some men very bad. Call Chinamen moon eyes—worse name."

The severe persecution of the Chinese in the United States was still several years away. Ah Ning and his countrymen were not easily intimidated, anyway. "Chinaman don't care. Get money. Live not much cost—go home [to] China [with] much money."

That was enough information for one letter—or at least enough to disclose to a persistent American journalist in a tongue that so poorly conveyed what Ah Ning was feeling. "No more," he concluded. He instructed his friend back home, "You write."[1]

Eight hundred miles down the coast from Portland, in a hinterland farming town too small to have a daily newspaper, the editor of the Los Angeles *Semi-Weekly Southern News* reprinted Ah Ning's letter. For a decade, his readers had spotted a handful of these foreigners from the Far East hurrying down the dirt streets, with their long pigtails and their incomprehensible language, their heavy bundles swinging from poles balanced across their shoulders. The town's Anglos, Latinos, Blacks, and Indians were not sure what to make of these newcomers. Fewer than thirty lived in the vicinity of Los Angeles, but their numbers were steadily increasing. And it looked as though they intended to stay.

Arrival

They left their villages before sun-up, under cover of darkness, so they would not encounter anyone who might speak inauspicious words that would spoil their journey. Each young man carried a bedroll and a bamboo basket filled with his most valuable belongings—a pair of shoes, a hat, a quilted jacket, perhaps some food. They were farmers and laborers of modest means who dreamed of the day they would return to the village, flaunting their newfound wealth. Most were only in their late teens or early twenties. In junks and sampans, they made their way over the waterways that led to Hong Kong, where the ship was waiting.

Those who could not afford the fifty-dollar fare borrowed their passage money. The luckier ones had brothers or cousins waiting to welcome them on the other side. The rest hoped to meet up with people from their home area who could help them navigate the complexities of living in the new land. After a voyage of two months, most of which was spent in cramped, fetid quarters below deck, they got their first glimpse of the rocky shoreline of northern California through a veil of gray fog. They anxiously inhaled the raw, damp air as they disembarked in San Francisco and braced themselves to meet the tall, fierce, hairy-faced barbarians who inhabited *Gum Saan* (Gold Mountain).

Contrary to popular belief, the earliest Chinese immigrants to America did not come to build the transcontinental railroad in the 1860s. Instead, it was the California Gold Rush of 1849 that brought the first large wave of Chinese to the West Coast. Most of them came from the villages of the Pearl River Delta, south and west of Canton (Guang-zhou). Like other foreigners, they migrated to California hoping to get rich quickly in *Gum Saan*. Many prospected for gold on their own; others went to work for mining companies. Those who had no luck in the gold fields found other jobs. The most entrepreneurial of them made a good living by catering to the miners, opening laundries in the remote mountain camps.

San Francisco became their home in America. As more Chinese arrived, however, they began to look for work elsewhere. In pairs or little groups, they traversed the continent in search of better opportu-nities. Some started their own businesses, washing clothes or peddling vegetables or fish. Those with no capital took positions as housekeepers, cooks, waiters, and farmhands. If they saved enough money and decided not to return to China right away, they might set up shop. Merchants, though inferior in status to the scholar-gentry class back home, were the elite among the Chinese in America, enjoying a level of respect and envy they could never attain in China.

A few Chinese wayfarers soon began trickling into the sunny, luxu-riant land of orchards, vineyards, and cattle ranches that surrounded the southern agricultural outpost known as Los Angeles, which settlers from Mexico had founded in 1781. The town's permanent Asian presence appears to date from 1850, when two Chinese house servants, Ah Fou and Ah Luce, showed up in the federal census.[2] Both managed to attract attention in a village of only 1,610 people, with their peculiar baggy trousers and bamboo basket hats and the long queues hanging from their shaved heads. No other Chinese were known to have arrived until 1854, when merchant Joseph Newmark brought his cook to Los Angeles.[3]

During the 1850s, the town's Chinese population increased very slowly; as handfuls of new migrant workers arrived, others departed. In 1857, the entire Chinese community consisted of three men, all of whom worked in the Los Angeles Laundry. That January, they held the town's inaugural Chinese New Year celebration. Though their festivities "were not of the most extensive character," according to a news report, the three representatives of China were not shy about taking to the streets in high spirits "to mark their respect for the great national holiday."[4]

The 1860 census of the town of Los Angeles listed fourteen Chinese men and two women out of a total population that had increased to 4,385. Their fledgling community saw its first real growth during the decade ahead. Twenty-one Chinese men were living in the vicinity of Los Angeles by the spring of 1861, and the number of women had increased to eight. Five Chinese laundries operated in Los Angeles at the time. In June of that year, another wave of Chinese immigrants arrived. By then, they worked not only as house servants and launderers but also as commercial fishermen. The Chinese population would reach 179 by the time of the 1870 census, comprising about 3 percent of the town's 5,728 residents.[5]

In Los Angeles, most Chinese worked in occupations that required them to interact with Americans on a regular basis, so they necessarily learned some spoken English and, to a lesser extent, Spanish. (Throughout this book, "American" refers to people who were US citizens, either by birth or naturalization—which excludes practically all Chinese immigrants, as they were denied citizenship.) Usually, the Chinese communicated with their non-Asian employers and customers via pidgin English, dispensing with the language's fussy articles and confusing its slippery consonants. The local press delighted in mocking and exaggerating the idiosyncrasies of their speech: "Melican malliage" (American marriage), "muchee talkee," "me no likee," "heap catchee China looman," and so forth. The immigrants aspired to do better, however. When a Los Angeles church offered classes in spoken and written English for Chinese newcomers in 1871, it drew ten eager men who studied hard and became fairly proficient with the alphabet. A Chinese cook who wrote a letter in English to his former employers proudly told them that he was "studying spell book most every day" and that he read the English-language newspapers. A few early Chinese, such as Los Angeles physician Chee Long "Gene" Tong, became fully fluent.[6]

The vast majority of Chinese who arrived in California during the 1850s and 1860s did not intend to settle there permanently. They planned to work for a few years, save at least several hundred dollars, and then return home to live with their families in relative luxury. Ah Ning, the Portland laundryman, admitted as much in his published letter of 1861: "Chinaman keep money for China land. . . . Go home China much money." In another letter, a man named Wo Kee warmly greeted a fellow Chinese immigrant with the salutation, "I trust that you . . . may early be able to return home to China." One laborer told a journalist, "Here I am a nobody, but in China, with three hundred dollars I am a big, very big gentleman." Ng Poon Chew, a Presbyterian minister in Los Angeles, also confirmed that a large proportion of his countrymen returned to China after accumulating about $1,000.[7] Few Chinese purchased property in the United States, and many relocated often, taking advantage of seasonal employment and localized economic booms.

Unlike those immigrants from Europe who pulled up stakes and essentially cut their ties with their pasts, the first Chinese who came to America remained closely connected with their kin back home. In the rural world of the Pearl River Delta, family was everything. A family's patriarch controlled its communal property, monitored its social behavior, and guarded its reputation. The next level of kinship was a person's clan or extended family, which consisted of distant relatives who shared a common paternal ancestor and surname. Sometimes entire villages were populated by members of no more than two or three lineages. The clans maintained the ancestral graves and temples and sponsored schools for their young.

In China, a man who spent most of his life working in a city always thought of his natal village as his real home and his faraway kinsmen as his most valued and reliable friends. He expected to spend his final, tranquil years among his family and old companions in the village. Chinese immigrants transported these attitudes to America, seeking out any distant relatives wherever they settled. If there were none, they associated with people from their home districts. Some made return visits to China whenever they were able. Those unfortunate souls who died while working in the United States were interred in foreign soil only temporarily. After their bodies had decayed, their bones were exhumed and shipped back to China for a proper burial, so that their relatives could tend to the needs of the spirits.[8]

Familial loyalty was not the only reason many Chinese left the United States after saving enough money. In nineteenth-century America, they met with strong resistance when they sought US citizenship. The Burlingame Treaty of 1868, while extending some legal protection to Chinese nationals residing in the United States, did not provide them with a path to naturalization. Ng Poon Chew suggested that many of his countrymen returned to China because they had no real home in America. Similarly, shopkeeper Lee Chew, having wearied of anti-Chinese prejudice, concluded, "[H]ow can I call this my home, and how can any one blame me if I take my money and go back to my village in China?" An Austrian archduke who visited Los Angeles in the 1870s also observed that it was "not surprising that people who are denied citizenship and equality before the law should return home."[9]

Nonetheless, some stayed longer than expected. By 1870, 44 percent of Los Angeles's Chinese males were age thirty or older. The town also had its first Chinese American, a three-year-old boy born in California and called Ah Tie. Many Chinese workers who extended their time abroad did so because they found that it took years rather than months to put aside a few hundred dollars—or they concluded that the few hundred dollars they had saved was not enough after all.

Changing attitudes also influenced their decisions. Otis Gibson, a Methodist missionary who worked among the Chinese immigrants, reported that some were becoming so attached to American ways that they were no longer content to live in China and wanted to settle permanently in the United States. He also thought their numbers were constantly increasing. Similarly, Los Angeles theater owner Jew Ah Mow said, "People come here and become accustomed to the ways of the country, and they like to remain here." Wong Ark, who operated a pawn shop in Los Angeles, announced, "I came here 17 years ago, and have never been back to China. I want to be a citizen here."[10] The efforts of numerous Chinese residents to improve their English also indicated that they were investing more than temporary labor in Los Angeles. Whether they felt welcome or not, some of them were starting to realize that this godless, isolated, unruly town was likely to remain their home.

A Town in Transition

Los Angeles looked better from a distance. As Chinese immigrants of the 1860s approached the town from the southern port at San Pedro, crossing the grassy cattle range where the Harbor (110) Freeway now runs, the first thing they would have seen was the lush, deep-green orchards of orange trees, whose hue became more golden as they got near enough to make out the abundant fruit among the glossy leaves. On the outskirts of town, the redwood houses were ornamented with ivy and vines. A profusion of jasmine, roses, and gillyflowers blossomed inside the fenced yards. Visitors to Los Angeles at the time described a series of gardens where "the perfume of myriads of plants and flowers diffuses itself through the air."[11]

As the immigrants made their way downtown, however, the air would have become less rarefied. People dumped their refuse anyplace convenient. Mongrel dogs roamed the streets. The open ditches that watered the town also served as laundry stations, hog wallows, and even latrines. Main and Spring Streets, which bordered the courthouse, reeked from the "green slimy ooze" that flowed down their gutters. One local newspaper complained, "Dead dogs and cats, with rotten fruit, slops and decaying vegetables, lie promiscuously about, and pass undisturbed through the successive stages of decomposition, making a picture of supreme nastiness."[12]

The small town of Los Angeles was suffering from growing pains. Its plaza, originally the town's central square and today a charming gathering spot across from Union Station, was described at that time as "an unsightly affair to everybody." In 1869, the city planted trees in the middle of it "to hide the ugliness of the old water tank." Much of the town's recent construction looked flimsy, scruffy, and utilitarian, and many of the newer houses remained unfinished. One writer described Los Angeles as "woefully bare of prettiness and even of neatness." Another traveler found its people "slovenly, lazy, and profane." Contrasting the town's slipshod appearance with its bountiful vegetation and temperate climate, he concluded, "Nature has done everything for it, and man very little."[13]

City services and amenities were at best primitive. On hot days, little shade could be found along the downtown streets. The unpaved roads, parched and dusty throughout the summer, suddenly turned into mud troughs when the rains came. Pedestrians who were not careful would sink into sticky muck as deep as two feet. Sometimes horses and carriages were forced to travel along the sidewalks, spattering passersby with filth. At the town's best hotel, the Bella Union, the leaky roof caused guests to slip on the dirt floors of their rooms. Privileged visitors were allowed to sleep on the billiard table. If they braved a meal at John La Rue's restaurant, the begrimed proprietor might pluck struggling flies from their soup using his coffee-colored fingers.[14]

The town's Chinese residents found themselves in the midst of a rapidly changing society. It is difficult to imagine how small Los Angeles was in the mid-nineteenth century. When house servants Ah Fou and Ah Luce arrived around 1850, the compact pueblo of 1,610 residents, which served primarily as a commercial and social center for the out-lying ranches, was still Mexican in character, similar in appearance to Santa Fe or Tucson. Most of the buildings were single-storied, white-washed adobes with flat roofs of gray asphalt. The writer and adventurer Horace Bell recalled that Los Angeles was "a nice looking place" when he arrived in 1852, with houses that "generally looked neat and clean."[15]

Within a few years, however, some of the Californios (the Spanish-speaking families of California prior to statehood) fell on hard times and lost their ranches through a devastating combination of floods, droughts, mortgage foreclosures, new taxes, and legal battles over land titles. Fruit production overtook cattle ranching as the most important agricultural enterprise. The population of Los Angeles grew nearly threefold during the 1850s, and Californios became a minority for the first time. In the 1860s, Los Angeles's Latino population declined from 47 to 38 percent of the town's total. By 1880, people with Spanish surnames would represent only 19 percent of Angelenos.[16] As the town became increasingly Anglo, the skyline also changed: the low, rambling adobes were outnumbered by two-storied brick buildings and frame houses.

The transition from Mexican to American Los Angeles was painful and contentious. From the time Anglos first took military control of the pueblo in 1846, Latinos, whose families had been living there for over three generations, resented being treated as conquered people and chafed at the injustices and inequalities they encountered. One prominent Californio remarked sadly, "If I were a younger man, I would take my boys and go to Mexico." Class divisions among the Latino population also became more pronounced after California was admitted as a state in 1850. Those Californios who had managed to hold on to their ranches and maintained close ties with the town's

Anglo elite did not want to risk trying to overthrow the new American power structure. In contrast, some of the recent, poorer immigrants from the Mexican state of Sonora, as well as the sons of those Californios who had lost everything, were more rebellious and even turned to banditry. Meanwhile, many Anglo newcomers distrusted practically all Latinos, fearing that they would stage a revolt and attempt to reunite the region with Mexico. Moreover, the Anglos who flocked to Los Angeles in the 1860s, unlike earlier arrivals such as Horace Bell, had no history of warm relations or intermarriage with the wealthy, genteel Californio families and regarded all Latinos with disdain.[17]

While the changes in the town's demographics caused friction between Anglos and Latinos, they worked in the Chinese immigrants' favor. More jobs became available, and the market for their services expanded. By the close of the 1860s, Los Angeles, previously unknown beyond California, was starting to flourish, even though it still had fewer than six thousand people. As outsiders became aware of the area's potential for cultivation and its suitability as a health resort, it enjoyed its first major real-estate boom. The old Mexican ranches were subdivided into high-yield farms that required lots of hands. New buildings were constantly under construction, and manual laborers were in demand. A local newspaper broadly welcomed immigrants in 1869, proclaiming: "Let them come and settle with us; there is room for them and many more."[18] Los Angeles's prosperity during the latter 1860s, at a time when northern California as well as much of the nation was suffering from an economic downturn and post–Civil War upheavals, no doubt contributed to the increase in the Chinese population—from about 30 in 1861 to 179 in 1870.

The abundance of decent-paying jobs in Los Angeles meant that many Chinese men who had not literally struck gold in America could nonetheless build up enough savings to avoid returning home in shame. Still, for some, the dream of succeeding in *Gum Saan* remained dismayingly out of reach. In the summer of 1870, Ah Gut, a thirty-three-year-old laundryman in Los Angeles, poisoned himself with strychnine. Along the route of his funeral procession to the City Cemetery, his friends scattered minute bits of paper, each of which represented some good deed that Ah Gut had done.[19]

The First Chinatown

The immigrants' determination to put aside a large portion of their earnings during their stay in America prompted them to seek the cheapest accommodations they could find. During the 1860s, Los Angeles's first Chinatown developed in a low-rent neighborhood immediately northeast of the principal business district, which was then centered at the three-way intersection of Main, Spring, and Temple Streets (approximately the junction of Main and Temple Streets today). Chinatown's focal point was Calle de los Negros, more commonly known among Angelenos by its English approximation, Negro Alley.[20] This unpaved lane, only about thirteen paces wide, ran five hundred feet from the intersection of Arcadia and Los Angeles Streets to the plaza. (The area now comprises the southeastern corner of El Pueblo de Los Angeles Historical Monument.) It was lined on both sides with single-storied adobes fronted by narrow, colonnaded verandas. By 1870, sixty-six Chinese had settled in Chinatown, while forty-six stayed with their Anglo or Latino employers. The remaining sixty-seven lived in scattered houses that they shared with their countrymen.

The Chinese of Los Angeles made their home in an old Mexican neighborhood. Calle de los Negros took its name from some dark-complexioned Californios who had once resided there. José Antonio Carrillo, a former Mexican congressman whom Horace Bell described as "full of humor and boiling over with sarcasm," reportedly gave the alley its name, which the original inhabitants thought was insulting. In its better days, the neighborhood had been home to some of Los Angeles's most substantial Californio families. In fact, Antonio F. Coronel, the California state treasurer and former Los Angeles mayor, owned the main block of adobe stores and apartments that the Chinese leased. Horace Bell recalled that the homes of the Californios were comfortable and well furnished, and that "a good deal of elegance, refinement and culture" had once existed in that part of Los Angeles.[21] Years before the Chinese settled there, however, the short block had deteriorated into a slum, a far cry from the bucolic world of orange, walnut, and olive groves and flowering gardens on the residential outskirts of town.

The Chinese laborers did not seem to care much, for they found that they could save a great deal on rent by cramming together in the worst part of town. Fifteen men sometimes shared a single room; seven Chinese occupied a seven-by-nine-foot cabin on Grasshopper (present-day Figueroa) Street. A Los Angeles policeman described the claustrophobic Chinese sleeping quarters as "shaped more like bunks on a steamer than anything else." Above the narrow beds, which were stacked three or four high, a set of steps led to another sleeping platform only two or three feet below the ceiling. The crowded conditions prompted a local health officer to denounce Chinatown as "the crying sanitary evil of Los Angeles."[22] Non-Asians were surprised to find that the Chinese people always appeared neat and clean despite the poor sanitation and overcrowding in their neighborhood.

The Chinese tenants of Calle de los Negros did their best to make the alley feel like home. They adorned the shabby, mud-walled houses with bright red posters and strung banners and lanterns from the sagging galleries. On the doorposts, small signs of red paper announced the names of the occupants, and shopkeepers placed large, blue signboards inscribed with gold Chinese characters above the lintels. The immigrants learned not to invest too much money in improving their rented premises, however. In the decades to come, the City of Los Angeles would repeatedly uproot their community in the name of civic progress.

Chinatown's Early Ambassadors

Although merchants eventually came to dominate Los Angeles's Chinatown, its earliest leader was an ambitious laundryman who used the English name John Tambolin. Described in the local press as a "man of parts," he arrived in town around 1856 at age thirty-six to operate a washhouse along with two younger men, Ah Chow and Ah Sook. A promoter of both his native culture and his people in America, Tambolin was the first Chinese known to have made overtures toward the larger population of Los Angeles. When he took a bride, Ah Qu, in 1862, they became the town's first Chinese couple to be married by an American justice of the peace.[23] Tambolin's efforts on behalf of his compatriots were likely responsible for the modest but noticeable increase in Los Angeles's Chinese population that occurred around 1861.

In 1866, hoping to win favorable publicity for his countrymen, John Tambolin invited a local journalist to participate in the Chinese New

Year festivities. He gave the newspaperman a personal tour of the Chinese quarters along Calle de los Negros, pointing out tables covered with cakes, fruits, and other delicacies. The reporter watched the Chinese men, with their long queues combed and braided and decorated with silk tassels, offering New Year's wishes to the friends they passed on the street. His host politely encouraged him to sample a cup of special liquor that had been procured at the exorbitant cost of fifteen dollars per pound. Tambolin proved to be an effective ambassador, for the journalist wrote that he was "agreeably surprised to find things so neatly arranged."[24] Afterward, however, the Los Angeles press resumed its usual practice of largely ignoring the Chinese. Readers of the English-language newspapers only seemed interested in those peculiarities of Chinese culture that could give them a few laughs.

For all the "kind attention" he showed the reporter, Tambolin could be hot tempered and tyrannical among his own people when his authority was challenged. A newspaper article noted that "all our Chinamen acknowledged John as chief mandarin, from whose decisions there was no appeal." In June 1861, the steamer that arrived at San Pedro harbor from San Francisco brought several more Chinese to Los Angeles, including one individual whom Tambolin feared might rival his power in Chinatown. He went before a magistrate and swore, apparently falsely, that this man had threatened his life. Although the interloper was arrested, he was released shortly afterward.

Tambolin, infuriated that his heavy-handed stratagem had failed, offered a police officer five dollars to place his enemy in jail. The officer refused, so Tambolin took matters into his own hands. That evening, he went to the house where the visitor from San Francisco was staying, chased off its occupants, and smashed the furniture. At a hearing the next day, he failed to prove his accusations against his opponent. Instead, the justice of the peace fined him for his churlish behavior the night before. Tambolin sprang up in the courtroom and shouted in broken English that he did not like the outcome one bit: "Why me pay, eh?" The justice answered that he was making him "pay for jealousy, John. That's all."[25]

Tambolin's last recorded appearance in Los Angeles occurred in 1868, when he was arrested for "threatening to do great bodily injury" to a fellow Chinese named Dung Loy. His stature among the non-Asian population had declined by then, for the press referred to him only as "a Chinaman," not by his name. According to news reports, the Chinese testimony at his arraignment "was of an extremely mixed and varied character, which speedily got the case into such a muddle as to place its merits beyond the comprehension of either the court or bar." Tambolin had no trouble coming up with his one hundred dollar bail, and the charge against him was dismissed.[26] But his influence in Chinatown was on the wane; he was no longer its "chief mandarin," as the newspapers had once called him. Other successful Chinese businessmen had established themselves in town. By the time of the 1870 census, he had disappeared.

One other Chinese trailblazer made a wholehearted effort during the early 1860s to reach out to the non-Asian population of Los Angeles. In the summer of 1861, a merchant named Chun Chick arrived from San Francisco and opened the first Chinese store in town. From the start, he attempted to lure non-Asian customers in addition to those from his own country. He located his firm not among the saloons and casinos of Calle de los Negros but in an adobe building on Spring Street opposite the courthouse. Chun Chick also took the unusual step of advertising in the English-language newspapers:

"A Chinese merchant!"

Then, even more breathlessly:

"To the public of Los Angeles!!!"

The shopkeeper invited Angelenos to come see his stock of tea, preserves, and other Chinese goods, "either to purchase or through curiosity." The local press did its best to help him gain a foothold, attesting that his store was well worth a visit and featured many unusual and useful things that could not be purchased elsewhere in town.[27] Having spent money on advertising and rented a building in a prime location, Chun Chick banked on the public at large developing a taste for Chinese delicacies.

Angelenos, however, were not interested in his wares. Indeed, across California, the early Chinese merchants found it hard to attract a non-Asian clientele and introduce Americans to the ways of the Far East. It was not for lack of trying. In Visalia, Chinese store owners gave the editor of the local newspaper a gift of tea, shell work, and white silk handkerchiefs to garner favorable attention in the press. But these efforts usually produced few results. Joseph Lamson, an artist who kept a diary while he was staying in California, recorded that the Chinese shops in Sacramento had "nothing that would attract the fancy of an American," finding "scarcely an article that would be worth sending home as an object of curiosity." Even in San Francisco's much larger Chinatown, the shops catered almost entirely to the Chinese during the 1860s. When some Chinese businessmen implored Governor John Bigler not to restrict immigration, they explained that a Chinese merchant's livelihood "chiefly depends upon Chinese consumption."[28]

In any case, the Chinese population of Los Angeles in 1861 was scarcely large enough to support a single store. Chun Chick found his name on the delinquent taxes list, and his establishment was soon gone.[29] Like John Tambolin, who had gone to great lengths to entertain a journalist during the New Year celebration, Chun Chick found that Angelenos were only marginally interested in learning how the Chinese among them lived.

Washing and Quarreling

Those Chinese who were looking to get ahead in Los Angeles had to find ways other than shopkeeping to attract non-Asian customers and tap into the town's booming economy. The laundry business gave them their first foothold. This American-born enterprise, entirely a product of happenstance and necessity, got its start in the mining camps. The Chinese who came to the West Coast during the Gold Rush discovered to their astonishment that their fellow miners were shipping their clothes all the way to the Sandwich Islands (Hawai'i) for washing and pressing, waiting several months for their return. Chinese men who had never worked in this occupation back home started operating hand laundries to provide faster service at a lower cost. The Chinese had no particular cultural affinity for the laundry trade; it was simply a ripe business opportunity that required little start-up capital. This experience would serve them well in the years to come, when Chinese were forced from other employment by discriminatory ordinances and hiring practices.[30]

Once they left the mining camps, these seasoned Chinese laundrymen set up their businesses all along the West Coast, reaching Los Angeles by the mid-1850s. In 1860, ten of the town's fourteen Chinese men worked in laundries. Eleven Chinese washhouses had opened in Los Angeles by the early 1870s, while only two non-Asian laundries competed with them. Although the employees of washhouses did not get wealthy, laundry jobs were relatively lucrative. A laborer who might have earned four dollars a month toiling in the tea and rice fields of China made fifteen to twenty dollars a month working in a Los Angeles laundry. Good ironers commanded even higher wages. Their method of sprinkling clothes was unique and efficient: the Chinese ironers would draw a large mouthful of water from a broad bowl and spray it evenly over a garment before pressing it.[31]

Although Angelenos came to depend on Chinese washmen, the laundry trade did not always foster good relations between the Asians and non-Asians of Los Angeles. Missing or damaged articles of clothing led to heated disputes, some of which ended up in court. In one case, Rosa Mariscal de Moreno charged Hop Chung with embezzling her underskirt, claiming that he tried to "feloniously convert the said petticoat to his own use." Although he denied ever receiving the garment, Hop Chung offered to pay $1.50 to settle the matter. His customer refused, saying the petticoat was a gift from her mother worth at least $12. Hop Chung's version of the events must have been more credible, for he was found not guilty of embezzlement. In another instance, Joseph Leventhal attempted to recover $2.50 for a missing shirt left with a Chinese laundryman. The justice of the peace, William H. Gray, caustically observed that "after much wrangling over one white shirt, the affair was finally settled by the Chinaman delivering said shirt."[32]

In another case, China Charley went to the home of Henry Brown to collect on a laundry bill of $1.75. Brown claimed he did not have the money on him at the moment. China Charley got mad and said he would not leave until he got it. Brown then "gently shoved him out of the house," according to those who witnessed the incident. The laundryman filed a criminal charge, accusing his customer of assault and battery. The prosecution was unsuccessful, as three witnesses testified that "no blows passed." Nonetheless, China Charley did get paid for the washing.[33] Like his colleagues in the laundry business, he was learning that American customers could be difficult.

The Scales of Justice

Popular culture has portrayed the early Chinese in the American West as docile, passive victims of bullies and unscrupulous bosses. However, the court records of Los Angeles County tell a strikingly different story. In addition to the laundry cases, the Chinese of Los Angeles went before local tribunals to settle a host of other complaints. More than any other immigrants to the region, they made efficient use of the local judiciary to redress the wrongs committed against them, despite the significant hurdles they faced in being allowed to testify. The legal documents also call into question another common assumption—that racial and ethnic minorities could not get a fair hearing in the courtrooms of the nineteenth-century American West. The surviving records, though too fragmentary to permit firm conclusions, reveal that the Chinese of Los Angeles won eleven of the thirteen civil suits they brought against non-Asians between 1869 and 1874. The persistency with which ordinary Chinese workers continued to file legal complaints over the years further suggests that they did not believe the scales of justice were weighted against them. In fact, the Chinese showed far greater confidence in the American legal system than in their own, for in China they had long associated the law with injustice.[34]

As early as 1864, Ah Tim sued Oliver Stearns, the water overseer and a member of an influential family, for "the unlawful violation of [his] personal liberty." In another case, Ah Wa was awarded one hundred dollars in 1869 on a bill of exchange against an American, Julius Chester. A man named Ah Mow recovered fifty dollars from John McDonald, who had knocked him down, kicked him, and threatened him with a knife. The sympathetic justice of the peace, the previously mentioned William H. Gray, thought that the days of work Ah Mow lost due to his injuries "would swell the amount considerably." In fact, Gray bemoaned his lack of authority to award a larger sum than Ah Mow had asked for in his complaint.[35]

As several cases indicate, Los Angeles judges could be surprisingly protective of Chinese newcomers who got cheated or injured by non-Asians. In that respect, Justice Gray, the town's lowliest jurist, was one of the unsung heroes of Los Angeles's judicial history. His court was restricted to hearing minor criminal cases and civil disputes involving less than $300—that is, the bulk of the Chinese controversies.[36] Horace Bell described him as "an able and an honest man," and the court records support that assessment. An older, partially disabled man of limited means, Gray needed to keep his elected office, because he was supporting a widowed daughter and her children.[37] Still, he did not hesitate to rule against some of the town's powerful people when aggrieved Chinese brought small claims against them.

In 1869, Wa Chung went to court to recover twenty dollars in rent money that he had overpaid to his landlord, Samuel Kearney. The landlord tried to get the case dismissed on the ground that Wa Chung, "being a Chinaman, was incompetent to swear to the complaint." Kearney's argument was bogus; although a blatantly discriminatory California statute prohibited Chinese witnesses from testifying against Anglos or Latinos of majority European ancestry,[38] it did not restrict their right to file lawsuits against whites if they could prove their cases using other evidence. Justice Gray was wise to any attempts to create distractions and skirt the merits of a case. In a pithy summary, he concluded that Kearney's only defense was "an ingenious resort to legal technicalities, behind which he seeks to screen himself from a just responsibility, and this court is urged to be a party thereto. Now, without arrogating to itself any profound knowledge of the law, the court is of the opinion that it was not created for any such purpose." Wa Chung recovered his money, and Kearney lost his appeal.[39]

After the passage of the federal Civil Rights Act of 1870, which provided that people of all races could give evidence, and the subsequent repeal of the California statute preventing Chinese witnesses from testifying against whites, several Chinese in Los Angeles successfully sued their American employers to get their unpaid wages as cooks, waiters, gardeners, and manual laborers. Of the seven surviving cases of this nature, the Chinese won five. In fact, some Chinese workers became quite belligerent when they felt their employers had treated them unfairly. In one instance, Sophia Goldstein refused to pay Lee Ock for his half-hour of work cleaning a chicken house, claiming he did not do a good job. The hired man became abusive and threatened her with a butcher knife, Mrs. Goldstein testified. She added, "I would have paid him had he not called me a son of a bitch." The county court fined Lee Ock twenty dollars for his aggressive behavior.[40]

Many non-Asians believed that the Chinese who lived among them resolved disputes between themselves under their own mysterious code, appealing to secret tribunals behind closed doors. Actually, the Chinese of Los Angeles were more apt to file civil suits and criminal charges against one another in American courts. Their claims ranged from theft to unpaid loans to attempted murder.

On one occasion, the truculent China Charley got crossways with Yo Hing, a railroad contractor and Chinatown kingpin of the 1870s who could usually be found at the center of any disturbances there. According to court testimony—one of the rare verbatim transcripts from the era that has survived in Los Angeles's judicial records—China Charley was smoking in Quan Ah How's opium hall when the two other patrons heard him fuming, "Yo Hing has turned my job off. I have to kill Yo Hing."

The three lethargic smokers were lying in narrow bunks, periodically lighting their pipes from lamps attached to the wall. One of them, Ah Fong, asked him, "Did the Chinese tell you or white people?"

China Charley growled, "I know myself. I am sure that Yo Hing turned my job off."

Late that night, Ah Fong went to Yo Hing's house and asked him, "What was the conversation between you and China Charley about?"

Yo Hing said, "I had no conversation with him at all. What is the matter?"

"He wants to kill you for turning his job off."

"I did not do such a thing," Yo Hing insisted.

Ah Fong warned, "I don't care whether you did or not. You'd better look out for your life and don't go on the street in the nighttime. China Charley is a very dangerous fellow."[41]

This matter made its way to county court. China Charley was tried for perjury after claiming under oath that he was absent from Los Angeles on the day he had supposedly made the threats. His accuser's story must have had some holes in it, for China Charley was acquitted.

In another squabble, Ah Quang confronted a laundryman, Chin Hing, at his washhouse and demanded that he repay a debt of $3.25. "I do not have the money but will pay you on next Saturday," Chin Hing told him. Ah Quang replied that he would not wait. He proceeded to help himself to two smoothing irons, two white shirts, and several bars of soap, then ran out of the room and up the street. The court fined him sixty dollars for taking the law into his own hands.[42]

Quarrels such as these would become increasingly common in the early 1870s, as regional differences and distrust that had divided people in the homeland started to splinter the local Chinese community. At this distance, given the meagerness of the surviving records, it is impossible to disentangle all the intricacies of the Chinese disputes of that era—or, in some instances, even to determine whether the testimony against accused malefactors was true or was just a means of trying to place an opponent behind bars. Whatever the case, the Chinese of Los Angeles were starting to show the town's other residents that they, like the Americans among whom they lived, were not afraid to stand up for themselves in court.

At the same time, the case of Ah Quang indicated that the Chinese were becoming more like their fellow Angelenos in another respect. Some of them were starting to settle their differences on the spot, using threats or actual violence rather than waiting for a tribunal to hear their grievances. That was bound to cause trouble. In a town rife with short-tempered, heavily-armed young men of all races, even trivial disagreements could result in bloodshed.

2

The Toughest Town of the Entire Nation

AS SEEN IN THE LAST chapter, the Chinese population of Los Angeles, though gradually on the rise, remained small throughout the 1850s and early 1860s. One reason was the abundance of jobs available to Chinese laborers in northern California, closer to their point of arrival and the heart of their society. The other was the town's reputation.

The original Chinese residents quickly found that they had chosen to try their luck in a notoriously violent environment. A temporary hangout for drifters, Los Angeles attracted aggressive young thugs who wandered into town from the mountains, mining camps, cattle-driving trails, and frontier forts. They did not plan to stay long, and they had neither relatives to shame nor good reputations to sully if they started a few fights while they were there. Fittingly, the first building erected with public funds in Los Angeles was the jail.[1]

One of the city's early historians, Charles Dwight Willard, characterized Los Angeles as "undoubtedly the toughest town of the entire nation" during the 1850s and 1860s. He claimed that it had a larger percentage of miscreants than any other American city and, for its size, also had the highest number of fights, murders, and robberies. Local merchant Harris Newmark confirmed that when he arrived in 1853, "Human life . . . was about the cheapest thing in Los Angeles, and killings were frequent." Many residents would not cross the plaza at night for fear of robbery. Former Los Angeles militiaman Horace Bell also recalled that during the 1850s, "there were more desperadoes in Los Angeles than in any place on the Pacific coast." The location suited them well, for if they needed to leave in a hurry, it was only a short ride to Mexico. According to Bell, "The slightest misunderstandings were settled on the spot with knife or bullet."[2]

These anecdotes may smack of hyperbole, but statistics bear them out. During 12 particularly lethal months in 1850–51, Los Angeles's per-capita homicide rate reached 12.4 per 1,000, the highest ever in American history. Between 1847 and 1870, the small town boasted an average annual murder rate of 1.58 per 1,000 or 13 killings each year—a much higher per-capita figure than New York, Chicago, or San Francisco. Historians of the city have put forth several plausible explanations for this carnage, reasons that were not in themselves unique to Los Angeles but nonetheless converged there in an explosive combination. Charles Dwight Willard contended that many of the "bad characters" who were driven out of San Francisco and the northern California mining camps during the Gold Rush drifted south to Los Angeles. Historian Robert W. Blew blamed the lack of police, effective courts, and a civic consciousness. Moreover, many newcomers were Southerners who thought any affront to their personal honor called for a duel. Leonard Pitt, a scholar of Mexican California, focused on the lingering wartime antagonism that placed Anglos and Latinos at odds with each other. UCLA professor Eric Monkkonen cited the problem of transiency in a "city of strangers," suggesting that the rapidly changing population prevented Angelenos from relying on any type of social commitment or responsibility.[3]

As Professor Monkkonen also observed, the sharp increase in murders during the 1850s coincided with the ready availability of Samuel Colt's new revolvers, especially the .31-caliber pocket pistol of 1849 and the popular Navy Model of 1851. With cylinders designed to hold five or six bullets, these handguns greatly increased their users' firepower and accuracy. Many Los Angeles residents, including the Chinese, habitually went around armed. One of them, Ah San, was fined in 1869 for carrying concealed weapons. The following year, a lone Chinese gunman went on a rampage along Calle de los Negros, brandishing his pistol and spewing profanities as his terrified neighbors disappeared through alleys and doorways. Indeed, Angelenos of all races and nationalities handled firearms recklessly. On one occasion around 1858, a white citizen named Gabe Allen was narrowly prevented from taking a random shot at an unsuspecting carpenter working on a roof just to test his marksmanship.[4]

The low-rent district where the Chinese had settled was not only shabby looking; it was also the deadliest section of Los Angeles. Harris Newmark recalled that by 1853, Calle de los Negros "was as tough a neighborhood . . . as could be found anywhere." The local press referred to it as the "Five Points" and "Barbary Coast" of Los Angeles—equating it with the roughest sections of two much larger cites, New York and San Francisco. Its adobes were home to saloons, casinos, and brothels that drew disorderly pleasure-seekers night and day—a diverse mix of Indians, Blacks, Latinos, and "the beetle-browed Caucasian, who, forgetting manhood, divides with his paramour the wages of her shame," in the purple prose of one reporter. Guitar music wafted through the open doors, regularly interrupted by noisy brawls and pistol shots. When Horace Bell arrived in 1852, he found that knifings and gunfights were commonplace, and the town's few law officers did not dare to attempt an arrest on Calle de los Negros. The infamous street was said to be the rendezvous of an unholy cadre of murderers, horse thieves, highwaymen, and burglars. A local newspaper maintained that "few decent men care to venture" there, even "when, in broad daylight, curiosity may lure them."[5] In order to survive, the Chinese who made Calle de los Negros their home quickly learned to be both tough and careful.

Bruisers of All Sorts

The perpetrators of violent crimes could not be linked to any particular place of upbringing or national origin. Rather, Los Angeles seemed to bring out the worst in everyone who came there. People of all races, both native born and foreign, took part in the scrapes that regularly resulted in bloodshed. Horace Bell recalled seeing "Americans, Spaniards, Indians and foreigners, rushing and crowding along from one gambling house to another" and getting into deadly confrontations along Calle de los Negros.[6]

Not all of Los Angeles's hotheads, bruisers, and killers were transient hooligans. Some of the town's most esteemed citizens set off violent confrontations on the slightest provocation. In fact, no one had a quicker temper than Horace Bell. An Indianan who had headed west during the Gold Rush, he blustered his way through a varied and controversial career as an army officer, volunteer militiaman, mercenary soldier, land speculator, lawyer, and writer. Tall, fearless, and highly opinionated, Bell cut a striking figure on the streets of Los Angeles, whether riding his black stallion or strolling with his cane, sporting a tight-fitting frock coat and a broad-brimmed black hat. For several years, he was the publisher of *The Porcupine*, which screenwriter Lanier Bartlett later described as a "prickly and dreaded little paper." Naturally, Bell made plenty of enemies in Los Angeles, one of whom charged that during his younger days he got drunk so often and "was such a perfect vagabond" that the local vigilance committee ran him out of town. His published memoirs, for all their exaggerations and inaccuracies, provide the most colorful glimpses into Los Angeles society during the 1850s and 1860s.[7]

Bell also had a reputation for ending arguments with brute force. He was charged with second-degree murder in 1867 after he struck the back of another man's head with his pistol, mortally wounding him. Bell used a horsewhip on his employee, Juan Trejo, in 1870; less than a month later, he lashed a neighbor whose mules had strayed onto his field. After the latter episode, Bell argued, preposterously, that he was essentially acting as a law officer and had the right to use force simply because he was taking the trespassing animals to the pound. Two years later, Bell struck another neighbor in the face with a willow switch when they got into a dispute over wandering hogs.[8]

Other prominent men of Los Angeles matched and sometimes surpassed Horace Bell in belligerence and vigilante inclinations. Councilman William Ferguson vigorously thrashed a druggist's clerk with a buggy whip in 1871 and was fined twenty-three dollars. Pharmacist Theodore Wollweber and grocer John Lazzarovich were both punished for assault and battery. J. J. Bell, a school teacher, accosted John Victoria at breakfast and threw him to the floor after overhearing that Victoria had called him a pimp and a swindler. Charles E. Beane, editor of the *Los Angeles News*, wounded John B. Wilson in a duel, which a competing newspaper described as a "foolish and very reprehensible affair." A spectacular shootout at the Bella Union Hotel in 1865 claimed the lives of

Robert Carlisle, owner of the huge Chino Ranch, and Frank King, brother of former California legislator Andrew J. King.[9]

The town's lawyers, judges, and peace officers could be even more recklessly violent and irresponsible. Attorney and former District Judge Robert M. Widney once drew a pistol on a courtroom witness whom he thought had insulted his honor. California's first attorney general, Edward J. C. Kewen, tried to shoot an opposing lawyer during a criminal trial in 1860, wounding a bystander and sending the jurors fleeing from the courtroom. A few years later, Kewen ambushed and shot an adversary on the streets of Los Angeles. A fatal confrontation occurred in 1869 between Charles Howard, the lawyer son of a congressman and judge, and Daniel Nichols, the son of a former Los Angeles mayor.[10] On several occasions, the town's lawmen injured or even killed each other in fits of rage.

The Chinese immigrants, taking their cue from the rough-hewn and quick-tempered people they met in Los Angeles, contributed their share of brawling. Henryk Sienkiewicz, the Polish journalist and author of *Quo Vadis?*, visited California in the 1870s and noted that the Chinese were usually "a peaceful and timid people, but amongst themselves they quarrel quite frequently and with equal frequency the quarrels end with a stabbing."[11] Los Angeles court records and news accounts indicate that Sienkiewicz's statement was only slightly exaggerated. Though the town's Chinese committed no murders prior to 1871, gunfights and knifings within their community often caused life-threatening injuries, and several Chinese men were accused of making threats to kill.

As early as March 1862, Tue Wy and Pui Wy were charged with assault when they fired their Colt six-shooters at a countryman, Ah Lom. Two other Chinese men got into a fistfight a month later. One of them, adopting the local method of settling disputes, drew his pistol and shot the other, badly wounding him in the neck. In a squabble that occurred in 1870, Ah Lim knifed Ah Choo, leaving a six-inch wound in his chest. When two Chinese men got into a loud argument one morning in 1871, the shorter fellow grabbed a bread knife and attacked the larger, who managed to fend off a blow aimed at the root of his queue but suffered a bad cut to his finger.[12]

A number of squalls erupted over gambling, a pastime far more popular than drinking among Chinese men. After working long hours in laundries, hotels, and fruit orchards, they congregated in bare adobe casinos where the air was thick with the blue smoke of opium and flavored tobacco. There they competed for each other's earnings in games of faro, fan-tan, and poker. Late one summer evening in 1871, a man named Ah Ching enjoyed a streak of luck in a gambling house on Calle de los Negros but found that his triumph was short lived. He had an outstanding bill to his physician, Ah Chuck, who vigorously tried to grab the money. A row broke out among the friends of each party, spilling into the street. Several of them drew pistols; the police appeared; Ah Ching was arrested. A month later, when an argument erupted between Ah Hog and Ah Yah over a poker game, they took up a stick and a lamp and went after each other. In August of the same year, another brouhaha over poker prompted Tin Chuen to attack Lay Yee with a hatchet.[13]

Gambling along Calle de los Negros not only provoked fights but also deteriorated a few laborers' work ethic, which most Chinese, as a matter of morality, would not tolerate. One spring afternoon in 1871, a crowd of Angelenos gathered in the street to watch a Chinese man attempt to uphold his family's honor by whipping his indolent nephew while two others held the boy down. When the man was arrested for assault and hauled before Mayor José Cristobal Aguilar, he explained in English that the "boy no work" because he "too much gamble." The mayor, unmoved, fined the uncle six dollars. His tirade against the evils of gambling had been wasted on the feckless spectators, who were seen "betting on the success or failure of the old man's little game."[14]

Not all of the brawls in Chinatown were confined to two or three people. Chinese from the same lineage, accustomed to defending their family's reputation back home, stood by one another and took up each other's feuds. Minor differences in language and customs were enough to divide the tiny Chinese community of Los Angeles into even tinier cliques, and these schisms made the clashes far-reaching. Shoving matches between individuals quickly escalated into free-for-alls as relatives and friends joined in the mayhem. A street row erupted among a group of Chinese in Calle de los Negros one summer evening in 1869 after "one took improper liberties in the house of another." In a fracas the following March, four Chinese men, one of whom was carrying a ten-inch knife, banded together to pummel one of their countrymen and rob him of five dollars. Late one night along Los Angeles Street, a fistfight broke out among several Chinese over some clothes that one of them had spoiled while working in a laundry. Merchant Quong Lee, perhaps in response to the unavoidable hazards of living in Chinatown, became the first Chinese in Los Angeles to apply for a life insurance policy in 1871.[15]

Whenever these scuffles occurred along Calle de los Negros, most Angelenos dismissed them as entertaining high jinks, and the press used them as fodder for cheap humor. Disputes that culminated in murder, on the other hand, periodically spurred the citizens of Los Angeles to take action. More often than not, that meant taking the law into their own hands.

Judge Lynch and "The Quibbles of Law"

In November 1870, after a year of deadly violence in which the Los Angeles legal system had produced more than a dozen murder indictments but no convictions, rumors circulated that a vigilance committee, consisting of over five hundred of the most influential citizens, was holding secret meetings in various parts of the county. A few weeks later, this group abandoned secrecy and placed a newspaper notice, advising the public that its members had agreed "under the high canopy of heaven, approved by our own consciences, approved by all good citizens, and above all by the laws of God and nature, to deal out justice impartially until the necessity no longer exists." This lofty rhetoric drew hoots from detractors. One letter writer wondered whether the proclamation was "most remarkable for impudence or ignorance." Another asked, "If an honest jury and learned judge mistake the law, is society any safer in the hands of an ignorant association of green grocers?"[16]

Los Angeles had a long tradition of mob "justice." Its citizens had organized California's earliest vigilance committee in 1836 to avenge a Latino man's murder at the hands of his wife and her lover. During the first two decades after California became a state in 1850, Angelenos witnessed nearly fifty lynchings of suspected criminals. One Yale-educated Los Angeles mayor, Stephen Clark Foster, had resigned his position to lead a mob that hanged a prisoner in 1855; eight years later, Angelenos had hanged an eighteen-year-old boy whose only known offense was stealing chickens. Although both Anglos and Latinos participated in these illegal executions, roughly three-quarters of the victims were Latinos, leading some historians to speculate that ethnicity and class were driving forces behind the vigilantes' killings.[17]

Popular opinion in southern California generally supported vigilantism, which was accepted as a disagreeable but necessary obligation of responsible citizens. Indeed, vigilance committees did not consist of revenge-crazed rabble but of successful tradesmen who believed that the legal system, through corruption or ineptness, had failed to bring order to the community in which they were investing their life's work. Their philosophy was simple: the rule of "the people" trumped the rule of law whenever the vigilantes agreed that quick, decisive action was necessary. They conducted their own popular tribunals, which mimicked the orderly ritual of a court trial, to determine a suspect's fate—usually hanging. The first Chinese immigrants to California, seeking to align themselves with respectable citizens, contributed to the funds of vigilance committees.[18]

For all their moral certitude, the vigilantes' assuredness vanished when they faced real challenges to their authority. While preparing to dispatch five prisoners in 1863, members of a Los Angeles lynch mob thought they heard federal soldiers approaching. They immediately scattered and ran off to hide.[19] At one point, the vigilance committee of 1870 determined that the Los Angeles criminal law firm of Kewen & Howard had been too successful in defending wrongdoers, and it voted to lynch the two attorneys. The following day, the committee's leader, an imposing French barber and former city councilman named Felix Signoret, encountered one of the firm's partners, James G. Howard, in the street. According to the memoir of local banker Jackson A. Graves, Howard said, "Signoret, I understand you are going to hang Kewen and Howard."

Shamefaced, the barber mumbled, "Yes, that was our intention last night."

"Come now, Signoret," Howard said. "We are old friends. Be generous. Let's compromise. Hang Kewen; he's the head of the firm."[20]

Only a month after the vigilance committee of 1870 was formed, Angelenos got their first chance in several years to find out whether the old vigilante mentality still prevailed in their evolving society, which by then had acquired many of the trappings of modern civilization. Around sundown on the evening of December 14, 1870, a giant of a man named Michel Lachenais rode his horse toward his farm south of town near the racetrack (present-day Exposition Park). Lachenais, who was about forty years old, had a reputation as a dangerous character, and people usually gave him the whole side of a street to himself. He had killed twice before but somehow had escaped punishment both times. For several months, he had carried on a dispute with his neighbor, an older man by the name of Jacob Bell, over the boundary line between their lands. That evening, he found Bell and his Mexican tenant plowing a field, preparing to plant barley. As soon as he arrived, he vented a tirade of abuse against his quiet and mild-mannered neighbor.

Finally, Lachenais rode off. But before he got very far, he wheeled his horse around and came back. He leveled his Colt six-shooter at the tenant, fired a warning shot, and told him, "Vamoose." The man hurried off. Glancing back in the twilight, the tenant saw Lachenais advance on his horse and start shooting rapidly at Bell. The older man returned two stray shots before he fell on his face. A few hours later, Deputy Sheriff Sam Bryant arrested Lachenais at a saloon on Commercial Street, still carrying the pistol that had recently discharged five shots.

Late that night, while a hard rain pounded the region, the vigilance committee convened to mull over the killing, which had greatly agitated the citizens of Los Angeles. Although Jacob Bell was not especially well known, his funeral the next afternoon drew an enormous crowd. The *Los Angeles News*, while decrying vigilantism, nonetheless railed against the legal system in general and local juries in particular for failing to punish accused murderers. It noted, "This state of affairs is interfering with the growth and progress of our city and county." Its competitor, the *Los Angeles Star*, also complained that "the quibbles of law could always defeat justice."

Three days after the murder, on the morning of December 17, about two hundred members of the vigilance committee, armed with shotguns, rifles, and pistols, assembled at Teutonia Hall on Los Angeles Street. They unanimously voted to hang Michel Lachenais. Around eleven o'clock, they divided into three companies and marched silently to the brick jail (southwest of the Spring Street entrance to present-day

City Hall). Jailor Frank Carpenter and Deputy Sheriff Henry C. Wiley stood guard on the street outside. Attorney George H. Smith and national guardsman John M. Baldwin, the only two citizens who volunteered to help the officers maintain law and order, kept watch inside the jail yard. The mob leaders approached Wiley, demanding the keys (which the jailor's wife had hidden).

The deputy tried to keep the vigilantes from entering, but they shoved him aside and poured into the jail yard. The heavy iron door of the jail was locked and barred in anticipation of the mob's arrival. The mob members used sledge hammers, pickaxes, crowbars, and even a huge beam to batter the door until the fastenings gave way. Then they rushed inside and up the narrow staircase. They found Lachenais in one of the cells. After breaking into it, they threw a rope around his neck and led him downstairs, manacled. As they stepped into the jail yard, the onlookers greeted the prisoner with triumphant yells, jeers, and epitaphs. Lachenais faced them stoically.

The mob marched him along Spring Street and then up Temple Street to the western gateway of Tomlinson's corral and lumber yard (approximately the junction of today's Spring and Temple Streets). They placed a dry-goods box under the transverse. The dense crowd of men, women, and children that had gathered there watched quietly from the tops of fences and housetops and the slopes of the nearby hills. According to some witnesses, Lachenais protested, "I am hung by a set of Jews and Germans, because I am a Frenchman." A Catholic priest administered last rites. By then it was a quarter to noon. The condemned man asked for a few minutes to make his will and provide for the education of his adopted child, but the vigilantes refused to give him any more time.

Resigned to his death, the prisoner stepped up onto the box. A mob member tied the rope to the overhead beam. Lachenais said in Spanish to those around him, "I am guiltless of murder. If I had not killed Mr. Bell, whom I liked and esteemed, he would have killed me. It was done in the excitement—"

Someone knocked the box out from under him. After he fell, not a muscle twitched. The vigilantes dispersed quietly, leaving the heavy, motionless body dangling from the beam. A large number of women continued to watch from the hillside, prompting the *Star* to object that they were gratifying "a morbid and depraved appetite for the horrible." An hour later, the dead man's friends cut him down.

The *Los Angeles News*, having mocked adherence to the "'quibbles and quiddits' of the law" only the day before, and having admonished its readers that the remedy "lies with the people," referred to the lynching of Lachenais as a "terrible tragedy," the hallmark of a "semi-civilized community."[21]

Partners in Crime

Whatever lessons the vigilantes hoped to instill by hanging Michel Lachenais were mostly lost on the reckless gunslingers of Los Angeles. Though tokens of civic improvement were increasingly visible around town—gaslights in 1867, piped water in 1868, a paid police force in 1869, and a three-storied, luxury hotel in 1870—fatal confrontations and disregard for human life persisted. What the men who dispatched Lachenais would have least expected, however, was that the first Angelenos to brandish firearms and draw blood after the lynching would be Chinese. Less than a week later, on December 22, 1870, a large group of excited Chinese men rallied at the corner of Main and Commercial Streets to try to prevent the arrest of one of their women. After chasing the carriage in which two law officers were riding with the woman, Chinese gunmen fired four wild shots into it, wounding a Chinese visitor from Santa Barbara.[22]

Though the early Chinese in America were often criticized for failing to assimilate, some Chinese adventurers had become readily enmeshed in one of the most notorious aspects of the town's culture, its pervasive violence and lawlessness. That was hardly surprising. The problems that afflicted Los Angeles as a whole—too many young, single men, too many gambling halls and pleasure palaces in close proximity, too many nefarious ways to earn a quick dollar—were even more prevalent in the male-dominated Chinese quarter.

As seen in the previous chapter, laundryman John Tambolin and merchant Chun Chick, the first two ambassadors of Chinatown in the early 1860s, had tried various respectable means of linking their countrymen with Los Angeles's non-Asian population. Angelenos had largely ignored their bridge-building efforts. Criminal activities, on the other hand, gave a few Chinese a more viable entrée into non-Asian society, as they formed lucrative alliances with disreputable Anglos and Latinos. The Los Angeles underworld was not demarcated by race or class but reached across all lines. In the casinos and whorehouses of Calle de los Negros, amid the illicit traffic in women and the scramble for contraband profits, the shadier portion of the town's racially and culturally diverse population found common ground and a reason to work together.

The people of Los Angeles may have taken little notice of John Tambolin and Chun Chick, but they paid a great deal of attention to those immigrants from the Far East who were engaged in high-profile criminal activities. When their escapades were reported in the press, Angelenos were left with the impression that the local Chinese community consisted of nothing but miscreants and racketeers. By the start of the 1870s, the men who made up the bulk of the town's Chinese population, those honest laborers who tidied the houses of the wealthy and cared for the vineyards and fruit orchards, found themselves reviled and harassed merely because they belonged to the same race as the outlaws who had fired into the law officers' carriage that winter night.

3

The Companies, the Tongs, and the Law

ON THE NIGHT OF MARCH 1, 1870, a seemingly senseless brawl took place in the heart of Los Angeles. A washman named Ah Wo went to the Bella Union Hotel on Main Street, only a block from Chinatown, to pick up some clothes from a customer. Along the way, some Chinese toughs jumped him and beat him up. A few hours later, after procuring a ten-inch knife and the help of three friends, the "pugnacious Chinaman," as one newspaper called him, took his revenge. To most Angelenos who read about it the next day, the "laundry affair" was just another street fight in a rough neighborhood.

Oddly, however, Ah Wo and his companions did not bother to track down the hooligans who had first pummeled him. Instead, they attacked an innocent passerby named Son Qua. They knocked him down, kicked him, and robbed him of five dollars in gold coin. When Ah Wo was arrested and brought before the justice of the peace, he readily admitted having assaulted a man who had done him no harm. Justice William H. Gray, who, as seen earlier, treated the Chinese fairly in his courtroom, asked him whether there was any reason why sentence should not be passed on him. The unrepentant Ah Wo had none, although he did offer an explanation for his misdirected vengeance. He said that he had sought satisfaction "by knocking down the first one of his countrymen whom he met that belonged to the same company with those who had whipped him."

The same *company*. When Ah Wo's story appeared in the papers, a new term entered the lexicon of Los Angeles journalists who wrote about Chinatown. Angelenos who read the news accounts critically became aware that some sort of dissension was brewing in the cramped Chinese quarters along Calle de los Negros, a deepening schism that was dividing this small community of immigrants. The *Los Angeles News* explained, "It seems that here, as elsewhere, the Chinamen recognize control by separate and rival 'companies,' having their headquarters at San Francisco."[1]

That term surfaced again during a legal tug-of-war the following month. A man named Ti Peo swore that Long Jim, a Chinese resident of Los Angeles, had murdered one of his countrymen in Tuolumne County, about three hundred miles to the north. Long Jim was arrested but quickly released, as it soon became obvious that Ti Peo's accusations of murder were bogus. A little investigating revealed that the trouble between him and Long Jim had something to do with the enigmatic Chinese associations known as "companies." The *News* explained that "open war" between two rival companies had been threatened as a result of this "bitter quarrel."[2]

Over the years, spats between individual Chinese laborers had often become collective, as immigrants from the same village or extended family came to one another's aid during a conflict. But these two news accounts in the early months of 1870 introduced the non-Asians of Los Angeles to a more formal line of demarcation running through the Chinese population, another type of division that would prevent the town's 179 Chinese residents from uniting as one people. The following year, it would culminate in an all-out war.

The *Huiguan*

"Companies," as the American newspapers called them, referred to the *huiguan* (literally "meeting hall"), the most visible type of Chinese organization operating in California. The Chinese who came to America, like immigrants from Germany, Sweden, and certain other European countries, found it useful to establish membership groups for their common benefit and protection. Founded along home-country geographic lines, these Chinese district associations functioned primarily as mutual aid fraternities. The Chinese-American journalist Fong Kum Ngon pointed out that "societies" would have been a more accurate English translation than "companies," as the *huiguan* were social rather than commercial entities.[3]

However they were characterized, their influence was extensive. When a ship arrived in San Francisco from Hong Kong, representatives of the various organizations came on board and registered the Chinese newcomers according to their home province. Thus, each man was automatically enrolled in his appropriate organization. (Chinese women were not included in their membership.) The *huiguan*—sometimes called "district associations"—helped their new members find work and loaned them money to travel from San Francisco to their ultimate destinations. In addition, they provided for ailing or impoverished immigrants who had no one else to care for them. If a Chinese worker died in America, his association collected money from its members to ship his remains back to his family in China. The functions of the *huiguan* were not entirely benevolent, however. They also acted as collection agencies for the immigrants' creditors, and they exerted a fair amount of control over their members through their power to extend or deny loans.

Since the *huiguan* sometimes advanced money for workers' passage overseas, many non-Asians believed that they acted as purveyors of Chinese slave labor. As early as 1861, a Los Angeles newspaper informed the public that thousands of Chinese "are being brought to California by their more wealthy countrymen, and are made to slave and work for their pecuniary benefit." Efforts to dispel this myth, which is essentially what it was, fell mostly on deaf ears. Sociologist Mary Roberts Coolidge tried to explain in her 1909 study of the Chinese in America that "ignorance and prejudice" sometimes caused people to wrongly accuse the district associations of "importing coolies and prostitutes under contract" and "extorting money illegally from their countrymen." Seid Back, a Chinese merchant of Portland, complained that non-Asians "do not know the facts. No Six Companies ever brought men over here that I know of."[4] Still, suspicion of the *huiguan* persisted for decades.

Technically, membership in a district association was voluntary, although at one time the *huiguan* had an agreement with the shipping companies under which a Chinese worker could not purchase a ticket back home without a certificate from his society verifying that he had settled all his debts. As a practical matter, there were very few Chinese in nineteenth-century America who did not pay the initiation fee of five to ten dollars and maintain membership in one of the *huiguan*. As Fong Kum Ngon pointed out, "Having been accustomed to live with people of his own clan in China, a Chinese naturally seeks for the people closely related to himself, or his immediate neighbors in the old country."[5] The provincial villagers also relied on the support of their district association if they got into a dispute with a member of another society. When these disagreements escalated to full-blown court battles, the *huiguan* sometimes hired American lawyers to represent their members.

Headquartered in San Francisco, the *huiguan* were nationwide organizations, operating through local branches in any city where a sufficient number of members settled. The mutual aid societies that were operating in the United States by the late 1850s formed a loosely organized federation called the Chinese Consolidated Benevolent Association, more commonly known among Americans as the Chinese Six Companies. In each town, local leaders of these organizations were influential merchants who usually spoke some English and unofficially represented the Chinese people to their non-Asian neighbors. The *huiguan* also served as a network connecting the scattered Chinese communities of California. The principals of the Los Angeles associations maintained close contact with their fellow company members in San Bernardino, Santa Barbara, and San Buenaventura (Ventura).

The first two *huiguan* to establish a presence in America were the Sam Yup Company and the See Yup Company (usually spelled "Sze Yup" today). Both were organized in San Francisco in 1851. The Sam Yups were better educated and more urbane people who came from the immediate vicinity of Canton. Experienced in commerce and well connected with shipping firms in the homeland, they owned the larger Chinese stores in San Francisco and ran the import-export businesses. They tended to look down on the far more numerous See Yups, whom they considered "uncouth bumpkins and social inferiors," in the words of historian Him Mark Lai. On the whole, the See Yups were poorer, less learned, more rural, and more gullible.[6] It was the working-class See Yup Company that dominated Los Angeles's Chinatown by the late 1860s.

Angelenos had a hard time grasping the nuances of the Chinese social order. During a murder trial, according to transcripts, Los Angeles prosecutor Frank Ganahl asked a witness named Chin Loey, "What company do you belong to?"

"See Yup," he replied.

"What company did Yo Hing belong to?" He was referring to the railroad contractor and strongman at the center of the Chinatown war in the early 1870s.

"Well, he belonged to the See Yup."

That response stumped the prosecutor. Yo Hing was well known as the leader of a breakaway *huiguan* called the Hong Chow Company, which also consisted of people from the Sze Yup district of China. The Chinese court interpreter explained, "He means by See Yup a province."

Ganahl then repeated, "What company does he belong to?"

This time Chin Loey said, "Kong Chow temple, they call it."

"Yo Hing, then, belonged to the Kong Chow?"

"Yes, sir, and he belonged to the See Yow. No relation."

By this point, Ganahl was completely confused. "Isn't this Kong Chow and See Yup all the same?"

"Kong Chow and See Yup all the same," agreed the witness.

The interpreter interjected, "Used to be the same; they are not now. They have divided off."[7]

In Los Angeles during the 1860s, the dominant See Yup Company's undisputed leader was Sing Lee, a prosperous merchant who had arrived in California around the beginning of the decade. The local press characterized him as "a 'big Tyee' [Taiyi] among the Chinese of this city" and a "boss Chinaman."[8] Less erudite than the average Chinese merchant in America, Sing Lee chose not to speak to non-Asians in English or Spanish but instead relied on his colleague, the controversial Yo Hing, to interpret.

For all the prominence he eventually enjoyed, Sing Lee's earliest appearances in Los Angeles's recorded history suggested a past as shady and violent as that of many of the non-Asians who drifted into the disorderly town. In 1864, a white woman accused him of petit larceny; the case was dismissed. Two years later, Sing Lee was charged with assault and battery, but the district attorney decided not to prosecute the matter. In 1867, a white man claimed that Sing Lee had hidden some stolen property in his house. However, a police search of Sing Lee's residence turned up nothing.[9] If Sing Lee was in fact a criminal, he was a lucky and successful one.

Though he frequently appeared in court on the wrong side of the law, Sing Lee also brought several suits of his own. In 1870, he filed a criminal complaint against an American, James Ganahan, who had apparently taken a pair of Sing Lee's pantaloons. Ganahan explained that Sing Lee had given him permission to change clothes in a back room while he was on his way to work. The room was dark, and he claimed that he mistook Sing Lee's garments for his own. After Ganahan returned the missing pantaloons, the charges were dismissed.[10]

A powerful man with many enemies, Sing Lee was the subject of a foiled assassination attempt in the fall of 1870. He received a telegram warning him that three Chinese cutthroats were on their way to Los Angeles. They had allegedly been paid to break into his store, gag his clerk, murder Sing Lee, and rob the firm. He obtained warrants for the men's arrest. One of them, Lee Fat, was captured and jailed shortly after he arrived in town.

Concerned that this sordid episode would soil his reputation among Angelenos, Sing Lee made a personal visit to the office of the *Los Angeles Star* to provide the newspaper with testimonials to his good character. He assured the editors that he was a "good Chinaman" who had "always behaved himself properly" and that he could not help it if a "bad Chinaman" was trying to take his life. At the same time, the See Yup Company placed a notice in the newspaper, affirming that its leader, Sing Lee, was "highly respectable" and "very well behaved" and had "constantly conducted himself in such a manner as to gain the respect and esteem of the entire community."[11]

That was not the impression he usually made on Angelenos, however, given the stories about him that appeared in the local newspapers. One summer night in 1871, the police went to Sing Lee's place on Calle de los Negros to investigate a report that he had severely beaten a Chinese woman. There they found the woman, bleeding from wounds to her face and surrounded by several Chinese men who shouted at the officers in English, "Away with her—she no good!" The lawmen arrested Sing Lee. He balked and refused to go with them until they drew their revolvers. Then he tried to bribe them, without success.

As the officers were leaving with their prisoner, the injured woman begged them to save her from Sing Lee's men. She claimed they would kill her and cut her body into small pieces all because she was the cause of their boss's incarceration. The woman explained that she belonged to Sing Lee and that he wanted to sell her for $500 to another man for use as a prostitute. When she refused to agree, Sing Lee attacked and beat her. Finding her story credible, the officers offered to take her to the jail for protection.

The following morning, the mayor, José Cristobal Aguilar, fined Sing Lee ten dollars for abusing the woman. Aguilar made no provision for the victim's safety, however. She refused to leave the jail, swearing that she would be murdered if she went back to Calle de los Negros. Some Chinese men tried to get the jailor to expel her, but he refused.[12]

In what was becoming a disturbing trend, the *Los Angeles News* used this deplorable incident as an excuse to lambaste the town's entire Chinese community: "The Chinese have no business here, and never can form part of our people; but being here, they must not be suffered to carry out their heathenish customs."[13] Despite the polite, carefully crafted advertisement that the See Yup Company had placed in the *Star*, and regardless of the consistently favorable impressions that Chinese laborers made on their employers, a growing segment of Los Angeles's population was starting to resent the presence of all Chinese who lived among them. Most of the news stories about their Chinese neighbors did not focus on their hard work or reliability in business dealings. Instead, the papers repeated lurid tales involving hired assassins and brutalized sex slaves.

Moreover, Angelenos never came to understand the true purposes of the *huiguan*, which were mostly benevolent. During the 1860s, northern Californians had developed a more balanced view of the Chinese Six Companies, whose merchant leaders in San Francisco made an effort to reach out to the city's elite and were also careful of their reputations. However, by the time the people of Los Angeles were introduced to the term "companies" in 1870, it was usually preceded by the modifier "rival." It did not help race relations that the unscrupulous See Yup leader Sing Lee became identified as the city's Chinese spokesman. Unfortunately for the Chinese people of Los Angeles, the town's non-Asians, from the time they first learned about Chinese "companies," associated the *huiguan* with immorality, intimidation, and violence.

"Bound Together by a Solemn Oath"

Perhaps because they were regarded as inferiors by their countrymen and held less of a stake in the overseas Chinese community, the See Yups, who made up the bulk of Los Angeles's Chinese population, were more susceptible than their compatriots to outside influences such as Christian mission societies. They were more readily lured into a radically different kind of organization as well. From the ranks of the See Yup Company came most of the recruits for the Chinese secret societies and their infamous offshoots, the mafia-like "fighting tongs."

Secret organizations had originated in the homeland as an outgrowth of what was known as the Triad Society. Named for the mystical connection between heaven, earth, and mankind, the Triad Society was formed in China in 1674 to overthrow the Manchu dynasty and restore the Ming house. In fact, many members of secret fraternal orders in California were refugees who had supported the Taiping rebellion, a widespread uprising against the Qing (Manchu) administration that had started in 1850. They fled China after it was crushed in 1864. Unlike the home-country counterparts, however, the secret societies in the United States were not politically oriented. In fact, the early Chinese in America rarely discussed their home country's politics, and few knew or cared much about anything in China beyond their home village.[14]

Like the *huiguan*, secret societies were originally formed in America for benevolent purposes. Whereas the district associations were organized along geographic lines, the fraternal orders admitted people from all lineages, regions, and classes. Their members were said to be "bound together by a solemn oath," swearing loyalty to one another and paying an initiation fee of ten dollars. By 1855, one secret society was estimated to have between three and four thousand members across California, approximately 10 percent of the thirty-eight thousand Chinese men in the state at the time.[15]

Within a few years after the secret societies were formed in America, some sects lost sight of their altruistic goals and became more interested in the profits they could reap from exploiting human weaknesses. The "fighting tongs" (so called to distinguish them from the nonviolent, charitable fraternities) came to dominate the three vice industries of California's Chinatowns—gambling, opium, and prostitution. A court interpreter testified in 1855 that the tongs' annual revenue from extortion exceeded $150,000. By the mid-1850s, Chinese prostitution in California had fallen under the domination of a nefarious organization called the Hip Yee Tong, a subsidiary of the I Hing ("Patriotic Rising") secret society. This group was originally founded to protect Chinese women from predators and racketeers. However, it soon became corrupted because of the high market prices that prostitutes commanded. The Hip Yees, who numbered about three hundred by the 1870s, reportedly brought six thousand Chinese women to the United States for the sex trade between 1852 and 1873.[16]

Competition for underworld revenue caused a great deal of friction in the Chinese communities of California. Although the general public did not become aware of the feuds between competing tongs until late in the nineteenth century, the San Francisco press reported as early as 1855 that several battles had been fought between secret societies in the interior of the state. One night a fight broke out in a Chinese brothel in San Francisco when five members of a secret society asked for a room where they could talk with the women. The proprietor refused their request, because they spoke a dialect different from the one used by his regular customers. Soon the parties were throwing bottles and earthen pots at each other and attacking one another with swords, knives, and clubs. A well-known San Francisco merchant, Tong Ah Chick, tried to mediate. However, he ended up leaping from a second-floor window, bringing the awning crashing down around him. This incident escalated into open warfare between members of two secret societies, and nearly all of them ended up bruised and wounded.[17]

The exploits of the secret societies have been sensationalized ever since the American press became aware of them in the late nineteenth century. Although the world of the fighting tongs represented only a small portion of the early Chinese experience in America, newspaper stories concerning professional killers and racketeers disproportionately influenced readers' opinions about all things Chinese. Non-Asians in California tended to lose sight of the fact that the overwhelming majority of the Chinese among them were ordinary people patiently seeking to improve their lot through honest labor. While it is true that the Chinese underworld in Los Angeles played a significant role in the troubles that erupted in 1870–71, it is also imperative to keep the influence of the Chinese criminal element in proper perspective.

Chinese immigrants in the United States had various reasons for joining secret societies. The less-worldly See Yup people were drawn to these fraternal orders for protection against ill use by their own people as well as the dangers of living in a foreign land.[18] Some recruits were aggrieved immigrants who felt alienated from the *huiguan*, believing that their district association had treated them unfairly. They hoped that their affiliation with the clandestine organizations would counteract the control that the *huiguan* exercised over their lives.

Not all tong members were disaffected outcasts, however. Some were daring, ambitious adventurers who thought the legitimate paths to wealth and power were too slow. In addition, a few successful Chinese businessmen, after getting involved in illicit side enterprises, became affiliated with the fighting tongs to take advantage of their cadre of hoodlums who could intimidate their competitors and recapture runaway prostitutes. Members of the notorious Hip Yee Tong reportedly included some of the most important Chinese merchants.[19]

The fighting tongs kept trained soldiers or "highbinders" on their payrolls to deliver threats and take revenge when necessary, even carrying out contract murders on occasion. The term "highbinder," which originally referred to Irish bandits, was first applied to Chinese cutthroats by policemen in New York. It appeared in the California press by 1876. According to Portland merchant Seid Back, the Chinese themselves did not use the word but instead called a tong henchman a "society man." Seid Back also admitted that he once belonged to the Boo Long Sing society, which purported to be a benevolent order. However, he dropped out when he learned that its members made their living by collecting tribute from brothels and casinos.[20]

"Secret" society was somewhat of a misnomer, because the fighting tongs operated fairly openly in the United States. A San Francisco police lieutenant, William Price, recalled that the highbinders were easily recognizable by the style of their hair ("not so neatly kept," "more fluffy") and the type of round, stiff-brimmed hats they wore. Journalist Charles Nordhoff, who visited California in the early 1870s, reported that when tong members testified in court, they made no attempt to conceal the fact that they were part of a commercial organization that brought young women from China to California for prostitution and received a share of the money they earned.[21] As long as this criminal system within the Chinese community remained internal, non-Asians were inclined to ignore it.

The tongs' professional killers were believed to have been Chinese criminals who had escaped to the United States. If a member of a secret society put up money to have an enemy dispatched, the tong's assassins were blindfolded and drew balls or buttons to determine who had to carry out the killing. Usually, two or three highbinders were selected to work in tandem. According to Police Lieutenant Price, "The society's rules are so binding that those chosen are bound to kill that man if there are twenty policemen about when he meets him." The secret society assured its assassins that it would pay their legal expenses were they apprehended. It would also compensate their families in China if they were imprisoned or hanged.[22]

Angelenos, with only a small group of Chinese among them, were not very familiar with the workings of secret societies. Nonetheless, they became aware of the tongs' practices in 1871, when assassins were enlisted to kill Yo Hing, by then one of Chinatown's most powerful figures. Yo Hing told the press that one of his enemies, Sam Yuen, had made an agreement with six men to murder him in exchange for $1,000. If any of the assassins were killed, the money would be divided among the survivors. If they were jailed, Sam Yuen promised to hire a lawyer and pay each of the hired killers two dollars a day while they were incarcerated. Yo Hing concluded, "They are bound to kill me, because they agreed to; they will kill me if they are killed just after, they don't care, will kill any body who tries to arrest them."[23]

Although the fighting tongs were heavily involved in the sex trade, they did not directly own or operate whorehouses as a rule. Instead, they made their profits by imposing an import fee of forty dollars for indentured women. In addition, they extorted weekly or monthly sums from both prostitutes and merchants, ostensibly for "protection" from other tongs. In the early days, the fees they sought were exorbitant. One secret society reportedly attempted to collect ten dollars per month from each prostitute (whose monthly earnings were about seventy dollars) and one hundred dollars from each merchant in 1854. The tongs' taxes had become more manageable by the early 1870s, when the Hip Yee Tong demanded one dollar per month from each woman.[24]

Constantly harassed, Chinese businessmen and prostitutes paid these amounts because they felt they had no choice. They lived in terror of the tongs' death threats, and they knew they could not turn for help to American policemen, who were bribed to look the other way while the extortion flourished. Most Chinese immigrants regarded secret societies with contempt. A few harried merchants privately furnished information to the authorities in an effort to destroy the fighting tongs' hold on California's Chinatowns. Nonetheless, fear of the tongs made it impossible to obtain Chinese testimony against them in open court.[25]

That fear was evident when an eighteen-year-old former prostitute named Ah Sing was called to testify in a San Francisco court. She had been rescued from a bordello and married to a man named Lun Yat Sung. Afterward, the Hip Yee Tong ordered him to pay $350 to compensate the brothel owners for their loss of his wife's services. Instead, he fled to a mission house for protection. The Hip Yees, perhaps leery of drawing the public's attention to their activities, and aware that their power had its limits, informed Lun Yat Sung that they were willing to negotiate: if he would pay only one hundred dollars, all would be "clear like ice melting before water." Still, he refused. Once his predicament came to light, eight Hip Yee men were charged with conspiracy.[26]

When his terrified bride, Ah Sing, took the witness stand at the tong members' trial, she kept her eyes fixed on them. The prosecutor asked her when she married Lun Yat Sung. Through a translator, she replied hesitantly, "I haven't any memory, and how can I remember?"

The judge then inquired, "Did you come from China?"

"It's so long ago, I can't remember."

"How long ago was it?"

"About seven months."

The prosecutor tried a different line of questioning. "Are you afraid to testify in this case?"

"Who says I'm afraid?"

"I say you are afraid. Is it not true?"

She hung her head, stared at the clock in the courtroom, glanced at the defendants, and finally blurted out, "Yes."

"Now then, tell the court who you are afraid of."

Ah Sing hesitated once more. "The people of the Hip Yee Tong."

"What has any of the defendants done or threatened to do to you?"

"I don't know."

"Do you know any of these men here?"

"I can't remember."

"Well, has anybody threatened you in regard to this case?"

"I don't know."

The prosecutor was unable to get the testimony he needed from Ah Sing. The Hip Yee racketeers were acquitted.[27]

Crossing the Lines

Naturally, the illicit goings-on within and between the fighting tongs drew much attention in California's newspapers, for the thrilling tales of vice and violence made terrific copy. A less publicized but equally interesting development was the way in which the boundary between law-abiding and law-breaking Chinese immigrants shifted. Those regular laborers who made up the bulk of the Chinese on the West Coast, the laundrymen and domestics and farmhands who spent most of their days toiling in thankless jobs and their nights enjoying the meager pleasures of the gambling halls, could be quick to take up arms whenever the interests of their extended family or district association were threatened. As Los Angeles Policeman Jesús Bilderrain explained, when the Chinese "expect any difficulty among themselves, they all get together and they all meet at their chief's house."[28]

The problems associated with clan loyalty became particularly obvious in Los Angeles's Chinatown during the early 1870s. When a fight was brewing in 1871 between members of two *huiguan*, the Caswell and Ellis merchandise store on the corner of Los Angeles and Arcadia Streets sold up to fifty pistols to Chinese customers over the course of a few days—that is, fifty handguns at a time when the city's entire Chinese population was probably no larger than two hundred.[29] Those fifty were in addition to the firearms that the Chinese already owned. In the rough-and-tumble world of Los Angeles, individual Chinese residents, like their non-Asian contemporaries, could not be neatly categorized as respectable or disreputable. Nor could all the shootouts be attributed to professional tong fighters. Even the humblest and most law-abiding Chinese laborers could be temporarily transformed into gunslingers when their kinsmen were wronged.

Likewise, the line between the criminal societies and the legitimate district associations tended to become blurred, at least in the minds of non-Asians. The belief that the companies essentially functioned as slave-trading organizations persisted despite the efforts of both the Chinese and their American defenders to distinguish between the beneficent *huiguan* and the fighting tongs. In 1909, sociologist Mary Roberts Coolidge chastised California journalists for mischaracterizing tong wars in San Francisco as disputes between the Sam Yup and See Yup organizations. Similarly, immigrant Lee Chew maintained, "Newspapers often say that [the fights among the Chinese] are feuds between the six companies, but that is a mistake."[30]

Most non-Asians remained unconvinced, however. A congressional subcommittee investigating Chinese immigration tried unsuccessfully to uncover some link between the *huiguan* and the secret societies, which many legislators felt certain existed but which the Chinese consistently denied. The subcommittee's chairman asked an interpreter named Carleton Rickards, "Do these Six Companies or any of them seem to approve of the existence of these highbinder associations?"

Rickards replied, "No, sir, they don't like to see these things existing, but they are not able to stop it." When another member of the subcommittee asked Rickards whether the Chinese Six Companies sometimes coerced members into repaying their debts by threatening to send highbinders after them, he stated, "I have not heard of it."

Subsequently, the congressmen asked San Francisco journalist A. B. Cromwell whether the *huiguan* ever engaged tong fighters. He responded, "I am not in a position to say that the Six Companies do, because they claim to aid the police in every case, and as far as I know they do."

The committee members pressed further: "Then you think the Six Companies don't use the highbinders in their business?"

"The Chinatown detectives say no," Cromwell replied. "I don't think the companies themselves would authorize murder, or would commit it, or tolerate it."

"You don't believe the highbinders have any connection with the Six Companies?"

"I think not," Cromwell concluded.

Later, the subcommittee asked Los Angeles Police Chief John M. Glass the same question: "Do you think the highbinders have any connection at all with the Six Companies?"

He replied, "I don't think they do. From what I know of the Six Companies, I think the intention of the Six Companies is to do what is right."[31]

At various times, the *huiguan* openly opposed the secret societies and tried to halt the traffic in prostitutes. Early on, in 1863, the Chinese Six Companies were partially successful in checking this trade and returned a large number of women to China. The San Francisco press declared the following year that the principal Chinese merchants were "all anxious and determined to stop . . . the outrages which are wrongly charged against them as a people." The *huiguan* combined forces again in 1868 to thwart the practice of selling women. They petitioned the California state government to instruct shipping companies not to allow Chinese women to disembark until *huiguan* representatives had verified that they were actually servants or wives. Writing to President Ulysses S. Grant in 1876, the leaders of the Chinese Six Companies castigated "unprincipled Chinamen" for bringing prostitutes to America.[32]

Although their functions were quite different, the *huiguan* and the fighting tongs did not have mutually exclusive enrollment lists. Since nearly all Chinese in the United States belonged to one of the district associations, membership in these two types of organizations overlapped. Nor were the *huiguan* and the criminal societies always distinguishable to outsiders when it came to the heavy-handed methods they used to get what they wanted. Interpreter Wo Ben testified that the *huiguan* did not bother to speak out against assassinations in San Francisco's Chinatown until 1876. Businessman Thomas H. King even contended that highbinders carried out contract murders under the direction of the Six Companies. One skeptical American journalist charged in 1869 that the Chinese Six Companies' attempt to stop the traffic in prostitutes "was nothing less than a cunningly devised scheme to effect precisely what was pretended to be opposed."[33]

These were most likely all overstatements. The surviving evidence does not indicate that any of the leaders of the Chinese Six Companies in San Francisco directed the activities of the fighting tongs or that the *huiguan*, as organizations, had anything to do with operating the brothels and casinos. Nonetheless, by the early 1870s, unscrupulous businessmen had infiltrated the upper levels of some local branches of the *huiguan*. One of them was Sing Lee, the previously described See Yup leader of Los Angeles who dealt in Chinese prostitutes and hired hoodlums to assist in this trade. As a result, the two types of Chinese associations, though supposedly competitors for power and control in Chinatown, sometimes appeared to be working in tandem. Los Angeles Policeman George Gard explained that "when any of the Chinamen get into trouble the leaders [of the *huiguan*] do the best they can for them."[34] That might mean retaining lawyers to defend them. Or it could mean hiring tong fighters to settle the score.

In Los Angeles's small but contentious Chinatown, legitimate and illicit Chinese enterprises often operated hand in hand. The local *huiguan*, which had fallen under the control of a few amoral and power-hungry men, did not even pretend to oppose the vice industries. Although the Los Angeles press never mentioned secret societies— indeed, the town's non-Asians were apparently unaware that such things existed—some of the city's most influential Chinese residents took part in activities usually associated with the fighting tongs. They also employed underlings who resorted to the intimidating tactics of high-binders. As early as 1866, the See Yup Company's three merchant leaders—Sing Lee, Yo Hing, and Sam Yuen—were jointly charged with "keeping, maintaining and residing in . . . a house of bawdy and ill fame." Sing Lee, the unofficial spokesman of Chinatown, was said to deal "extensively in human flesh." Over a period of several years, these three *huiguan* magnates, the men who came to serve as the ambassadors of Chinatown to Los Angeles's non-Asian population in the early 1870s, were all directly involved in the hostilities that periodically erupted over the possession of Chinese women. The unfortunate result was that Angelenos began, in the plaintive words of the leaders of one Chinese association, to "hold all of us accountable for the villainy of a few."[35]

The Machinery of the Courts

As seen previously, the Chinese of Los Angeles learned as early as 1864 that they could use the local courts to resist maltreatment and right the injustices committed against them. At the same time, some men who were involved in the vice businesses discovered an equally valuable corollary to that lesson: the American legal system could be manipulated to thwart one's enemies and facilitate illicit transactions. The Chinese did not necessarily regard these shenanigans as an abuse of the courts. At home, the mandarins had administered edicts so unfairly that it had almost become a virtue in their eyes to obstruct the execution of the laws.[36] Los Angeles's Chinese residents used civil lawsuits and criminal complaints as vehicles of both liberation and oppression, of righteous redress and wrongful retaliation, with the complacent cooperation of American lawyers and judges who either did not know or did not care about the litigants' underlying motives.

Chinatown's first leader, John Tambolin, set the precedent by lodging a dubious charge in 1861 that a visitor from San Francisco had threatened his life in order to land the man in jail. In the years that followed, the court records are replete with examples of this type of legal maneuvering. In 1869, Tung Say accused Ah Song of stealing a pair of gold earrings, but the testimony of several Chinese witnesses showed that the case was baseless. A cook named Que Ma was arrested and brought to Los Angeles on a false charge of horse theft to prevent him from testifying in a legitimate criminal proceeding in San Bernardino. Justice Gray dismissed other Chinese cases involving murder threats as "purely malicious" and "without foundation," stemming from the parties' "competitions and jealousies." The leaders of the See Yup Company accused members of other *huiguan* of having "moved all the machinery of the courts to compass the destruction" of several unfortunate victims. Chinese litigants also used the legal remedy of attachment as a means of appropriating a rival's property, and they leveled false charges of theft to effect the capture and return of runaway prostitutes. Sometimes the threat of going to court was enough to coerce an adversary to capitulate. When Tung Soy accused three Chinese men of assault, he soon announced "that after a full explanation of the whole matter, he had become satisfied that he had been laboring under a mistake, and asked to withdraw the complaint, he paying the costs."[37]

The judiciary of Los Angeles often did not know what to make of the Chinese controversies before them and found it very difficult to arrive at the truth. The local press derided Chinese witnesses as unreliable. "Their thousand and one friends tell five hundred and one lies," according to the *Los Angeles Star*. In one case in which several Chinese were present in the courtroom, County Judge Harvey K. S. O'Melveny declined to let the lawyers examine every witness, because he felt certain they would all testify alike.[38]

Part of the problem for jurists was, in the words of the *Los Angeles News*, "the culpable want of proficiency of our officers in the Chinese language." Most Chinese witnesses testified through interpreters, who, according to memoirist Eng Ying Gong, "were bribed and brow-beaten" and "confused testimony" that often depended on "nuances of meaning." In one court case, a Los Angeles newspaper quipped that "two interpreters were necessary—one to watch the other, we suppose." Also, judges required Chinese witnesses to swear on a Bible, which meant nothing to them. Li Gui, a visiting official from China, said the Chinese thought that swearing on a book was nonsense. Reverend Otis Gibson, the Methodist missionary, confirmed that the Chinese did not take American oaths very seriously and sometimes got together prior to a court hearing to "manufacture or arrange the testimony of their witnesses."[39]

The judiciary was slow to recognize the most effective way to prevent Chinese witnesses from committing perjury: requiring them to swear on the head of a chicken that had been chopped off in open court. The Chinese considered this oath to be binding and sacred. During Ah Sing's case in San Francisco, one of the accused Hip Yee tong members dared a witness for the prosecution to cut off a chicken's head and then testify against him. In Los Angeles, a justice of the peace first allowed this form of attestation in an 1864 contract dispute. One of the witnesses for the aggrieved party substantiated his testimony by solemnly severing a chicken's head and invoking on himself the chicken's fate if he spoke falsely. The accused "immediately succumbed and had no more to say."[40]

A Mutually Beneficial Relationship

The vice industries of nineteenth-century Chinatowns could not have flourished for so long without the acquiescence—and, in some cases, the direct assistance—of American policemen, lawyers, and judges. California's law officers came under particularly harsh condemnation for their role in perpetuating the prostitution and gambling businesses. In a letter to President Grant in 1876, the Chinese Six Companies complained, "If officers would refuse bribes, then unprincipled Chinamen could no longer purchase immunity from the punishment of their crimes." The same year, interpreter Wo Ben testified "that a few officers could keep the gambling-houses in check, but the men detailed for that purpose are not anxious to perform their duties, as they make money by neglecting them." One policeman in San Francisco reportedly received five dollars per week for every Chinese casino and fifty cents for each prostitute on his beat. Reverend Otis Gibson also reported that part of the "blood-money" that the Hip Yee Tong collected from prostitutes went into the pockets of policemen.[41]

Los Angeles's early police department was too small, and was staffed by men too inexperienced or indifferent to their responsibilities, to be very effective in keeping order. Transformed from a volunteer organization to a paid city division in 1869, the initial force consisted of only six officers—roughly one per one thousand residents in the nation's most unruly town. From its inception, the Los Angeles Police Department had a checkered reputation. Its patrolmen were often at odds with the city's councilmen. One council member, William Ferguson, complained in 1871 that on various occasions he had seen police officers gambling. He opined "that it was wrong, that Policemen are paid by the city to guard its citizens and should not be found in gambling houses." On Sundays, Policemen George Gard and Jesús Bilderrain regularly staged cockfights on Calle de los Negros. The Common Council (the predecessor of today's City Council) discharged Officer Esteban Sanchez in 1872, finding him to have been derelict in his duty. Later that year, Policeman George Gard resigned following a report that he had habitually neglected his responsibilities, although he eventually became chief of police and then a US marshal. The committee on police later recommended discharging Officer Emil Harris for leaving the city on several occasions and disobeying the chief's orders. However, two councilmen vigorously defended him, and he kept his job.[42]

The Los Angeles lawmen of the 1860s and early 1870s did their part to uphold the town's reputation for reckless violence. In fact, their most dangerous confrontations were not with the hardened desperadoes they pursued but with each other. As will be seen later, Officer Joseph F. Dye, who had a history of violent assaults, got in a shootout with City Marshal William C. Warren in 1870 over reward money offered by the See Yup Company for a missing prostitute. Policeman Emil Harris pled guilty to a charge of assault and battery lodged by another city marshal, R. J. Wolf. The hotheaded Officer Dye once approached the sheriff, William R. Rowland, grabbed him by the beard with his left hand, and with his other held a cocked, cut-off five-shooter to the sheriff's chest. Their trouble stemmed from some remarks Dye had made at a political meeting that Rowland claimed were lies. After a struggle, both lawmen were charged with assault.[43]

The patrolmen of the latter 1860s took their cue from the man at the top, William C. Warren. He was only in his late twenties in 1865 when he was first elected city marshal, a predecessor position to chief of police. Warren remained popular among the public throughout his time in office. The *Los Angeles Star* praised him as "one of the most capable, efficient and successful officers in the State," neglecting to mention that he was also impulsive and trigger-happy. During his first term, Warren got in a gunfight at his home with the deputy provost marshal, Frederick Morris. Prior to this affray, the two men had been close friends; in fact, Morris and his family had been living at Warren's house for several months. Both lawmen shot and wounded each other. Morris died from his injuries two weeks later. Their quarrel, never fully explained, reportedly arose out of a business dispute. The following year, the people of Los Angeles responded to Warren's killing of a fellow officer by reelecting him, and the Common Council even approved his request to increase his salary.[44]

Warren had a penchant for shooting before he asked many questions, regardless of whether he was dealing with a criminal suspect or an innocent passerby. One night in 1867, the marshal was lost in the countryside and stopped a Mexican man, Rafael Oyos, to ask him for directions back to Los Angeles. Oyos, according to his testimony, offered to lead the lawman to the main road while Warren followed in his buggy. Along the way, the skittish marshal made Oyos get off his horse and searched him at gunpoint, saying that there were "a good many rascals around here." When they reached the road and heard a voice from a nearby wagon, the terrified marshal pointed his pistol to Oyos's head and said, "Traitor! You have people there to kill me." The two men scuffled by a bridge. Warren shot his harmless guide as the man tried to flee, badly wounding him. The next day, the marshal told people that he had been attacked.[45]

Corruption became increasingly open among Los Angeles's police force during the early 1870s. Along Calle de los Negros, where the local patrolmen seemed entirely willing to partner with the town's Chinese bosses, payment to the lawmen took several forms: gifts that were openly bestowed, rewards that were publicly advertised, and bribes that were offered in private. At that time, officers' salaries ranged from eighty to one hundred dollars per month—not paltry wages in an era when manual laborers earned less than two dollars per day of work, but modest enough to make graft a constant temptation. As early as 1862, a Chinese brothel owner in Los Angeles admitted that he paid policemen for the "privilege" of keeping a disorderly house. Following an examination of the force that finally occurred in 1877, policemen who were found guilty of taking bribes from Chinese gamblers were discharged.[46]

The local lawmen were particularly eager to help capture runaway Chinese women and collect the reward money offered by their keepers, as will be seen in the next chapter. On one occasion, several officers invaded the Tie Long laundry, where a Chinese woman reportedly had been chained to a stake behind the building and starved for four days. They surrounded the laundry and rushed through it with their pistols drawn. The lawmen were not so much concerned about rescuing the abused victim as receiving a twenty-five dollar reward offered by her brother, Ah Me. The Los Angeles Star mocked the "'indefatigable' and ever energetic 'authorities'" for their "zeal and anxiety to capture the 'fiendish perpetrators' of this heathen cruelty." But the officers soon discovered, to their disappointment, that they had been outmaneuvered. The woman was gone, and the reward went uncollected.[47]

The Chinese businessmen of Los Angeles understood perfectly the importance of maintaining a mutually beneficial relationship with the police force. One news account observed wryly that the Chinese were "choice in their selection of officers." By March 1871, one of the new district associations, the Hong Chow Company, had managed to secure the goodwill of some unnamed police officers, who reportedly prevented several members of the See Yup Company from testifying in a controversy before the district judge.[48]

At one point, Policemen Emil Harris and George Gard, who regularly patrolled Chinatown, received a gift of Chinese embroidery from some merchants who belonged to the Nin Yung Company, "as a testimonial of their appreciation of services rendered from time to time," according to the press. Subsequently, the *Los Angeles News* reported a "suspicious negligence" on the part of the police force to serve a warrant for the arrest of a Chinese businessman whose colleagues had presented the embroidery. Officer Jesús Bilderrain, who was assigned to enforce the warrant, claimed to have lost the document. When the justice of the peace issued a second arrest warrant, neither Bilderrain nor the officers who had received the gift—Harris and Gard—were willing to carry it out; in fact, they exhibited "a suspicious disinclination to do so." The newspaper clamored for their immediate dismissal from the police force.[49]

But they were not dismissed—at least not for forming surreptitious partnerships with the Chinatown magnates who headed the local branches of the *huiguan*. By the start of the 1870s, corruption was rampant in all the organizations intended to keep order and administer justice in Los Angeles. The local branches of the Chinese district associations, originally formed to protect the foreign workers from exploitation in a hostile land, were led by men who trafficked in enslaved prostitutes. The Los Angeles judiciary was uninterested in prying deeply enough to put an end to their transparent schemes. And the town's lawmen profited from carrying them out. By the time City Marshal William Warren and Police Officer Joe Dye had their fatal shootout over Chinese reward money in 1870, some Angelenos must have wondered how law enforcement in their town had come to this: its policemen were literally killing each other in their eagerness to do the bidding of a handful of Chinese racketeers.

4

Daughters of the Sun and Moon

ANGELENOS GOT THEIR FIRST GLIMPSE of a Chinese woman in October 1859, a full decade after the earliest men from the Far East had appeared. According to the *Los Angeles Star*, her arrival "caused great sensation in Chinadom," as "the fair one was conducted to her home with all due ceremony." The Chinese men were "out in full fig." Local curiosity-seekers also hovered around her in the streets, following the procession and boorishly raising "much din and tumult." The *Star's* reporter did not manage to find out who the woman was. However, the joyous, festive reception that marked her journey's end, as well as the *Star's* reference to "her home," suggested that she was a mail-order bride for one of the town's more successful Chinese businessmen.

A month later, the *Star* ran a news item about a Chinese female named Hop Path—most likely the same woman, although others may have arrived by then. She tried to kill herself by taking opium. An American doctor saved her from death. The *Star* cited "family squabbles" as the cause of Hop Path's misery.[1]

Whatever the true reason, life in America was bitter and harrowing for the West Coast's earliest Chinese women. The lucky ones—and Hop Path may have been one of them, if she was in fact a bride—spent lives of lonely seclusion in their husbands' quarters. The less fortunate, after being traded like livestock several times and forced daily to sell their bodies to abusive drunkards for a quarter, might wind up addicted to opium and dying alone in a back alley.

Women in a Bachelor Society

Though they had little political power or social standing, women were often the center of attention in America's first Chinatowns. Many of the troubles that arose within Los Angeles's Chinese community in the 1860s and early 1870s were rooted in a pronounced gender imbalance. By 1870, only 34 of the town's 179 Chinese residents were women. That proportion was higher than the national average. The US census that year showed 78 Chinese women for every 1,000 Chinese men.

Although Chinese America in the mid-nineteenth century was often described as a "bachelor society," the lopsided ratio between the sexes did not necessarily mean that most of the Chinese men in the country were unmarried. The families of many migrant workers who sought their fortunes in the United States had arranged marriages for them shortly before they left China. That cemented their ties to their clans and villages and ensured that they would send part of their overseas earnings back home. Ng June, a partner in a merchandise business in Port Townsend, Washington, estimated that about half of the five hundred Chinese men who lived there were married, but not one had brought his wife to the United States. Seid Back, the previously mentioned Chinese merchant of Portland, reported that about 70 percent of the town's five thousand Chinese men had wives. However, only about one hundred of those estimated thirty-five hundred wives lived in America.[2]

As a rule, young Chinese men chose to leave their wives at their parents' home because of traditional values as well as the dangers they associated with living in America. In China, a married woman was expected to perform duties for her husband's family under the direction of her mother-in-law. Abandoning those responsibilities to venture abroad would have been scandalous. According to Li Gui, a visiting official, Chinese men wanted their wives to be submissive and unobtrusive. They even had a saying, "Only a woman without accomplishments is virtuous."[3]

Several Chinese merchants of San Francisco explained to Governor John Bigler in 1855 that the wives of China's better families lived "in the utmost privacy." Moreover, men had not brought their families to

California because of the warnings that were issued in China against journeying to the United States. According to a report prepared by the Chinese Six Companies in 1876, the wives remained behind "because it is contrary to the custom and against the inclination of virtuous Chinese women to go so far from home, and because the frequent outbursts of popular indignation against our people have not encouraged us to bring our families with us against their will."[4]

Methodist missionary Otis Gibson claimed that about 90 percent of the married Chinese women in the United States were second wives; first wives living overseas were a "rare article." Chinese society tolerated polygamy, though it was not widely practiced. While marriage shielded a Chinese woman from the savagery of California's flesh trade, the solitary, tedious life of a merchant's wife in Los Angeles was hardly enviable. Closely guarded, she was kept indoors at her husband's house and was largely isolated from both non-Asian society and the Chinese community. It was considered immodest for her to be seen very often on the streets, especially a street as rowdy and disreputable as Calle de los Negros. There were few other Chinese women of her social standing in Los Angeles who could call on her at home. As one local journalist reported, "She seldom goes out, and does not receive visitors until she has been a wife for at least two years. Even then, if she has no child, she is supposed to hide herself." Her peers back home considered her fortunate in one respect, however: she was not subject to the demands of her mother-in-law.[5]

Other, less-privileged Chinese women, after being brought to America against their wills and forced to work for some time in brothels, eventually wed laborers and helped their husbands in their trades. Chinese working men were less likely than non-Asians to stigmatize prostitutes, since they knew that most of these women had not chosen their occupation. Augustus Ward Loomis, a Presbyterian missionary, referred to these marriages between immigrant men and prostitutes as "a returning to virtue." He described the groom in these cases as a "quasi husband," suggesting that the Chinese did not take these American marriages of convenience as seriously as a proper wedding back home.[6] Though these brides were less isolated than their countrywomen who married into Chinatown's elite households, working-class wives had no time for leisure. They toiled long hours in physically demanding jobs. In addition, they were sometimes responsible for taking care of boarders at home.

Nor did these marriages necessarily bring happiness to either party. Chinese men and women, longing for companionship in an alien land, sometimes made poor choices. Reverend Loomis indicated that "the greater portion of these alliances, it is to be feared, are merely temporary." Sometimes the woman would leave the man, though more often it was the other way around; he might even barter her away. The *Los Angeles Star* was blunter, stating that Chinese matches did not often prove congenial, particularly after the wife learned that in America she could marry anyone she liked.[7]

On Calle de los Negros, Angelenos saw a Chinese man take a broomstick to his wife, ostensibly because he did not like the food she had cooked. The mayor fined another Chinese man when he "somewhat severely chastised his affectionate spouse." However, one Chinese couple's fight on the streets of Los Angeles resulted in the woman being jailed, as she proved to be the aggressor.[8]

The people of Los Angeles County witnessed a very public Chinese marital spat in the summer of 1866. Late one afternoon, just before the steamer was about to leave for San Francisco, a laundryman named Wing Sing was seen rushing through the streets of Wilmington (near San Pedro harbor), frantically searching for the justice of the peace. He explained excitedly that his errant wife, Sing Toy, had left him and run off with his money and jewelry. He obtained a warrant for her arrest. The constable found the woman at the wharf, clutching a white dog in her arms and preparing to board the steamer. Her husband thanked the constable, calling him a "very good man." The news report said that Wing Sing was "once more a happy man." However, the journalist neglected to find out whether Sing Toy, who was taken back to preside "over the washtub mansion as in former days," shared in his joy.[9]

"The Majority, if Not All"

From the time Chinese women first arrived on the West Coast, they were regularly maligned in the American press. California newspapers perpetuated the widely held belief that "the majority, if not all," of the Chinese women who came to the United States had been brought for the purpose of prostitution. To some extent, Chinese men fostered this stereotype when they spoke to reporters. "The Chinese laugh at the absurdity of supposing that any of their countrywomen of respectable position ever come here," reported one journalist. Ling Ming How, the nationwide president of the Sam Yap Company, estimated that only one in every eleven of the Chinese women living in San Francisco was respectable.[10] Consequently, many non-Asians came to assume that practically every Chinese female in the United States was a woman for hire.

However, American journalists overlooked one critical fact: "respectable" Chinese women were rarely encountered on the streets, because they lived cloistered lives and seldom appeared in public. In fact, contemporary scholars have produced convincing evidence that a significant proportion of Chinese women in nineteenth-century America became wives or laborers in other occupations. In Los Angeles, several of the most influential Chinese men had wives in town by the early 1870s: Chee Long "Gene" Tong, a popular physician; *huiguan* leaders Yo Hing and Sam Yuen; and businessmen Hing Sing, Quong Lee, and Charley Shew. According to the Los Angeles census of 1870, two of the town's Chinese women, Ah Lee and Wa Sug, worked in laundries. That census also indicated that three of the town's Chinese households consisted of one man and one woman. Another nine mixed dwellings may have housed as many as fifteen couples. Thus, more than half of the thirty-four Chinese women living in Los Angeles may have been laborers or wives.[11]

Still, American newspapermen never acknowledged that possibility when they covered events in Chinatown. In one instance, trouble arose in Los Angeles when some Chinese adversaries of a middle-aged woman named Zouk Nai accused her of keeping a house of ill fame. Journalists automatically assumed the charge was true. One paper delighted in describing the purported madam as having fingernails "an inch long and dyed with the juice of henna." She was arrested and taken to jail but was not charged. During the two hours she was away from home, three men named Wah Hing, Ah Son, and Ah Shoah went to her "den" on Sanchez Street and harassed two of the teenage "inmates" of the "bagnio," according to the *Evening Express*.

When those two girls, Ah Choy and Ty Choy, were called to testify, their consistent accounts were strikingly different from the newspaper's racy story. Ah Choy was married. Zouk Nai was her mother, and the other girl, Ty Choy, was her sister. The four members of the family shared the house, where both girls worked as seamstresses. The charge against their mother was apparently false. While Zouk Nai was at the jail clearing her name, the three visitors used the opportunity to threaten the girls and steal their jewelry. A police officer who had arrested their mother even helped Wah Hing drag one of the girls, Ah Choy, outside the house. When asked if she feared Wah Hing, she replied: "I was afraid he would take me away and sell me."[12] Considering the seamy escapades the girl must have witnessed in Los Angeles, her fears were well founded.

The Sex Trade in Los Angeles

While the local press certainly overstated the proportion of Chinese women who were prostitutes, there is no doubt that the sex trade in Los Angeles, both Chinese and non-Asian, was thriving by the early 1860s. No one really knows how many of the town's women worked in brothels, since the early censuses did not list prostitution as an occupation. John Tambolin told a local reporter that the eight Chinese women living in Los Angeles in the spring of 1861 were "no very good." Seven or eight more women arrived that June. Their occupations were unknown.[13]

By 1862, there were several brothels in various parts of the city, including a Chinese bordello on Main Street near San Pedro that was reportedly a nuisance to the neighbors in that prime residential location. Its proprietor readily admitted that he paid policemen so they would allow him to keep it open. Although Chinese women apparently made up only a modest proportion of the town's sex workers in the 1860s, they initially bore the brunt of criminal prosecutions. Later in 1862, the Los Angeles court of sessions fined sixteen Chinese residents twenty-six dollars each for "keeping and residing in a house of ill fame." District Attorney Ezra Drown, not bothering to find out the women's true names, amused himself by giving them pseudonyms such as "Chick," "Lick," "Rum," "Bum," "Clap," and "Pox."[14]

The number of whorehouses in Los Angeles was rapidly increasing by 1864. One newspaper recommended restricting them to specific zones. That spring, three Chinese women and one man accused of keeping brothels were each required to post one hundred dollar bonds. Prostitution had become a big business in Chinatown by 1866, when

Los Angeles's three most notable Chinese entrepreneurs were charged with keeping a brothel. They pleaded guilty to the lesser offense of disturbing the peace and were fined fifty cents each.[15]

After 1866, criminal prosecutions of Chinese brothels in Los Angeles fell off considerably for several years. One of the few citizens' complaints was brought not by an irritated American neighbor or reformer but by a Chinese man named See Jo, who charged his countryman, Ah Sy, and "and a bevy of Chinese nymphs" with running a brothel on Calle de los Negros in 1870. The complaint was probably See Jo's way of retaliating against an adversary. The *Star* blithely pointed out that Ah Sy's bawdy establishment was "endangering the health of the classic precinct of Negro Alley."[16]

Despite these periodic criminal suits, Los Angeles officials usually took a casual attitude toward prostitution. Perhaps that was not surprising, considering that they had their hands full pursuing cutthroats and thieves. The city did not even bother to pass an ordinance regulating the sex trade until 1874. Even then, the restrictions on solicitation applied only to certain parts of town; an amendment to outlaw prostitution citywide was voted down.[17]

In 1870, a group of concerned citizens petitioned the Los Angeles Common Council to address the problem of prostitution along Bath (present-day North Main) Street, where several non-Asian bordellos were located north of the plaza. The council's committee on police responded that they could do nothing to convince the property owners to clean up the neighborhood. Instead, they recommended that every prostitute who appeared on the street "to induce men to enter her house by obscene language or act" should be fined ten dollars. Councilman Andrew A. Boyle, the namesake of Boyle Heights, set off a big round of laughter when he objected, "They must go out of doors sometimes. We could not shut them up always." The *Los Angeles News* chided the council for making a "burlesque report" while its members "aired their wit and indulged in facetious remarks."[18]

The Chinese sex establishments in Los Angeles were relatively tame in comparison with the vile American whorehouses on Bath Street. There, according to reporters, prostitutes would "sit at windows and in front of open doors, nude or seminaked, exhibiting themselves to passers, or seeking to attract attention by indulgence in lascivious gestures and acts." The worst sex offender, however, was not a prostitute but a Basque deviant named Pierre Basange, who was in the habit of "exposing his person in the most beastly manner" to children walking along Alameda Street on their way to parochial school. At his trial, Basange admitted that he was naked at the time but kept insisting that he meant no harm. In sentencing him to six months in jail, Justice of the Peace William H. Gray told Basange that "for the first time since I have acted as a magistrate do I regret the limited jurisdiction of my Court, for that alone prevents me from placing you where you would have no opportunity of following your brutal practices."[19]

Compared to Pierre Basange and the lewd women who aggressively peddled their favors on Bath Street, Chinese prostitutes seemed fairly innocuous. In fact, several non-Asian observers marveled at their naiveté. As one remarked, "They are ignorant of the disgrace of their calling: if the term may be allowed, they pursue it innocently." According to another, the Chinese streetwalkers of Los Angeles seemed like "lost children," wandering from one doorway to another. Albert S. Evans, a journalist who toured San Francisco in the early 1870s, wrote sympathetically, if patronizingly, that Chinese prostitutes "are intellectually only children, and are more to be pitied and less condemned than the fallen of their sex of any other race." He reported that they had no trace of modesty, no education, and no experience of the world outside of the brothels where they lived. They were often seen walking hand-in-hand on the streets, laughing and exchanging compliments "like little Caucasian sisters going home from school."[20]

Although Chinese working girls formed friendships with each other, the intense competition for clients, gifts, and potential husbands sometimes provoked violent outbursts among them. A fight between two women, Ah Sing Quay and Ah Sing Foy, resulted in their arrest in Los Angeles in 1869. Another two Chinese women, one of whom had recently secured a husband, were arrested and fined six dollars each in 1871 after they tried "to disfigure each other's countenances" along Calle de los Negros. In one terrific street fight among Chinese women in Santa Barbara, the combatants used knives, sad-irons, and bludgeons. The city marshal declined to intervene.[21]

The Los Angeles press, in a feeble attempt at sarcastic humor, referred to Chinese sex workers as "almond-eyed beauties," "daughters of the sun and moon," "heavenly maidens of the Flowery Kingdom," and so on. The reality was quite different. Women of uncommon beauty, pedigree, or charm were taken as wives or girlfriends when they arrived in America. Those who went to work in brothels tended to be plain peasant girls. Sacramento diarist Joseph Lamson described them as "short, broad-shouldered, coarse-featured, and dark-complexioned." Since their feet had not been bound, they walked "freely and unconstrainedly, though without grace or dignity."[22]

Chinese streetwalkers wore wide, straight, cotton trousers of blue or black that reached to their feet. They clothed their upper bodies with either broadcloth jackets or loose silk tunics that hung down to their knees. Their hair was braided in two strands. When they went out, they covered their heads with striped gingham handkerchiefs, and they clad their feet in blue satin shoes embroidered with bullion. They adorned their wrists and ankles with bracelets of gold, silver, or jade.[23]

These young women may not have been "heavenly maidens," as the papers mockingly described them, but they seemed like godsends to homesick Chinese laborers nonetheless. Immigrant Lee Chew defended his countrymen who patronized bordellos, remarking, "What other set of men so isolated and so surrounded by alien and prejudiced people are more moral? Men, wherever they may be, need the society of women." The word "society," as Lee Chew used it, was not simply a euphemism for copulation. As another immigrant, Ah Quin, indicated in his diary, Chinese men went to brothels not just for sexual gratification but also to relax and socialize in the company of women from their homeland. Like the Chinese casinos, opium parlors, and theaters, bawdy houses offered a few hours of escape from the loneliness and harshness of a foreign land. However, just as an evening of revelry in a gambling hall sometimes ended in a brawl, a visit to a bordello did not always bring comfort. One Sunday evening, after attending a Presbyterian church service and a Bible study, diarist Ah Quin ended up in a "bad Chinese woman['s] room, only fuck once. So mad [at] her."[24]

Chinese disorderly houses attracted non-Asian as well as Chinese clients. Many Chinese men believed that the most debased thing a woman could do was to take a "barbarian" to her bed. Consequently, the higher-class brothels in Chinatown catered to Chinese men only, while the seediest cribs welcomed non-Asians. According to Reverend Otis

Gibson, whites were charged lower rates than Chinese, probably because the establishments that were open to men of all races housed the less desirable women. In one of his odder observations about race relations, Gibson opined that the fact that "dissolute [white] men and depraved boys" visited Chinese prostitutes proved that there was "no impassable abyss preventing the mingling and assimilation of the two races." The clergyman's reference to "depraved boys" was telling. According to interpreter Wo Ben, non-Asian boys only ten or twelve years old were frequent visitors to the Chinese houses of ill fame in California. Moreover, a San Francisco doctor testified that he had treated boys as young as eight for venereal diseases contracted in Chinatown.[25]

In Los Angeles, the fact that an astonishing sixteen Chinese were charged with "keeping and residing in a house of ill fame" in 1862, when the town's entire Chinese population probably numbered no more than sixty, suggested that the bulk of the women's customers were non-Asians. As mentioned earlier, at least one Chinese brothel was located in an American residential district. A couple of Los Angeles court cases provide rare glimpses into the world of the city's Chinese bordellos and their white patrons during the 1870s. In the late hours of a slow business night, a prostitute named Ah Hoo made the mistake of soliciting an undercover policeman, John Fonck, on Sanchez Street behind the Pico House Hotel (one of the few buildings from that era still standing on the plaza). According to his testimony, she called to him, grabbed his coat through a hole in the fence, and asked, "How do you like it?"

He said, "What do you mean?"

"You fuck me for two bits."

"What then?"

Thinking he was haggling, she unlatched the gate, grabbed him by the clothes, and made a more generous offer. "You come in, me give you two fucks for two bits."

Two other women, Ah Choy and Ah Lee, appeared and tried to lure him inside. He entered the hallway of the house, then opened his coat to reveal his badge. As he was arresting the three women, the proprietor, a man named Ah Hoy, ran up, took hold of two of the women, and tried to stop him. Ah Hoy asked, "How much you will take and let the women go?" His attempt to settle the matter on the spot was fruitless.

They were all hauled before the county justices court and fined a total of eighty-five dollars.[26]

In another case, a thirty-two-year-old baker named Henry Armbruster leveled charges that a Chinese prostitute had stolen his money. He had come to the courthouse in Los Angeles to get his naturalization papers, downed some beer at a nearby saloon, and then wandered through Chinatown, where a woman beckoned him inside one of the brothels. She asked for fifty cents, which he gave her. He claimed that she asked for two bits more, then reached around him and took a wad of bills totaling $380 from his back pocket. She ran out of the house. He followed her around a large brick building, but lost her when she disappeared into a basement. The woman's defense attorney questioned him carefully:

"What did you give the four bits to the China woman for?"

"She wanted me to go into her room with her to sleep with her. I gave it to her because she wanted it, but I did not get anything for it. I discovered my money was gone and she went out."

"Did you get into bed with her?"

"I stood by the side of the bed, and she stood right in front of me with both her hands round me. I cannot say which hand she had in my pocket."

Indeed, many of the details were difficult for Armbruster to recall. The court dismissed the charges against the woman. It found instead that Henry Armbruster was "a gambler, was drunk and in the act of visiting a house of prostitution." Therefore, he was not to be believed.[27]

Servitude in a Free Country

How did modest, unsullied young women from China end up selling their bodies for twenty-five cents to any passerby in California's Chinatowns? For the most part, unmarried girls did not willingly leave their homeland or enter the sex trade. Although some Chinese prostitutes worked as free agents in California during the Gold Rush that started in 1849, involuntary servitude soon became the norm.

Some girls were sold into bondage by their families. In times of war or famine, desperately poor parents in China traded their daughters to procurers as the only way of providing for their other children. Orphans were especially likely to be bartered by their relatives. The girls had no say in the decision. The lack of shame that Chinese streetwalkers reportedly displayed may be better explained by their sense of familial duty than by their unawareness of their fallen estate. Although the Chinese did not consider prostitution an honorable occupation, some of these women were secure in the knowledge that they were saving their families in China from starvation.

Other young women were lured by false promises of marriage or jobs. Agents would travel through the rural areas of China, pretending to want the women as second wives. Later, they would sell them to procurers. Some girls were kidnapped by pirates or taken captive during civil warfare. According to the Chinese Six Companies, most of these women came from "decent families," but they were "purchased by racketeers and forced to be prostitutes."[28]

Brothel owners in America imported these young women under contracts of indentured servitude or outright sale. The contracts of service usually required a woman to provide her body for use as a prostitute for four years. During that time, she received no wages, although she got to keep any jewelry, silk, or extra cash that her regular customers gave her as gifts. If she ran away before the end of her term, she had to repay the brothel owner's expenses in locating her. If she got sick and could not work for more ten to fifteen days, an extra month was added to her term of service.

These contracts were highly favorable to the brothel owners. According to one estimate, a prostitute could earn about $850 per year, while the annual cost of her upkeep was not more than $96. Merchant Thomas H. King of San Francisco explained that one method proprietors used to keep women in bondage beyond their term of service was to lend them money for gambling. They often lost the money and thus remained in debt. Their short careers offered little security. Women who caught diseases might be expelled from the bordello and left alone to die. Those who got too old to attract customers sometimes found work as cooks or laundresses.[29]

For many years after the Thirteenth Amendment forbidding involuntary servitude was ratified in 1865, a type of overt slavery still flourished in the brothels of California, which American authorities tolerated and even abetted. The Los Angeles newspapers occasionally railed against the traffic in prostitutes, not so much to defend the rights of the enslaved women as to portray all the Chinese people as venal. However, most Angelenos were indifferent toward the sale of Chinese women in their city. To them, the matter was an internal affair of a foreign community. Moreover, Angelenos were hardly outraged by the concept of slave labor. As recently as the 1850s, they had auctioned off Native Americans in a similar manner, getting them drunk and then bidding for their services once they were incarcerated.[30]

Like other enslaved people, Chinese sex workers were badly treated by both their customers and their keepers. As early as 1863, Los Angeles resident Ah Luce was accused of assault and battery on a Chinese woman. In May 1871, a Chinese woman applied to the city marshal for protection and was lodged in jail, where she remained at her own request. As seen in the previous chapter, the See Yup leader Sing Lee was arrested in July of the same year for beating a woman, who also begged to be housed in jail for safekeeping. A month later, Sam Wing got in a fight with a woman he had purchased named Quang Kong, whom he claimed had taken some of his money and run away. According to the *News*, "He choked her and she clawed him." The mayor fined him eight dollars, which Sam Wing considered an affront to his rights of ownership. A San Francisco streetwalker named Sing Kum claimed that her former mistress used to whip her, pull her hair, and pinch the inside of her cheeks. Another prostitute in that city, Ah Goom, said that even though her keepers had never prohibited her from going outside the brothel, she was afraid to leave for fear that they would punish her.[31]

Not surprisingly, a few desperate prostitutes chose suicide. In 1871, a Los Angeles woman named Sing Hi swallowed half an ounce of opium that she had purchased from an apothecary. According to a news report, the dead woman had become infatuated with a man who refused to marry her. The local press, not missing a chance to mock the Chinese even at a time of sorrow, quipped that Sing Hi had "determined to 'shuffle off this mortal coil,' and reascend to the 'Hi' estate from which she had fallen." In death, Sing Hi was more fortunate than some streetwalkers in that her body was not simply discarded in the street. Her funeral at the City Cemetery "excited much attention from the curious, by the paper-strewing, cracker-firing, and Josh-stick-burning ceremonies."[32]

For all the abuse they endured, women such as Sing Hi often preferred to remain with their Chinese masters rather than risk falling into the hands of non-Asians, who terrified them much more. When the San Francisco police raided the bordello of a madam named Ah Tai, the young women she employed became very uneasy once they were separated from her. A Chinese assistant to Reverend Gibson explained to the three oldest women that they were free to go and would be assisted if they wanted to lead honest lives. However, they all chose to return to Ah Tai. Two younger girls were forced to go to a mission house until guardians could be appointed for them. There, they were miserable and cried bitterly that they wanted to go back to Ah Tai. Gibson posited that the girls were misled into believing that their American rescuers were actually sex traffickers themselves. Most likely, however, these young women simply succumbed to a more general fear that had been instilled in them before they left China: they believed that Westerners were "wild and fierce and wicked" barbarians who "loved to beat people and to rob and murder," in the words of immigrant Lee Chew.[33]

"The Aid of the Law"

For indentured or enslaved Chinese sex workers in America, the avenues of escape were limited. A few fled to mission houses for protection. Others absconded with a lover to start a new life in another town. When a prostitute ran off, however, her owner or his friends in his district association would go to great lengths to recover her, for several reasons—the high profits she earned, the owner's vindictive feelings toward her, and the precedent she would set for others if she were successful. Journalist Albert S. Evans claimed that an owner would spend ten times a prostitute's market value to get her back. He concluded that the young women's chances of avoiding recapture were "very slim indeed."[34]

One of the main reasons Chinese prostitutes were unable to escape was because American lawmen bent over backward to help restore them to sexual slavery. The *Los Angeles News* explained the legal machinations that Chinese flesh traffickers used to get a runaway woman back or to steal a prostitute from another agent. They would swear out a complaint charging her with grand larceny, claiming she had stolen some money or jewelry. Then they would wait until she was arrested, put up bail to get her out of jail, and thereby get her released into their custody—which was "the object of the proceeding."[35] This system was not unique to Los Angeles. Throughout California, dealers in Chinese women leveled false charges of theft against escaped prostitutes and offered rewards to encourage police officers to track them down and bring them back.

Angelenos first witnessed this type of subterfuge in the summer of 1870. On August 25, Sing Lee, the notorious head of the See Yup Company, swore out a warrant for the arrest of a missing prostitute named Sing Yu, whom he described as "full faced and about twenty years old." He claimed that she had broken into a trunk and stolen $500 in jewelry and cash. Chinatown was "thrown into a fever of excitement" over the woman's disappearance.

As Sing Yu's story came to light, it turned out to be much more complicated than a simple case of theft and flight. The previous evening, revelers along Calle de los Negros had seen Juan Espinosa, a regular in the town's roughest neighborhood, waiting with his buggy outside one of the Chinese apartments. Espinosa was not a man to be trifled with; he had once slashed a rival's neck in a fight over a woman.[36] Two Chinese men, Ah Chu and Ah Chung, emerged from the adobe dwelling with Sing Yu and forced the unwilling woman into the buggy. Then Espinosa drove off to his house on First Street.

The See Yup Company offered a one hundred dollar reward for Sing Yu's return. Then the race was on. Three policemen—one of whom, Joe Dye, had a violent temper—got wind that Juan Espinosa had kidnapped the woman. The officers' boss, City Marshal William C. Warren, opened a competing investigation with the help of Deputy Sheriff Sam Bryant. From their sources, Warren and Bryant also learned that Sing Yu was being hidden by Espinosa. Dye's group was "close on the trail," but Warren and Bryant got to Espinosa's house first. They arrested Sing Yu and collected the reward money from her See Yup masters. Policeman Dye had been bested by his boss, and he did not take this defeat lightly.

When Sing Yu was brought before Justice Gray, she maintained that she was innocent, "the victim of conspiracy." If any money was stolen, she said, her kidnappers must have taken it. Justice Gray granted her request to get witnesses for her defense and set her bail at $500. Meanwhile, the city's non-Asian population followed the case closely. The *News* offered its take on the dispute: "There are two China Companies in this city. It is well understood, throughout California, that the ordinary Chinese laborers who visit this country are simply serfs, owing allegiance to these companies. The women are, for the most part, prostitutes, to be sold at a certain price, or rented."[37]

As was typical, this news account of Chinese life in Los Angeles was only about half accurate. For starters, at least five *huiguan* had established a presence in Los Angeles, not two. Much worse, this story reinforced the familiar misconception that Chinese working men were "serfs," even though they had come to America willingly. While they tended to stick by their relatives and the people from their home villages when troubles flared, they did not owe "allegiance" to the district associations. Furthermore, the census of 1870 suggested that fewer than half of the Chinese women in town were prostitutes. Nonetheless, Angelenos who read the papers came to believe that the principal business of the Chinese in their city was procuring and selling women.

Sing Yu's court case resumed on August 27. The See Yup leader Sing Lee appeared again in Justice Gray's court, declaring that he had investigated her kidnapping, and asked that the case be dismissed at his cost. The court records do not indicate what happened to Sing Yu, who was apparently returned to her owner in the See Yup Company. According to news reports, she had "been kidnapped more than once by the rival dealers in prostitution," and her possession "often changed from one company to that of another."

Sing Lee swore out another complaint for the arrest of Sing Yu's abductors, including Juan Espinosa, charging them with the theft. When Espinosa was brought into court, he admitted that Ah Chu and Ah Chung had hired him to take the woman to his house and hide her. From there, he was supposed to convey her to Visalia and deliver her to another dealer in women. For his services in this lucrative transaction, he was to receive $200—twice the monthly salary of Los Angeles's highest paid policemen. Since there was no evidence linking him to the theft of jewelry and cash, Espinosa was discharged.[38] Apparently, kidnapping a foreign prostitute and transferring her from one owner to another did not warrant prosecution in Los Angeles. Disreputable Angelenos who did business with the Chinese underworld bosses found that crime paid handsomely and was likely to go unpunished as long as no Americans were harmed.

Sing Yu vanished a second time seven weeks later, on the night of October 14, 1870. This time she left town of her own free will, and in the company of a Chinese man—possibly a lover. Once more, her master accused her of stealing a gold watch and $130 in gold coin, and, once again, Justice Gray issued a warrant for her arrest. The *Los Angeles News* expressed outrage that the escaped woman might be returned to bondage through "the aid of the law."[39]

For the second time in two months, Sing Lee offered a one hundred dollar reward for Sing Yu's capture. City Marshal William Warren and one of his police officers, José Redona, traced her to Wilmington and then to Anaheim, where "she had hired a Mexican with a stylish turnout." They finally apprehended her in San Buenaventura. They got back to Los Angeles with their prisoner at two o'clock on the morning of October 31, 1870.

That afternoon, Sing Yu was brought before Gray for a hearing. Afterward, Marshal Warren and Policeman Redona started escorting her back to jail. They were in the middle of the street when, according to eyewitness accounts, an angry voice called out from the crowd, "Warren!" Policeman Joe Dye approached the city marshal in a rage. "Warren, what are you going to do about this matter? About the reward? I want my rights."

Warren said, "I don't wish to have any trouble with you. I won't say anything more about it."

That made Dye even madder. "I want that money. You have robbed me of that money." They stood only a few feet apart. The two officers loathed each other. Only two months had passed since Warren had outmaneuvered Dye and received the previous one hundred dollar reward for the same woman. This time around, Warren and Redona had done the legwork and located Sing Yu. However, Dye had telegraphed the warrant to the marshal of San Buenaventura, authorizing him to detain her. Each lawman thought he deserved the money.

"I don't want anything to do with you," the marshal told Dye. "Go away." A crowd of both Chinese and non-Asian men surrounded them, drawn by the shouting.

"You know you have not treated me right."

"Dye, I know you want to fight."

"I don't care if you are city marshal. Do you think I'm going to be swindled out of my money?"

Several bystanders noticed that Warren was holding a derringer in his left hand, hiding it behind his back. All day Warren had been on edge; several people had warned him that Dye was threatening to kill him. He told one man, "If Joe Dye ever crooks his finger at me, I'll shoot him like a dog."

Dye leaned on the small cane he held in his right hand. "You have wronged me and defrauded me out of my rights," he roared. "If you don't do me right, I'll go and expose you in the courts."

Warren snarled, "If you say that I've defrauded you out of your rights, you are a damned dirty liar."

Dye raised his cane as if to strike. Immediately, Warren's left arm shot out from behind him. He thrust the derringer forward and fired at Dye's head.

The policeman jumped back and staggered a little. Then he stood up straight. The bullet had grazed his face at the corner of his left eye.

Dye released his cane and reached beneath his coat. Warren dropped his derringer. Both peace officers drew six-shooters and started firing rapidly at each other. The spectators jumped back as the lawmen's wild shots—eight or ten in all—struck at random. Officer Redona was shot through his right arm above the elbow, and Deputy Constable Robert Hester was hit in his right hand. Another bullet shattered the jaw of a Chinese onlooker.

Warren fell backward, clutching his revolver in both hands. "I'm killed," he groaned. Dye, though shot in the thigh, rushed to his wounded superior, struck at his head with his pistol, grabbed him with both hands, and bit him. Several men from the crowd seized Dye by the throat and pulled him off. Warren tried to get up, but he was too badly hurt. The bullet was lodged in his groin and had pierced his bladder.

The city marshal died the next morning, the first member of the Los Angeles Police Department killed in the line of duty—albeit at the hands of his own officer. William Warren's funeral at the Catholic Church was one of the largest ever seen in Los Angeles at that time, with a procession of nearly one hundred carriages following the horse-drawn hearse to the cemetery. His widow, Juana Lopez Warren, lashed out at his killer: "Base, ungrateful wretch, who so often has received the gratuitous help and kind assistance of the very man whom he wantonly followed up, and forced into a difficulty which deprived him of life." But Joe Dye was cleared of manslaughter charges. The witnesses agreed that Warren had fired first.[40]

Meanwhile, Sing Yu was released for lack of evidence, and her master spirited her away. A journalist for the *News* suggested that "she, like other maidens, had been the victim of the cruel men, who took both her and the property."[41] Which "cruel men" did the writer mean? The Chinese racketeers who kept her in bondage, or the American law officers who repeatedly brought her back to them?

"Any Sum in Reason"

For women in Sing Yu's situation, the most promising way out of the flesh trade was marriage. When a brothel customer took his favorite girl as his bride, however, one major problem remained: either the woman or her new husband would have to buy out her contract. Otherwise, they would face harassment, even death threats, from the tong henchmen hired by her keepers. In many cases, neither husband nor wife had enough money. Some couples tried running away to another town, but brothel owners pursued them ruthlessly and persecuted them. These couples knew they could not turn for help to American policemen, who would be all too willing to return the wives to their keepers in exchange for a reward.

Thus, even those Chinese women who married laborers often had a hard time escaping bondage, as illustrated by a high-profile case in San Diego. The girl in this instance was Sing Yee, who had been born into a wealthy family in China. Rebels kidnapped her when they burned her family's homestead and killed her parents. At age sixteen, she was sold to sex traf-fickers, who sent her to California. At first, she was placed in a brothel on Calle de los Negros in Los Angeles; then she was forced to work in San Diego. Her purchasers beat her, leaving a deep scar on her left temple.

She had been in San Diego only a couple of weeks when Ah Quock, a small, "square-built" domestic in the household of George P. and Harriett Marston, met the "bright and intelligent" young woman and learned about her predicament. He told his employers how pretty Sing Yee was and that he was determined to marry her. "It is evidently a real love affair," Mrs. Marston wrote. After persuading the Marstons to let him bring Sing Yee to their home for safety, Ah Quock sneaked her out of the gambling hall where she worked. Sing Yee had been traumatized by her entire experience in California, and staying in the home of American "barbarians" gave her little relief. At the Marston residence, "she exhibited uncontrollable terror."

The groom, Ah Quock, planned their wedding for four o'clock the following afternoon. However, the woman's owners, Sin Lee and Ah Won, succeeded in getting an order for her to appear in court at nine o'clock the next morning. They leveled the usual charges of grand larceny of a skirt and some trinkets. Ah Quock prudently decided to move up the wedding. At half past eight the following morning, he and Sing Yee were married in the Presbyterian Church. The sanctuary was overflowing with a huge crowd of the town's American elite, for this was the first time a Chinese couple in San Diego had married in a Christian church. The bride was dressed in dark, full trousers and a matching blouse buttoned up to her throat. She wore a pair of gold earrings strung with shell circlets, and her hair, brushed flat against her head, was topped with an orange wreath. San Diego's non-Asian population followed the love story with great interest; there was unprecedented demand for the Sunday newspaper that told it.

After the wedding, the couple went to the judge's office to respond to the charge against Sing Yee. At first, the woman's owners were willing to resolve the dispute for $150, but later they reneged. The groom, Ah Quock, was "anxious to settle" and was willing to pay "any sum in reason," because he feared that otherwise they would kill him. They finally negotiated a fee agreeable to everyone, and Ah Quock paid it. He took his bride to live in his room at the Marston home, which Sing Yee kept "perfectly clean" while she learned "to work and read," reported Harriett Marston. She also commented, "They seem as happy as two kittens."

However, their troubles were not yet over. Less than two months after the wedding, a man named Ah Pot swore out a complaint in Los Angeles charging the new bride, Sing Yee, with stealing jewelry and coins worth $290. A warrant was placed in the hands of a local policeman, Emil Harris, "whose jurisdiction, it would seem . . ., extends even to San Diego," quipped the *Evening Express*.

Four days later, Harris arrived in San Diego on the steamer *Orizaba* and quietly asked where Sing Yee was staying. Realizing that her arrest would cause an uproar, he thought it best to wait until just before the boat was scheduled to depart the next afternoon at two o'clock. He obtained the help of the city marshal. At half past noon the following day, they showed up at the Marston residence. The household was thrown into turmoil by the officers' arrival, with both the family and the newlyweds trying to prevent the arrest. George Marston hurried off to find a lawyer. Sing Yee "was dissolved in terror, and her screams were heartrending," according to newspaper accounts. She was "borne shrieking" to the *Orizaba*, "sobbing her heart out." During the trip to Los Angeles, several passengers were upset by the cries they heard coming from a stateroom near the bar.

The people of San Diego were up in arms. A local newspaper noted in disgust, "A woman legally married is torn away from her husband to be made an enforced prostitute." George P. Marston hired a lawyer in Los Angeles on the woman's behalf, and his twenty-two-year-old son, George W. Marston (who later became a well-known philanthropist), took the stagecoach to attend the hearing there. Finally, the controversy was resolved. Justice of the Peace John Trafford released Sing Yee after determining that she had committed no crime, and she returned safely to her husband in San Diego. Unlike many women in her situation, her story had a happy ending—although it left newspaper readers with the impression that virtually all Chinese were corrupt and immoral.[42]

American Marriage

Ah Quock and Sing Yee married in a church, because the groom was a Christian convert. Most couples favored traditional Chinese ceremonies. Others would simply "live together as husband and wife," according to Reverend Augustus Ward Loomis. Only a few of the early Chinese couples in the United States sought a civil marriage under American law and took out a license.

That changed abruptly in Los Angeles in the fall of 1871, when five Chinese couples married before a justice of the peace during a five-month period. The local press took notice. The *Star* speculated that these couples wanted marriage licenses to thwart brothel owners if they filed lawsuits claiming that the brides belonged to them and had broken their contracts of service. Similarly, the *News* observed that the weddings may have been a way to avoid paying the purchase money to the woman's owner. The same newspaper also noted, "The Chinese have found that by going through the form of marriage as required by the law of the country, they can defy their rivals."[43]

Not all of these civil marriages were voluntary on the woman's part. In some cases, the purported "bride" was actually an enslaved sex worker who had been kidnapped by her owner's competitors. For a brief period starting in 1871, forced marriage supplanted bogus charges of theft as the primary means of procuring Chinese women from members of other *huiguan* in Los Angeles. One observer explained that "in order for a Chinaman to hold a prostitute, he goes to a white justice of the peace or minister and gets married." This happened not only to prostitutes. A few women who were stolen and forced into these sham marriages were already wives.[44]

Other weddings were genuine love matches. While these civil marriages were entitled to the protection of American law, they did not necessarily give legitimate Chinese couples the peace they hoped for. When One Za wed a Los Angeles prostitute named Sing Hee, the affair set off a bitter quarrel in Chinatown that lasted several days. The episode began one night when Charley Chung, a principal in Yo Hing's Hong Chow Company, hired a hack and tried to rescue Sing Hee from a brothel on Alameda Street. He failed to secure her, but later that night the bride-to-be managed to flee to Yo Hing's house. Her owners approached Police Officers Emil Harris, George Gard, and Jesús Bilderrain, all of whom regularly patrolled China-town. They claimed, as usual, that Sing Hee had been "enticed away" and had taken with her "certain articles that belonged to other parties."

The officers searched the home of Yo Hing, who protested vehe-
mently. Yo Hing claimed that "his bedroom was invaded, and the
clothes stripped from himself and wife . . ., and every nook and corner
of his domicile peered into—even the boxes broken open for inspection."
However, there was no sign of the missing woman. Frustrated, the
police arrested Charley Chung for attempting to steal Sing Hee from
her keepers—that is, they charged him with the "crime" of trying to
help an enslaved prostitute escape. (Incidentally, Sing Hee belonged to
members of the See Yup and Nin Yung Companies. Less than a month
earlier, the Nin Yung Company had given Officers Harris and Gard a
gift in appreciation of their "services," as discussed previously.)

As it turned out, Sing Hee had fled to the home of a rival policeman,
the infamous Joe Dye, where she spent the night in hiding. Early the
next morning, she and One Za were married before Justice of the Peace
John Trafford. While the wedding was underway, Yo Hing appeared on
the street, loudly complaining about the police assault on his home the
night before. Officers Harris and Bilderrain arrested him for his "noisy,
boisterous and threatening conduct." His wild outburst was most likely
a calculated effort to deflect attention from the marriage ceremony,
which proceeded uninterrupted.

The *News* interviewed Yo Hing after his release from jail. He provided a pithy summary of the recent events in Chinatown, and the
newspaper delighted in playing up his pidgin English: "Chinaman very
smart; heap stealee woman. Woman no likee be bad; woman she get
married—bad Chinaman he likee sell woman. Police likee money—
he heap catchee woman—big pay."[45]

Yo Hing's candid assessment of the Los Angeles flesh trade omitted
only one major group of players in this sordid charade: the local judges
and lawyers who chose not to inquire very thoroughly into the true
circumstances of the indentured or enslaved Chinese women brought
before them. One member of the Los Angeles judiciary, Justice of the
Peace William H. Gray, finally got tired of hearing cases that involved
the sale and exploitation of women. He was called on to settle a contract
dispute in which Ah Chu was supposed to receive $300 for locating and
retrieving a missing woman who was the "servant" of Fong Chong. Ah
Chu found the woman in a laundry and bought her from the owner for
$125, then delivered her to Fong Chong. Justice Gray exploded:

On inquiry as to the present whereabouts of the woman, witness coolly stated that Fong Chong had sold her to a man in Bakersfield! Plaintiff having closed his testimony, defendant[']s attorney moved that this cause be dismissed on the ground that the law does not recognize slavery and that the contract between the parties is not only null and void but criminal. . . . [T]he court, . . . in dismissing the cause, regrets its want of power to punish both parties as they deserve, for the violation of the Laws of the Land, and afterward, for contempt of this Court in attempting to make it a party to the transaction.[46]

However, Justice Gray's duties required him to continue hearing these cases for several years. His courtroom was subsequently the scene of yet another suit in which "an old hag" claimed ownership of "a woman purchased for vile purposes, but who has managed to escape from her clutches to try to lead a decent life."[47] Ironically, the Chinese women who were forced into prostitution, the only blameless participants in the sex traffic, were the ones most often accused of crimes if they managed to escape from their shadowy adobe prisons along Calle de los Negros.

5

"Us" and "Them"

DURING THE LATE HOURS OF March 2, 1864, a gang of local thugs amused themselves by terrorizing the Chinese prostitutes of Los Angeles. They broke into several brothels where the women lived, demolishing their furniture and generally wrecking their quarters. According to the news report, they acted "in pure viciousness." They were never identified or brought to justice. Instead, the law was invoked to punish the victims. Ten days afterward, three Chinese women and one man were prosecuted for keeping houses of "bawdy and ill fame" and fined one hundred dollars each.[1]

The annals of the American West are full of similar stories about racially motivated attacks on Chinese immigrants and the injustices they faced. What set this episode apart was the reaction in the press. The *Los Angeles Star* reported the incident with none of the sneering, juvenile humor that later attended all local news stories about the Chinese. Instead, the newspaper described the perpetrators as "unmanly" and "evil disposed persons" whose actions warranted "public execration." In the *Star*'s view, this single occurrence was "enough to stain the character of any community."

More surprisingly, the news account was exceedingly delicate in characterizing the Chinese women and their occupation. The article never used terms such as "prostitute," "house of ill fame," or "disorderly house."

Instead, it described the women's "domiciles" as "humble and unobtrusive establishments." Though it acknowledged that some Angelenos thought the brothels were annoyances, the *Star* maintained that as long as the women "keep within the limits prescribed by law, they are not nuisances, and are entitled to the protection of the law in their persons and property."[2] This 1864 article, one of only a handful about the local Chinese that appeared in the Los Angeles press between 1857 and 1868, set a benchmark for measuring how drastically Angelenos' attitudes toward the town's Chinese residents would change in just a few years.

Early Contacts

The brothel article was not just a fluke. In the early 1860s, the few references to the Chinese in the Los Angeles press were typically neutral in tone. More significantly, very few attacks on Chinese residents were mentioned in the town's newspapers and court records during the 1850s and 1860s. While the atmosphere of violence that permeated Los Angeles would not seem conducive to racial tolerance, it appears that non-Asian Angelenos more or less ignored their Chinese neighbors, adhering to a "live and let live" philosophy.

In a sense, that was not surprising. Though Los Angeles was still a small, remote place with a tough reputation, its citizens, by and large, were not provincial. Indeed, the town boasted a cosmopolitan mix of cultures and peoples. On the streets, one could hear English, Spanish, French, German, Italian, and Chinese spoken. Ludwig Louis Salvator, the Austrian archduke who visited Los Angeles in the 1870s, thought that the "idea of equality" was "highly developed" there. He noted, "Any stranger, provided he shows good breeding, is looked upon with favor."[3]

Initially, that included the Chinese. In 1852, one newspaper predicted rapid assimilation of the Chinese in California: "The China Boys will yet vote at the same polls, study at the same schools, and bow at the same altar as our own countrymen." The early Los Angeles historian James Miller Guinn wrote that when they first arrived, the Chinese were "flattered and complimented by the presence of distinguished citizens at their meetings." The admiration was mutual. An American correspondent traveling in Asia reported in 1871 that Los Angeles enjoyed an "enviable reputation" in the Far East. The *Los Angeles Star* went so far as to express hope that successful Chinese businessmen would choose southern California as a place to retire: "Let them all come. There is room enough, and to spare for all such." Some Chinese in Los Angeles even married Europeans.[4]

For the most part, non-Asians in California who engaged Chinese laborers spoke very highly of them. Charles Nordhoff, a journalist who visited the state in the early 1870s, suggested that employers held their Chinese workers in high regard because they were industrious, patient, dependable, and quick to learn. Another writer, Charles Loring Brace, said that Chinese laborers were the neatest and most respectable group of working men he had ever seen, with faces "of scholars and gentlemen." L. J. Rose, Jr., whose father owned a vineyard near Los Angeles, recalled that the family's Chinese employees rarely missed a day's work.[5]

Only a minority of Angelenos regularly interacted with the Chinese and learned much about their customs. The 1870 census suggested that about thirty Chinese men worked alongside, and lived under the same roof as, Anglo or Latino farm laborers, domestics, and hotel or restaurant employees. Although they did not get to know each other well, Chinese and non-Asians who worked together fraternized and enjoyed teaching each other a few words of their respective languages, according to Rose. In addition, thirty-seven Los Angeles households employed Chinese domestics in 1870. Many of the town's most substantial citizens hired Chinese house servants and cooks. Even the kitchen of the local jail was run by a Chinese cook named Ah Sum, who was admired for his culinary skill.[6]

The average Angeleno dealt only with Chinese manual laborers, launderers, and vegetable peddlers. However, some of the more affluent residents visited Chinese physicians, because American medicine during the nineteenth century was largely ineffectual in treating some types of injuries and infections. One Chinese doctor, Chee Long "Gene" Tong, sought to attract a non-Asian clientele in 1870 by setting up a drugstore and examining room in the house of William Abbott, who built the Merced Theatre south of the plaza (still standing today). The enterprising Dr. Tong also operated an employment-brokerage business at the same location, so that his patients could arrange to hire Chinese cooks and farmhands when they came for treatment. Another Chinese doctor in Los Angeles, Ah Poo Ji Tong, advertised for patients in both English and Spanish.[7]

The services of Chinese herbalists were comparatively expensive. Consequently, their non-Asian clients in Los Angeles tended to be "well-to-do people, many women, business men, capitalists, and a few professional men,—lawyers, journalists, and even physicians," according to newsman William M. Tisdale. Most of them sought out Chinese medicine as a last resort in treating chronic disorders. The reverse also occurred occasionally. Yo Hing's wife visited an American physician, John S. Griffin, who treated her for curvature of the spine. Tisdale further noted that the Angelenos who consulted Chinese doctors were impressed by their abilities: "Some are loud in their praises, and freely assert that the Chinese system of medicine is more rational, more thoroughly in accord with nature, and more successful than any other. 'I am sorry,' said one of these, 'for what I know of Chinese medicine; sorry to think that these degraded heathen can do things with their herbs which our own doctors, with all their skill and knowledge, cannot do.'"[8]

The epithet "degraded heathen" fell in the middle of a very backhanded compliment. Indeed, Angelenos showed a peculiar mix of tolerant restraint and offhand bigotry toward the Chinese in the 1860s. They recognized the immigrants' right to be there and thought they should be protected by law. At the same time, they looked down on them and often made fun of their ways. They referred to the Chinese as "Celestials," a nod to the Celestial Empire, or as sons and daughters of the "Flowery Kingdom." Both titles emphasized their foreignness. They called individual Chinese men "John" and women "Mary" (or "Maly")—names that sounded harmless enough but were used with pejorative intent, much like "Sambo."

Sometimes the Chinese resisted. Writer Sidney Andrews recalled a time when he was staying at a San Francisco hotel and needed some clothes laundered. Standing in the door of his room, he called to a Chinese man walking down the hall, "John! John! Oh John!" The man ignored him, and Andrews followed. In the next hall, he called again, "John! Oh John! Washing!" The man kept going. Andrews ran down the hall and overtook him on the stairway. "I want you to do some washing for me, John," he said. "Me not John!" the man finally replied.

He handed Andrews a card that read "Hop Long." As they walked back to Andrews's room, Hop Long admonished the hotel guest at length that Chinese, like Americans, preferred to be called by their proper names. Andrews concluded, "That's how this washerman from Canton taught me good manners."[9]

Other confrontations did not end so harmoniously. Two Los Angeles teenagers, Guillermo Moreno and Abran Bareles, were once passing Lee Ying and another Chinese man on Main Street when Moreno asked them, "Where you going, John?" One of the Chinese men replied in perfect English, "Go to hell, you son of a bitch." The boys asked, "What did you call us sons of bitches for?" A fight broke out. Bareles claimed that he got hit in the head with a rock, and Lee Ying swore that Moreno stole his watch.[10]

Two stories recorded by non-Asians who immigrated to California during the 1860s illustrate the ambivalence they felt toward the Chinese they met. The first is a letter that Ezra Gregg wrote to his siblings from the northern California mining town of Downieville in 1863:

> We are living by ourselves at present in the woods six miles from D'vile and our neighbors and associates are Chinamen and other *varmints* that inhabit this part of the world we are thronged with China reptiles most, they are in my cabin every night talking their lingo and it would make you think of a flock of black birds if you could only hear them but I get along with them very well. I have been with them so much that sometimes I think that I am a Chinaman they are very good neighbors they will do anything *for me.* Using a California phrase they are *stuck after* me I have to do the most of their business among the Whites and anything I tell them they think is so. I have to eat with them some times and drink whiskey with them (which goes very much against my stomach you know) and we make things as agreeable as the circumstances will permit . . . .[11]

After his initial references to "varmints" and "reptiles," it comes as a surprise that Gregg got along "very well" with his "very good" Chinese neighbors. In fact, he seemed to enjoy a warm acquaintance with them, even if their communication was limited. Like the Los Angeles patient who marveled at the wonderful things the "degraded heathen" doctors could do, Gregg—perhaps to satisfy his readers' expectations or to ease his own embarrassment about enjoying the company of these much-maligned foreigners—seemed to find it necessary to cloak his affection for the Chinese behind disparaging terms.

A second chronicler, Elizabeth Fitzgerald B. Knowlton, described her encounter with some Chinese gold miners on an overland journey west in 1866. Her traveling party was running low on food when they camped near the miners along a river one evening. While the men in her group were taking care of the horses, Knowlton's husband asked her to go to the "Chiney Camp" and buy some rice for their supper. When she arrived, the Chinese miners were seated at a long table. "I could not make them understand what I wanted," she related. "They would not give me anything but fixed a place at the table and told me to eat." Knowlton inspected the pinkish meat and feared that "it was rats or young Pups," as she "had been told they ate them." The miners insisted that she join them and served her a generous portion. They also poured her some brandy. She wrote, "What could I do but eat? I was afraid not to." Afterward, she finally made them understand that she wanted to buy rice. She did so, and one of the Chinese men accompanied her back to her camp. However, he refused to sample the food she cooked, which left her "quite provoked," as she had eaten "something of everything they had."[12]

A People Apart

Unlike recent immigrants from Europe or Mexico, the Chinese found it difficult to blend into their California communities. Language and cultural barriers made it hard for them to mix casually with non-Asians. Consequently, they tended to remain a people apart. They bought most of their supplies at Chinese-owned stores and limited their social outings to the restaurants and gambling halls of Chinatown.

Americans, who did little to welcome the Chinese into their society, were also quick to criticize the newcomers for failing to assimilate. Journalist Albert S. Evans wrote, "What a strange, peculiar people are these Chinese! Dwelling among us, they are not of us." Reverend Gibson thought that their assimilation was slow because "the Chinese are extremely conservative, and it takes a long time to permeate the thought of a whole Chinese community with a favorable notion of any change in their national customs."[13]

According to Gibson, the men's practice of wearing long, braided queues was the biggest single obstacle to their assimilation. He explained that this fashion had nothing to do with religion but instead signaled their loyalty to the reigning dynasty. Indeed, the tradition dated back to the early seventeenth century, when the Manchus compelled all Chinese men to wear queues as an open sign of allegiance. Gibson observed that "Chinese dandies" paid "great attention to this part of their toilet," neatly combing and braiding their hair and attaching a silk tassel at the end. Another writer explained that the queue was considered sacrosanct: "Never can a Chinaman be persuaded that he can survive the loss of that emblem of dignity." Since queues got in the way when the men were working, laborers would wind them close around their heads, "but gentry, scholars, men of leisure and society, never."[14]

Their clothes also set them apart. When they first arrived in America, Chinese men wore petticoat trousers that reached to the knees, large quilted jackets lined with sheepskin, blue stockings, shoes of thick cotton cloth, and huge basket hats made of split bamboo. Soon, however, they adopted American attire. Artist and diarist Joseph Lamson thought they made this accommodation mostly out of necessity, as their clothes from home soon wore out and Chinese tailors were a rarity in the United States. The first American garb that caught their fancy was coarse, heavy cowhide boots. Eventually, most Chinese abandoned their loose pantaloons for broadcloth trousers and purchased broad-brimmed black felt hats. One sea captain who had visited many places where overseas Chinese lived remarked that the United States was the only country in which Chinese men concealed their queues and dressed like the locals.[15]

Over the years, the Chinese of California became increasingly mindful that American labor agitators were looking for any excuse to expel them from the country, so they stepped up their efforts to fit in. When John Tambolin invited journalists to attend the Chinese New Year festivities in Los Angeles in 1866, one reporter, impressed by the finery and hospitality, admitted that he "left with a better opinion and feelings towards the Moon Eyed race." By 1871, the Chinese of Bakersfield showed "a disposition to appear as much like Americans, and as

little like Chinamen, as possible." The officers of the Chinese Six Companies in San Francisco maintained friendly relations with prominent
citizens and occasionally invited distinguished visitors to a grand
Chinese dinner.[16]

Even more impressive were the newcomers' strenuous efforts to
master English. Nineteenth-century ethnographer Stewart Culin
remarked that the desire "to learn the language of his adopted country
seems to be one of the highest ambitions of the Chinese immigrant." Wo
Kee, a laborer in Santa Barbara, wrote to a friend in Pasadena, "I, a thousand times, think it very important for our countrymen in California to
learn English." It did not help that American journalists loved to
ridicule their English usages and missteps. However, given the short
time most Chinese had been in America, Reverend Gibson thought the
surprising thing was "not that they know so little, but that they know
so much of our language."[17] Testimony that several Chinese merchants
gave before Congress in 1890—though a generation after the events of
this book—demonstrated that they had become completely fluent in
English.

For all their deliberate attempts to appear less foreign, the Chinese
showed no more inclination to mingle socially with people outside their
own community than non-Asians did. One writer maintained that they
seldom accepted invitations from non-Asians, other than to make "cer-
emonious" visits, and rarely asked Americans to their homes. As a
result, non-Asians had few opportunities to see the Chinese in their
"social relaxations." Even Chinese laborers who worked on remote
farms or ranches, cut off from the company of their countrymen,
usually seemed to prefer solitude to socializing with the Americans
around them. According to one observer, Chinese servants appeared
"content to be alone in a house," and loneliness did not "make them
seek the companionship of other races." It was also said that the Chinese
wife, unlike other immigrant women, made "no attempt to know us."[18]

Early California historians attributed the reticence of the Chinese
immigrants to the mistreatment they suffered at the hands of non-
Asians. According to Hubert Howe Bancroft, the Chinese "exhibited a
disposition to hold aloof from the white race . . . as much from choice
as from recognition of the unfriendliness visible in the looks and acts
of their American or European neighbors." James Miller Guinn posited

that the Chinese despised the "white devils" among whom they lived, but added that this was unsurprising given how badly they were treated. Memoirist Samuel Bowles also contended that non-Asians' harassment of the Chinese had "driven them back upon their naturally self-contained natures and habits."[19]

While persecution by non-Asians was the most significant factor, the Chinese immigrants' aloofness also stemmed from their national pride and their initial disdain for the people they met in America. Chinese citizens, no matter how humble their circumstances, were heirs to one of the great ancient civilizations, a fact that seemed to help them maintain their self-esteem and dignity in a land where they were frequently called "heathen," "inferior," "filthy," "depraved," and "repulsive." After California Governor John Bigler tried to restrict immigration in 1852, Chinese merchant Norman Asing responded indignantly, "[W]e would beg to remind you that when your nation was a wilderness, and the nation from which you sprung *barbarous*, we exercised most of the arts and virtues of civilized life." When immigrant Lee Chew was growing up in his village in China, his grandfather told him to remember that the Chinese "had invented and discovered everything that was good."[20]

Even ordinary Chinese laborers with little education or property could claim an extended family, a village, and a national history as their own.[21] No matter how long he stayed in America, each man had a specific place on the Pearl River Delta where he could always feel he belonged and would be welcomed back, because his relatives were long-established there. They looked down on the rootless non-Asian opportunists and transient riffraff they encountered in California, people who did not even know their great-grandparents' names and whose only concern was the here and now. An early immigrant named Lu Chong expounded on this deficiency in the American character when he wrote to a friend back home, "These people have no national genealogy; their history is spanned within four-score years, and their ancestry is tinged with the blood of every nationality of Europe." He observed that Americans had no "past for them to recur to, and their hearts and hopes are thus dependent on the present and the future."[22]

By and large, the early Chinese found American customs and values unappealing. Zhang Deyi, a Chinese diplomat who visited the United States in 1868, thought that American food tasted "like the rank odor of sheep" and that the practice of blowing a kiss to a member of the opposite sex was "wanton in the extreme." When the "barbarian women" ate their meal, he observed, "A cacophony of *dingdang* noises was the sound of all the people wielding their knives and forks." Lee Chew disclosed that some of his countrymen living in the United States believed "that there is no marriage in this country, that the land is infested with demons and that all the people are given over to general wickedness."[23]

Even though Chinese merchants such as John Tambolin made an effort to befriend the prominent Anglo and Latino men of their California towns, they had little desire to get to know ordinary white Americans. Samuel Bowles remarked, "They look down even with contempt upon our newer and rougher civilization, regarding us barbaric in fact, and calling us in their hearts, if not in speech, 'the foreign devils.'" Clergyman and newspaper editor Ng Poon Chew admitted that, on the whole, few Chinese would mingle "with the lower classes of Italians and other European races," because they felt superior to them "in morality." Lee Chew was even more bluntly dismissive of his white fellow immigrants in New York: "Irish fill the almshouses and prisons and orphan asylums, Italians are among the most dangerous of men, Jews are unclean and ignorant."[24]

The Chinese bristled whenever whites lumped them into the same generic "non-white" racial classification as African Americans and Native Americans. In Norman Asing's rebuttal to Governor Bigler, he complained that the Chinese "are as much allied to the *African* race and the red man as you are yourself." The Chinese merchants of San Francisco were outraged that whites treated them "as if we were the same as Indians" and viewed them "as equals with this uncivilized race of men." As these comments demonstrated, some Chinese living in America adopted the bigoted attitudes of the locals with whom they did business. Journalist Liang Qichao even subscribed to white Americans' ugliest prejudices about African Americans, writing that black men "would die nine times over without regret if they could possess a white woman's flesh."[25]

In the end, the contacts between the early Chinese immigrants and people of all other races living in the United States remained limited and superficial. Both the Chinese and their non-Asian neighbors bore some responsibility for not bothering to get to know each other. Reverend Huie Kin, who emigrated from China to California as a teenager in 1868, reflected late in life on the racial prejudice that he encountered in the United States. "As I now look back," he wrote, "I feel that we ourselves were partly to blame." He thought that his fellow Chinese "were too slow in adapting ourselves to the life of the people among whom we lived, moved, and had our material well-being." And the Americans, rather than trying to understand the difficulties faced by newcomers in a strange land, simply came to believe that the Chinese "have no business here, and never can form part of our people."[26]

"A Horde of Idolatrous Barbarians"

In January 1869, the *Los Angeles News*, until then a semiweekly publication, became the town's first daily newspaper. The publishers, Andrew J. King and R. H. Offutt, were staunchly Democratic, pro-white-labor men. That meant their paper was highly sympathetic to the anti-Chinese demagogues who had become increasingly vocal in San Francisco. Up to that point, the Los Angeles press had voiced few objections to Chinese labor—aside from a passing reference to "Chinese slavery" or to "being troubled with the outcasts of the Flowery Kingdom," or an isolated column in 1867 decrying the wages at which they were willing to work.[27] However, most of the local coverage of the Chinese prior to 1869 had ranged from neutral to somewhat positive.

Things changed abruptly that year when the nascent daily *News* launched a prolonged series of vitriolic editorials railing against Chinese immigration. They recited the standard arguments that the Chinese, who lived "like rats in one tenement," were too frugal and servile for American and European laborers in California to compete with. According to one editorial, the Chinese laborer's habits were such that he could live at one-fifth the cost of a white man. The *News* opined that cheap Chinese labor would encourage capitalists to trample the rights of white laborers, decimating "the working classes of the superior races." The editors predicted that the influx of Chinese to California would eventually force the American middle class "back to a brutish, mere physical existence." Furthermore, according to the *News*, the Chinese immigrants' entire purpose in life was to save money and send it back to China, and they added "nothing but vice and prostitution to society."[28]

These diatribes were motivated not only by the perceived threat from Chinese labor in California but also by fear that the impending passage of the Fifteenth Amendment ("The right of citizens of the United States to vote shall not be denied or abridged by the United States or by any State on account of race, color, or previous condition of servitude") might pave the way for Chinese citizenship and suffrage. The *News* proclaimed that if the Amendment guaranteeing voting rights for all races were ratified, the next step would be naturalization for the Chinese. "Permit the hordes of pagans that are daily seeking our shores to come here," exclaimed one editorial, and "they will avail themselves of the right to become citizens and voters." The expansion of voting rights would enable the Chinese to flood the country with "a horde of idolatrous barbarians." Even the California Supreme Court, the state's bastion of justice, was alarmed by the "actual and present danger," as it put it, that "we might soon see them at the polls, in the jury box, upon the bench, and in our legislative halls." Significantly, the California legislature rejected the Fifteenth Amendment and did not ratify it until 1962.[29]

The hysterical fear of a "Chinese invasion" seemed quite real to many Californians in the 1870s. The number of Chinese arrivals in the United States increased from 2,242 in 1866 to 18,021 in 1875. In 1876, a California farmer named John Mellon testified before Congress, "If Chinese immigration continues for twenty years as it has for the last two years, the Chinese will be telling us to get up and leave. . . . This is 1876, is it not? In 1976, if Chinese immigration continues, the Chinese will be celebrating the anniversary of their independence from the United States."[30]

The torrent of anti-Chinese, pro-white-labor rhetoric that the *News* unleashed in 1869 does not appear to have been sparked by changes in Los Angeles's demographics or economy. While the local Chinese population was growing, it made up only about 3 percent of the town's total by 1870. Moreover, the *News* welcomed non-Asian newcomers, proclaiming "there is room for them and many more." The fact that the editors targeted only Chinese immigrants, not those from Europe, Mexico, or other states in the union, belied the idea that Los Angeles was getting too many new workers for the number of jobs available.[31]

In fact, despite the economic downturn in northern California, Los Angeles was booming in 1869. New buildings were springing up, and carpenters and masons were in high demand. Almost two thousand new houses were built in the small town between 1869 and 1872.[32] Rather than commenting on the local labor situation, the editors of the *News* seem to have been aping the anti-Chinese sentiment filtering down from northern California, which had intensified since 1867.

The stance taken by the *News* was by no means a universal trend in the California press. Newspaper editors in Bakersfield, about one hundred miles northwest of Los Angeles, complained about receiving written rants from "the demagogues in San Francisco" that were "designed to bias us unfavorably" toward Chinese immigrants. In Los Angeles, the *News*'s main competitor, the *Star*, attacked the "inflammatory language" used by anti-Chinese agitators in San Francisco, warning portentously in 1870 that this kind of rhetoric could lead to "violence and mob law." The *Santa Barbara Press* also thought that anti-Chinese journals such as the *News* could provoke actual harm, "inciting ignorant and desperate men to oppress and maltreat Chinamen."[33]

The primary objection to Chinese laborers—that they undercut the wages paid to white workers and would eventually displace them—was open to question, at least in some occupations. Lee Chew, for one, claimed that the cry of cheap labor was a falsehood. Similarly, Ng Poon Chew pointed out that, as a rule, the Chinese were paid fairly good wages. Journalist Charles Nordhoff also contended that the Chinese received just as high wages as anyone else and that they did not deprive white men of work. California historian Hubert Howe Bancroft maintained that the increase in the number of foreign-born workers from 1865 to 1875 resulted in "no great reduction in the price of labor. Even the influx of Chinese laborers made no perceptible change in the labor market for a period of from six to ten years, and then not because labor was too abundant, but because money was more scarce."[34]

It was true that Chinese farmhands, factory employees, and railroad crews in California typically worked for lower wages than their white counterparts. In 1870, after Irish factory workers in San Francisco went on strike in an effort to increase their earnings from $3 to $4 per day, management replaced them with Chinese who worked for a daily rate of $1. Chinese farm laborers of that era also drew $1 per day, while

Latinos and Anglos averaged $1.25 and $1.50 respectively, plus board valued at 60 cents. In Los Angeles County, Chinese who worked in vineyards made $1.10 per day, as compared to $1.25 for Latinos. However, these raw figures require nuanced analysis, because some of the disparities in pay at least partly reflected legitimate differences in skill levels. For instance, when the San Fernando railroad tunnel was constructed near Los Angeles, Chinese diggers were paid $1 per day, while skilled white mechanics and carpenters earned an average of $2.60.[35]

A more critical factor in the Los Angeles labor market of the 1870s was that the local Chinese who worked for non-Asians were employed mainly as domestics, a position that gave them much greater bargaining power over wages than general laborers could command. Charles Nordhoff reported that the amount earned by Chinese cooks and waiters kept pace with non-Asian wages. Reverend Gibson also claimed that Chinese house servants would strike for the highest wages they could get. Wong Ark, who worked as a domestic in Los Angeles, confirmed these reports when he was asked how much he was paid: "When I didn't know anything, $15 a month, and then after I understood everything I got generally $30 a month."[36]

Nonetheless, the *Los Angeles News* made no attempt to investigate the veracity of the cheap labor cry and determine whether the town's Chinese, on the whole, were really working for lower wages than non-Asians in comparable jobs. Furthermore, it went much farther in its attacks than simply complaining about the increased number of Chinese laborers in California's workforce. The newspaper relentlessly castigated the Chinese: "degraded beings"; "an alien, an inferior and idolatrous race"; "filthy and disgusting"; "without truth, honor, or religion"; "without one single redeeming feature"; "a people who are so utterly depraved and debased that no single thought of virtue or honesty ever entered their heads"; "a curse to our country, and a foul blot upon our civilization." It called the Chinese "animals" and reinforced that impression by constantly referring to their homes and shops as "dens." Even Chinese streetwalkers were vilified. Although they were probably the least brazen practitioners of their profession in California, the *News* asserted that Chinese prostitution was the most degrading of any on earth.[37] The highly publicized rows over the possession of the prostitute Sing Yu in 1870 also gave the *News* a convenient excuse to portray the entire Chinese community as immoral. While the vast majority of Chinese in Los Angeles were ordinary laborers living uneventful lives, non-Asians' attitudes toward them were colored by these sensational news stories.

Meanwhile, what about those residents of Los Angeles who spoke glowingly of their Chinese employees? How did they respond to this barrage of anti-Chinese animosity in the *News*?

In short, they did nothing. The educated elite and the successful tradesmen of the community never raised their voices in protest. Citizens who relied heavily on Chinese house servants and launderers wrote no letters to the *News* or its competitors complaining about the vicious editorials. Furthermore, the editors of the town's other newspapers rarely voiced alternative views. The city's many lawyers, who profited from representing Chinese clients in their numerous court cases, also remained silent. So did local clergy and teachers. Elected officials chose not to speak out against the anti-Chinese rabble. Historian Hubert Howe Bancroft maintained that the Chinese were "protected by the better sentiment of the intelligent and right-minded,"[38] but the intelligent and right-minded of Los Angeles were noticeably shy about offering their Chinese neighbors any kind of protection. The whole time the *News* portrayed the Chinese people as venal and bestial, the hatemongering went unopposed.

"I Hit a Chinaman Because I Wanted To"

The first attacks were fairly mild. In the summer of 1869, a "ragged urchin" hurled a rotten egg at a Chinese man who was walking down the street. It smashed into the pavement and spattered the man's trousers. A white man was found guilty of running his wagon, which was loaded with bricks, into a Chinese man's cart, "mashing it to pieces." Things soon started getting uglier. In August 1869, another Angeleno pleaded guilty to assault and battery on Quong Lee.[39]

Unprovoked attacks on the Chinese were on the rise by the spring of 1870. A Chinese man was shot through the leg at a laundry on Calle de los Negros. That summer, another Chinese man was knocked down at the corner of Commercial and Los Angeles Streets. A policeman caught some men throwing stones into a Chinese house. An inebriated Native American woman wandered into some Chinese shoemakers' shop and started a ruckus. When they made her leave, she grabbed a stick of firewood and smashed their window. Another Native American woman stole a hat from a Chinese man's head. A drunken white man demolished a window in a Chinese house on Los Angeles Street.[40]

By the fall of 1870, the anti-Chinese outbursts were becoming even more frequent and violent. When Yo Hing and a friend stopped for a drink at an El Monte hotel, an Anglo man grabbed a chair and tried to batter them with it. Another white man was fined twelve dollars for assaulting a Chinese. Ah Lo was driving his vegetable wagon in Los Angeles when teenager Santiago Arguello, a member of one of southern California's oldest families, approached him and for no apparent reason struck him across the head and face with a heavy whip. When Ah Tom tried to retrieve an umbrella from two white men who had stolen it, they kicked him severely. Juan Alipaz was arrested when he got into a fistfight with Ah Fy along Calle de los Negros.[41]

This pattern of unchecked violence continued into 1871. A white man was fined seven dollars for striking a Chinese woman. A Latino shot a Chinese man in the neck and hip during a botched robbery. Irish immigrant Pat Gleason, irate because a Chinese cook had "called him hard names" while he was in jail, severely thrashed the first Chinese man he saw after his release because he had "a great antipathy to the Chinese race." Some boys on the corner of Aliso and Los Angeles Streets threw stones at a passing Chinese woman, then turned a water hose on her bruised body. In the early hours of a summer morning, a party of drunken Latino "serenaders" pounded three Chinese men on Commercial Street. A white man "hit a Chinaman on the head because I wanted to." A Latino boy tried to steal a watermelon from a young Chinese man, who ended up with a bruised head. A white youth hit a Chinese boy on the head with a club when they got into an argument on Aliso Street. One Saturday night in September, "a party of roughs" chased down a Chinese man on Main Street, and "one of them commenced to pelt the unoffending heathen with stones." A young African American lashed out at Ah Goff and "subjected him for a time to severe lapidation." Late that year, Andy Sharkey pleaded guilty to beating and kicking a Chinese man "without provocation."[42]

Other assaults on the Chinese of Los Angeles were indirect. In Sonoratown, the barrio north of the plaza where poorer Mexican immigrants lived, someone posted a warning in 1871 that no "Heathen Chinee" would be allowed to settle in that ward. A new American laundry proudly advertised that Chinese were barred from employment there. Another washhouse attempted to attract customers who were "not partial to Chinese labor." The *Los Angeles News* rejoiced that the work would be done by whites. In announcing that Jacob Vogelsdorff had opened a cigar factory on Spring Street, the *News* commented, "Persons purchasing at this place will have the gratification of being free from suspicion of contact with loathsome disease, which must naturally haunt the imagination of the smoker of cigars made by the Chinese."[43]

While it is impossible at this late date to determine how great a role the *News* editorials may have played in fomenting these attacks on the Chinese, the timing cannot be dismissed as coincidental, especially since the assaults were not sparked by a decline in the local economy. The *News* pieces seemed to reflect some Angelenos' dubitable but readily embraced belief that Chinese labor was, or would become, a threat to the working class of southern California. Moreover, people tended to talk about what they had seen in the press, so the influence of the *News* editorials spread beyond the paper's actual readership. A combination of fear, rumors, willful ignorance, and racial prejudice caused a sizable segment of the local population to accept unquestioningly the anti-Chinese rancor that was emanating from San Francisco. Similar episodes occurred in other towns of southern California. In 1868, some residents of Santa Barbara cut off the queue of a Chinese man suspected of stealing groceries. Vandals attempted to set fire to a Chinese house in San Bernardino in 1870.[44]

Most significantly, nothing in the news accounts indicated that any of the non-Asian perpetrators of these attacks were competing for the same types of jobs as those held by the Chinese they assaulted. Nor were they avenging personal grievances against specific Chinese. Rather, it seems that they were eagerly willing to believe the increasingly common and uncontested talk, both in the press and on the streets, that the Chinese were depraved, degraded, and subhuman. An early history of Los Angeles pointed out that "public sentiment at the time placed a very low estimate on the value of the life of a Chinaman." In later years, Reverend Huie Kin reflected on the "sudden change of public sentiment" toward his people: "The useful and steady Chinese worker became overnight the mysterious Chinaman, an object of unknown dread."[45]

The escalation in violent episodes caused the *News* to retreat temporarily from its anti-Chinese rants in the summer of 1871 and even to fret that the Chinese "seem to be made especial objects of attack." In the same sentence, however, it characterized assaults on the Chinese as a form of "cruelty to animals." Only a month later, the *News* reaffirmed its views about the "natural antipathy . . . inherent in persons of the white race against the hideous and repulsive Mongolians." This remark was prompted by an incident in which two young boys were observed "shaking their little fists at a passing Chinaman."[46]

On the streets of Los Angeles, the Chinese faced the most vehement opposition from lower-income laborers who saw them as competitors and the cause of their troubles, whether or not that was really the case: poor Southern whites who had drifted to California, dispossessed Californios, recent immigrants from Europe and Mexico who were struggling to gain a foothold, and African Americans and Native Americans whose employment options were few. Both the racial animosity and the pervasive xenophobia among less-privileged Angelenos were evident in an altercation that occurred on Los Angeles Street in 1867. A Mexican man took up a huge club and loudly proclaimed his superiority over all "niggers." A black man responded by reaching for his pistol and announcing that he was an American and was therefore a "right smart better" than anyone who was not. When a visiting Englishman tried to separate them, the black man curtly informed him that he was no American and should get away if he did not want to get hurt.[47]

Charles Nordhoff described the friction in California between the Chinese and the "Pike," or poor Southern white, whom he called "the Chinaman's enemy": "He does little work himself, and naturally he hates the patient industry of the Chinese. Of course, if you ask him, he tells you that he is 'ruined by Chinese cheap labor.' 'You could no more get these fellows to work than you could get grasshoppers out of a vineyard,' said a farmer to me; 'but they sit in the saloons, and growl about the unfair competition of the Chinese. One Chinaman is worth a regiment of them.'" James Miller Guinn contended that certain working-class

European immigrants who "had always been kept in a state of servility" back home were the harshest persecutors of the Chinese.[48]

Tension between poorer Mexican Americans and Chinese laborers was exacerbated by close proximity. The barrio of Sonoratown, where many disappointed gold prospectors from the Mexican state of Sonora had settled, was located just across the plaza from Chinatown. In 1871, a Chinese washman got into a heated argument with a resident of Sonoratown who refused to pay his bill. The customer drew his revolver and started beating the laundryman over the head with the butt end of it. The gun went off, shooting the assailant in his own hand.[49]

African Americans also held the Chinese in low esteem. In jockeying for status after the Civil War, they took care to distinguish themselves from the "pagan foreigners," touting their own American birth and citizenship as well as their Christianity and military service. However, one contributor to a black newspaper in San Francisco denounced the instigators of the anti-Chinese movement as "demagogues and blatherskites." He further argued that it was "disgusting" that "some of our race should be found among this motley throng, following some of the very men that led the New York riots of '63"—referring to the Draft Riots, in which white laborers who resented the class inequities of Civil War conscription had vented their rage on African Americans. The writer thought it was reprehensible that "the same people that have been pelted, scourged, abused, outraged and murdered" by these "Human Hyenas" could be willing to help them victimize the Chinese.[50] Pity that so few of his colleagues in the California press joined him in raising the specter of mob violence against the Chinese as a logical outgrowth of the incessant, frenzied propaganda.

Fighting Back

In response to the brutalities, the Chinese did not withdraw but instead grew more aggressive in their dealings with others. One Saturday evening in the early part of 1869, a "lively row" occurred in a laundry on Main Street between six Chinese and one white man. The white man "retreated in good order after the first skirmish." A year later, a Chinese man reportedly entered a German's house and, for reasons unknown, knocked down his two young children, proceeding to kick them.

When several Chinese men living on Grasshopper (present-day Figueroa) Street awoke to find bandits leading their horses from the stable, "one discharged a rusty shotgun, and the thieves incontinently vamoosed." In October 1870, José Juan Moreno accused a Chinese man of assault and battery, while another was fined seven dollars for beating a little boy. That December, some Chinese men "roughly handled" an African American whom they believed had stolen an umbrella. The next year, Gin Seng and Gim Lee were convicted of assault for striking Mary Fritz and spitting in her face after she "refused to submit to an attempted extortion." When a Native American woman and a Chinese woman got into a "desperate fight" on Calle de los Negros, "the 'celestial' won the fight."[51]

Mirroring the abuses perpetrated by non-Asians, Chinese assaults also became more serious over time. Juan Tapia, a ranch hand who worked for Eulogio de Celis, returned home in the early morning hours of October 17, 1871, and told the Chinese cook to get up and make him a cup of coffee. The cook said it was too late. Tapia threatened and chased him. Cornered, the cook drew a pistol and shot Tapia in the hand.[52]

The most impressive show of Chinese resistance in Los Angeles came on the night of December 22, 1870, during the third highly publicized row over the prostitute Sing Yu. Earlier that day, the deputy sheriff of Santa Barbara County had arrived in town with a warrant for her arrest on a false charge of grand larceny. He rented a carriage and a team of horses from the stage agent, George Fall, to use in transporting the woman. Accompanied by a deputy US marshal and a Chinese man from Santa Barbara who was there to identify Sing Yu, he went to Calle de los Negros to search for her. A guide led them to her apartment. The driver waited outside with the carriage. Around eight o'clock that night, the officers found Sing Yu in bed. They roused her and told her to dress quickly.

News of her arrest spread rapidly along Calle de los Negros. When the Chinese learned what was happening, about one hundred rallied in the street, brandishing knives and six-shooters. They shouted excitedly that no American should "catch" a Chinese woman. When the officers emerged from the adobe building with Sing Yu, they had to force their way through the dense throng. Then they put Sing Yu into their carriage and started off. The crowd followed close behind.

Although non-Asians did not realize it, something highly unusual was going on. Sing Yu's owner was a member of the See Yup Company, so the people trying to prevent her arrest on false charges would normally have been members of that organization. Oddly, however, the crowd also included members of the competing Hong Chow Company. On this rare occasion, the fractious Chinese community of Los Angeles apparently came together and collectively tried to prevent the American officers from interfering in their affairs by taking one of their women out of town.

When the lawmen got to the intersection of Commercial and Main Streets, the Chinese mob caught up with them and forced them to stop. Yo Hing, the Hong Chow leader, smashed the front of the carriage. The Chinese forcibly tried to recapture Sing Yu. The officers used their pistols as clubs, trying to beat them back.

Then the unthinkable occurred: Chinese gunmen fired four shots into the carriage in which the American lawmen were riding with Sing Yu. One bullet struck the Chinese informant from Santa Barbara in the shoulder, badly wounding him. Another bullet, reportedly aimed at the deputy sheriff, instead hit one of the horses. It died a short distance from town. Although gunfights in the street between Chinese toughs were not unheard of, this was the first time the Chinese of Los Angeles had ever turned their weapons on American law officers. It was a bold new development, one that would result in terrible consequences down the road.[53]

"A Frightful Dream"

In the summer of 1870, a San Francisco newspaper published a strange editorial titled "A Dream of an Anti-Chinese Riot," which merits lengthy quotation:

> We had a dream. We saw that most horrid of horrors, a mob in their frenzy, drunk with blood and whisky, headed by two notorious demagogues, who called upon the multitude in the name of Christianity and civilization to drive the Chinamen from San Francisco. The mob, blinded by prejudice, answered to their calls with demoniac screams of approving rage, and asked to be led on. . . . A scene of

indescribable confusion and fury followed. The Chinamen rushed out and pleaded for mercy but in vain. They were shot down as if they had been enemies of the human race. . . . Even the little boys, who had been taught by their parents to stone the wicked Mongolians, were there armed with long knives, with which they dispatched the wounded Celestials, still in the agonies of death. For hour after hour the massacre went on. . . . All [the Chinese] houses were broken open, their furniture destroyed, their goods thrown into the street, and the ruins set on fire. . . . The police attempted to stop the riot, but were powerless. . . . Night came, and there was a meeting of congratulation. The leaders of the mob said the day had been a splendid success. . . . The name of the city bore a stain that never could be washed out.[54]

The writer concluded with confidence that this mob, which had "really been proposed," would never actually be formed and that his "frightful dream" would never come to pass. Yet little more than a year later, the very scenario he described would unfold not in San Francisco but four hundred miles down the coast.

PART II

STRIFE BEGETS STRIFE

6

Hating Each Other Like Christians

Sing Ye

Sixty miles east of Los Angeles, on the level expanse outside San Bernardino, four Chinese outlaws forced a barefooted woman named Sing Ye across a marsh. It was around noon on a crisp autumn day, November 1, 1870. One of the men dragged her through the wet grass. Another kept hold of her hair, punching her now and then. When the men were far enough from town so they would not be seen, they stopped near a walnut tree. A fifth outlaw, known as Ah Ohn or "Scald Neck," joined them there. The men roughly stripped off Sing Ye's dress. Then they bound her to the tree, tying her so that her toes barely touched the ground. Using sticks, they started beating her from her shoulders to her heels. One climbed the tree and yanked the rope that held her. From his perch, he thrashed her for about fifteen minutes. Another lit some paper with a match and touched the flame to her breast. She shrieked in agony. Finally, Sing Ye's captors untied her and put her dress back on her. The woman's breathing was labored.

All this concerned a small sum of money. The men claimed she had stolen it. She refused to give it up. Sing Ye was a prostitute in San Bernardino, purchased for $340 in San Francisco and brought there by the same racketeers who were tormenting her.

After a while, her captors started walking off. Sing Ye, weeping and barely able to walk, tried to follow them, apparently terrified that she might fall into the hands of Americans. She acted like she wanted one of the men to lead her. Catching up to them, she grabbed hold of Ah Ohn.

It all began again. A man known as "Charley" jerked her away and ripped off her dress once more. Then he got the ropes. Charley and another man grabbed her hands. They tied her arms behind her as tightly as they could, while Sing Ye twisted and cried. With the remaining length of rope, Charley dragged her to an elder and bound her to it, tying her hair to a limb. They took off her underclothes. The men gathered some brush and lit a fire nearby, piling on wood until it roared. Then they surrounded Sing Ye with blazing sticks and started searing her bare skin. One man thrust his fingers in her mouth as she moaned. She kicked and twisted, the limb bobbing every time her hair yanked it.

The torture continued off and on for an hour and a half before they finally untied her. She slumped against the tree, unable to walk. Her tormentors sat around the fire, talking and laughing. Then they left her there.

Late that afternoon, some passersby found Sing Ye and brought the traumatized woman into town. Her persecutors were found and arrested. The people of San Bernardino were irate and immediately passed a resolution that no Chinese could work there after thirty days, not even harmless launderers and domestics. A local newspaper railed hysterically against the "idolatrous, degraded, unelevating, impoverishing heathens."

The story of Sing Ye's torture caused a stir far beyond San Bernardino. In San Francisco, the press reported that she had been burned to death at the stake. The *New York Times* repeated this falsehood on its front page. However, the *Alta California* announced that it looked on the report "with suspicion." The *Los Angeles Star*, miffed that the story had its doubters, embellished it further by claiming that the victim's back had also been cut with a knife in several places.

The five perpetrators were tried in the county court of San Bernardino. Four of them were convicted of assault and sentenced to two years in the state prison at San Quentin. The following month, however, they would be discharged when the California Supreme

Court overturned their convictions. "Assault to commit great bodily injury" was merely a misdemeanor, not punishable by imprisonment. The *Star* protested that the convicted men had "roasted for two hours one of their countrywomen, for which crime, it appears, there is no punishment by law."

The sole witness to Sing Ye's ordeal was a fifteen-year-old white farmhand. Hiding in the bushes about thirty-five yards away, he watched the whipping and burning for nearly two hours without intervening or going for help. A provocative letter to a Los Angeles newspaper queried, "Who was the most barbarous, the Chinamen who committed the deed, or the man who could witness the atrocity, without an effort to prevent it?" The *San Bernardino Guardian* was outraged that this writer compared the white witness to the Chinese gangsters. It attributed the farmhand's voyeurism to "boyish curiosity." The Los Angeles letter-writer replied, tongue-in-cheek, that he was merely trying "to show the degrading effect, upon the noble Caucasians, caused by their contact with the inferior Mongolian race." Had it not been for this "demoralizing influence," the writer sardonically explained, the young witness would have taken some action rather than merely satisfying his "prurient curiosity" and "feasting his morbid appetite."[1]

The sarcastic letter-writer was J. J. Warner, a prominent Los Angeles newspaperman and politician. Warner was only trying to goad complacent American readers, but this would be the last time he would make pointed jokes about the mistreatment of Chinese immigrants. A year later, he would serve as foreman of the grand jury that had to decide whether to indict the accused instigators of the most gruesome anti-Chinese violence the nation had ever seen. And during that mass murder, some of the town's most substantial citizens, just like the white teenager of San Bernardino whom Warner had chastised, would "witness the atrocity without an effort to prevent it."

A Split in the *Huiguan*

The spate of excitement that the torture of Sing Ye stirred up in San Bernardino soon dissipated. Among the Chinese of Los Angeles, however, the incident resonated much more deeply. Although Sing Ye and her tormentors had no direct connection with the town's Chinese community, the San Bernardino affair indirectly set off a vengeful feud along Calle de los Negros.

At the center of the turmoil was Yo Hing, Chinatown's most affable rogue and also its most sinister troublemaker. An extroverted, ambitious man, he had settled in Los Angeles around 1863, when he was about twenty-four years old. Local banker and memoirist Jackson A. Graves described him as "a huge man, not so tall, but thick, heavy, while not fat. . . . He had extremely long arms, and a voice that fairly rumbled when he talked." Yo Hing built a vast network of social connections in Los Angeles and also brought his relatives there. He had a wife who suffered from curvature of the spine, and they were unable to have any children. He also had a brother-in-law in town, a laundryman named Sin You.[2]

Yo Hing began his career as a cook in the household of attorney Andrew J. King, who later became co-publisher of the rabidly anti-Chinese *Los Angeles News*. King in turn served Yo Hing as his lawyer. From his humble first job as a domestic, Yo Hing quickly worked his way up as an entrepreneur. He leased a farm from former mayor John G. Nichols and ran a vegetable business. Afterward, he owned a cigar factory and store on Los Angeles Street, served as a court interpreter, and acted as a railroad contractor. Within three years of his arrival in Los Angeles, Yo Hing had become one of the three most influential Chinese men in town, together with Sing Lee and Sam Yuen. Not all of his enterprises were legitimate, however. In 1866, he was charged with "keeping, maintaining and residing in a house of ill-fame."[3]

Unlike the Chinatown magnate Sing Lee, who, as noted previously, spoke little English and interacted mostly with his countrymen, Yo Hing actively engaged with the larger community. By his own admission, his business was mostly with Americans. At one point, he reportedly adopted the English name Joseph Hinton. Yo Hing forged friendships with several well-known Americans, and his efforts paid off bountifully. The local press lauded him as "a good and upright man," claiming that "many of our best citizens stand ready to testify to the good character he has always borne." Years later, Horace Bell praised him as "a fine fellow." On the other hand, C. P. Dorland, an early president of the Historical Society of Southern California, remembered Yo Hing as upholding the "reputation of his race for ways that are dark."

More succinctly, a Chinese physician named Fung Chong described Yo Hing as "one big rascal."[4]

The first hint of trouble between the emerging leaders of Chinatown surfaced in 1868, when Yo Hing and Sam Yuen were among five Chinese cited for rioting after they got into a street fight with each other. Both men were up-and-comers in Sing Lee's dominant See Yup Company. A few days later, Yo Hing filed a complaint charging Sam Yuen with threatening to whip him, professing his fear that his See Yup colleague would carry out this threat. The accused was released after he gave a $300 bond to keep the peace, with Sing Lee acting as surety. Sam Yuen did not have a reputation for losing his temper; instead, it is likely that Yo Hing simply needled him until he reached his breaking point. This pattern continued for several years: Yo Hing would stir up dissension behind the scenes in Chinatown, then run crying to the American police or the English-language press that his Chinese enemies were threatening to harm him. In one of those instances, Sam Yuen mockingly retorted that this "brave fellow Yo Hing" was terrified that he might be dispatched "by those whom he has hunted and injured."[5]

The rift in the local Chinese leadership grew more severe over time, and it involved more than petty rivalries and jealousies between individuals such as Sam Yuen and Yo Hing. At least four major Chinese street fights occurred between May 27 and July 13, 1870. Around that time, the dominant See Yup Company of Los Angeles broke apart, and several new splinter associations emerged. Yo Hing became the leader of one of them, the Hong Chow Company. Sam Yuen assumed control of another, the Nin Yung Company. The original See Yup Company, still headed by Sing Lee, continued to exist as a separate *huiguan*, although its membership was greatly reduced.[6]

The reason for the breakup of the See Yup Company in Los Angeles is unknown, but it appears to have been the product of a major power struggle. One Chinese writer, Fong Kum Ngon, explained that there was originally only one *huiguan* for all Chinese in America, but that after more immigrants arrived they started to resent its monopoly and formed other district associations. As early as 1853, a faction broke off from the See Yup Company in San Francisco and formed a Nin Yung organization there. Subsequently, the Hong Chow Company supplanted the See Yup Company in San Francisco, which eventually became defunct.[7] Members of all three of these *huiguan* came from the Sze Yup region of China, which consisted of four counties in southern Guangdong Province.

In Los Angeles, the split in the See Yup Company was far from amicable, especially since *huiguan* leaders Sing Lee, Yo Hing, and Sam Yuen all competed in the prostitution traffic. A fight for control of Chinatown soon followed. By the spring of 1871, Yo Hing had turned his upstart Hong Chow Company into the most powerful Chinese association in the city. Sing Lee publicly denounced the aggressive newcomer as a rogue organization formed "for the purpose of plundering and oppressing" Chinese workers. In an American newspaper, he accused Yo Hing's Hong Chow Company of operating more like the notorious fighting tongs than the beneficent *huiguan*. He further claimed that it was "not one of the old established Chinese companies" but a new organization formed in Los Angeles "for the purpose of trading upon the fears and necessities of friendless Chinamen, and of levying black mail."[8]

As of May 1871, nearly a year after the breakup, the Hong Chow Company's chief competitor was still Sing Lee's long-established See Yup Company. Within a few months, however, the See Yup organization was surpassed in prominence by another splinter *huiguan*, Sam Yuen's Nin Yung Company. Surprisingly, there was no reported friction between these two associations; in fact, the See Yup and Nin Yung Companies seem to have been allied. In one instance, a newspaper article indicated that a single prostitute was held jointly by the managers of the two organizations. It appears that Sing Lee, who was planning to return to China in the summer of 1871, was winding down his affairs in Los Angeles and transferring his business interests to members of the ascendant Nin Yung organization. Police Officer Emil Harris would later identify Sing Lee as a "former" proprietor of the Wing Chung store, which Sam Yuen and his Nin Yung colleagues had acquired by the fall of 1871.[9] It is also possible that the See Yup and Nin Yung headmen thought an alliance was necessary to counter the increasing influence of Yo Hing and his Hong Chow association.

Sam Yuen, like Yo Hing, had a great many relations in Los Angeles, including a brother named Cum Yun. He and his business partners in the nascent Nin Yung Company ran the Wing Chung store, which operated a restaurant and sold a variety of Chinese merchandise.[10] It was located toward the western end of the southern wing of China-town's Coronel block, a rambling, L-shaped strip of dilapidated adobe apartments that occupied the corner of Calle de los Negros and Arcadia Street (the present-day intersection of North Los Angeles Street and the Hollywood Freeway). The average passerby would not have realized from the store's outward appearance that it was prospering. The build-ing's whitewashed walls were flaking badly, the floor of its raised gallery was missing several planks, and the roof over the veranda had buckled in waves, making the homely structure look as besotted and unsteady as most of the revelers who congregated along Calle de los Negros.

The neglected tenement belonged to State Treasurer Antonio F. Coronel, one of the town's most distinguished citizens and a former mayor. As owner of the Coronel building, he was also one of Los Ange-les's chief slumlords. He was certainly not the only one, however. The property along Calle de los Negros was owned by some of Los Angeles's most prominent citizens, including Prudent Beaudry, a future mayor who rented out his rundown adobe strip at the corner of Los Angeles and Aliso Streets. When Antonio Coronel briefly considered demol-ishing his deteriorating adobe in 1870 and replacing it with a modern, three-storied brick building, the *Los Angeles News*, for one, was elated that he would be "forcing the numerous Chinese bagnios . . . to find quarters in some less prominent locality."[11]

With a limited market of fewer than two hundred Chinese in the town of Los Angeles, competition among the Chinese merchants was cutthroat. The leaders of the various *huiguan* resorted to heavy-handed tactics on behalf of their members. In one instance, a shopkeeper who belonged to Yo Hing's Hong Chow Company was renting a commercial space in Prudent Beaudry's adobe for $15 a month. Sam Yuen, as Nin Yung kingpin, reportedly leased the entire Beaudry building for $169 and raised the hapless shopkeeper's rent to $50 in an effort to drive him out of business. Yo Hing told the shopkeeper to keep paying Sam Yuen the old rate of $15. The Nin Yung leader threatened to evict the man but finally relented, apparently believing that Yo Hing would prevail if they took the controversy to court.[12]

Indeed, Yo Hing was looking for an opportunity to test the extent of his newfound clout. The San Bernardino case in the fall of 1870 gave him his first chance. The five men who were charged with brutalizing Sing Ye belonged to the same *huiguan* as Yo Hing, and he did his best to protect them. His association spent a large sum of money on their legal defense.

More than simply protecting his associates, Yo Hing interfered directly with the administration of justice in the case. A week after Sing Ye's whipping and burning, he accused a See Yup man named Que Ma of stealing his white horse and taking off to San Bernardino. A warrant was issued in Los Angeles for the man's arrest. Policeman Joe Dye, who had killed the city marshal less than two weeks before, traveled to San Bernardino and brought the accused thief to town.

When the prisoner appeared in court, a different story emerged. Through an interpreter, Que Ma argued convincingly that he had never set foot in Los Angeles County before. Instead, he worked as a cook in San Bernardino. His arrest was a ruse to ensure that he would be absent from San Bernardino and therefore could not testify against the five defendants in Sing Ye's case. Indeed, neither Yo Hing nor any other witness appeared against Que Ma, who was discharged. Nonetheless, according to the See Yup Company, the unfortunate cook had to spend most of his modest savings employing lawyers and, though innocent, was financially ruined by the baseless prosecution.[13]

Even without Que Ma's testimony, four of Sing Ye's accused torturers were convicted in San Bernardino. Yo Hing did not take this defeat in stride. Instead, he turned his wrathful attention to those Chinese individuals who had provided evidence against the convicted men. He devised a plot to take revenge on the informers one by one. In doing so, he would show the Chinese of southern California what they could expect if they crossed him.

Retaliation

January–March 1871

In January 1871, a prosperous and well-known San Bernardino laundryman named Wong Hing and his wife, Ah Mouie, planned to pass through Los Angeles on their way back to China. The couple had managed to accumulate enough of a fortune over the years to enable them to return home and enjoy their newfound wealth in their own country. Wong Hing was also suspected of having given information to the authorities in Sing Ye's case. Yo Hing located the couple as soon as they got to Los Angeles. He demanded that they reimburse him for the Hong Chow Company's costs in defending the woman's abusers. They refused. Yo Hing threatened to get even.

On the morning of January 23, Wong Hing and Ah Mouie went to the railroad depot at the corner of Alameda and Commercial Streets to board a train for the short ride to the southern harbor at San Pedro. There they planned to catch a steamer to San Francisco and then continue on to China. Just before the train left the station, Policeman William Sands stepped into the car and, to their astonishment, arrested them on a charge of grand larceny.

At the jail, they were both searched. Jailor Frank Carpenter, following his usual practice, took their property for safekeeping—$694 in gold and silver coin, plus a large trunk, silver watch, knife, and pocket chest. Ah Mouie was greatly distressed when Carpenter took the money from her, and she tried to resist. Although she spoke only a few words of English, he understood her to say that the coins were her "Chinese God." Her husband, who spoke English, confirmed that was what she meant. By this time, Wong Hing must have suspected what was going on and who was behind their arrest. He asked desperately whether he could get out of jail and recover his property if he put up bail. That afternoon, when Wong Hing and Ah Mouie were brought before the justice of the peace, their accuser withdrew his charge, stating that it was all a mistake and that the money had been found.

In the meantime, one of Yo Hing's men, Lay Yee, had filed a bogus civil action against Wong Hing, claiming he had defaulted on a $600 loan made two years earlier. As evidence, Lay Yee produced a document purporting to require "the payment of $600, coupled with the condition that the drawer of the note should not leave for China, until the note was paid." The court, hearing the evidence, was influenced by the fact that Wong Hing was on his way to board the steamer when he was apprehended. Concluding that he was trying to flee without repaying his debt, the district judge issued a writ of attachment. The innocent couple's money and other personal property that the jailor was holding ended up in Hong Chow hands.[14]

Word of Yo Hing's devious and heavy-handed tactics spread quickly. A few days later, armed members of the See Yup and Hong Chow associations lined both sides of Calle de los Negros. The leaders of each company stood arguing with each other in the middle of the street. The police arrived, dispersing the agitated crowd before any shots were fired.[15]

Yo Hing's next victim was Choo Chee, a merchant from San Francisco who visited Los Angeles in March 1871. The Hong Chow people mistakenly thought he had come to town to assist his fellow *huiguan* member Wong Hing, who was still in Los Angeles trying to recover the money taken from him and his wife at the county jail two months earlier. In an effort to get Choo Chee imprisoned, two Hong Chow men, Lay Yee and Quang Yu, swore out a complaint before Justice of the Peace William H. Gray falsely alleging that the visitor from San Francisco had paid an assassin $400 to kill them.

When the matter was heard, the courtroom was packed with spectators who listened very attentively. The case took two full days because, as Justice Gray noted in his minutes, the first day was "consumed by the respective attorneys in badgering one another" and by the two Chinese accusers, through an interpreter, prattling on and on without "eliciting a single particle of testimony bearing upon the case." The second day was spent in the same manner, and by the end of it, Gray wrote that he was "completely exhausted." The following morning, Justice Gray curtly dismissed the prosecution, noting that it grew out of the "competitions and jealousies which characterize these Chinese Companies, and with which the Courts are so frequently annoyed." He ordered Yo Hing's men to pay the court costs of twenty-eight dollars.[16]

Incensed by this defeat, Yo Hing opted for a more direct method of retaliation. On March 9, 1871, Wong Hing, the San Bernardino laundryman, was walking arm-in-arm with a friend when the Hong Chow Company's main henchman, Lay Yee, approached them and fired his pistol. The bullet missed Wong Hing but struck the other man in the hand. Lay Yee was held to answer before the grand jury. After a $500 bond was posted, he was discharged. Two days later, Yo Hing attached and closed the laundry of Sam Gut Gee, another See Yup member, claiming that he had failed to pay $17.50 for goods sold and delivered.[17]

Yo Hing had not yet secured a clear-cut victory in the widening feud. Early on, he had succeeded in bullying the San Bernardino cook, Que Ma, and the laundryman, Wong Hing. However, the results of his schemes since then had been mixed. He still needed to stage a triumphant coup in Chinatown, some daring escapade that would serve as a warning to his countrymen in Los Angeles that he was not a man to be trifled with. That would finally happen in March 1871. This time, his victim was a woman.

"An Old Man's Darling"

On the morning of March 7, 1871, a daring young man named Lee Yong arrived in a carriage on Calle de los Negros with three of his friends. Lee Yong was a cook in a local household and a member of Yo Hing's *huiguan*. He stopped the carriage in front of the house of Hing Sing, an older, wealthy member of the See Yup Company who was away from home at the time. Lee Yong brazenly entered the older man's residence and brought out his wife, Yut Ho.[18] He and his helpers put her in the carriage and took off.

Once Hing Sing's friends realized what had happened, they chased the carriage on foot. The pursuers followed it all the way to the office of Justice of the Peace John Trafford, where it stopped. Lee Yong banged on the door. He and Yut Ho were admitted. Four days earlier, Lee Yong had quietly obtained a legal certificate to wed the woman. They were married quickly. Afterward, the couple escaped through a back door and fled in the carriage.

The Los Angeles newspapers had tremendous fun with this story. Journalists delighted in portraying the whole affair as a romantic caper, creating an imaginative scenario in which the "lovely Yut Ho" had "wearied of being an old man's darling" and willingly escaped with the dashing Lee Yong. According to the news accounts, Hing Sing was "a very wealthy but most infernally ugly old heathen" who "neither feared his enemies nor envied his friends." Yut Ho was his "pet lamb." He and Lee Yong "belonged to rival companies, which hated each other like Christians."

In a fanciful story that the *Los Angeles News* concocted, Hing Sing had given a masked ball during Chinese New Year. At that time, Lee Yong, a "handsome cavalier of the rival faction," stole serpent-like into Hing Sing's house and "penetrated even to the boudoir of the fair Yut. He saw her just in the prime of her matronly beauty, he loved her, and he told his love. She listened to his honied words, refused, relented, and agreed to fly from the home that sheltered her to seek a refuge in his commodious bosom."[19]

These colorful newspaper accounts were pure fiction, but Hing Sing's fury was quite real. Enraged by his wife's abduction, he filed suit in county court the same day, alleging that Yut Ho had been illegally detained under a forced marriage. He lodged a separate petition before the justice of the peace against Yo Hing and six other men. Hing Sing charged them with kidnapping his wife and, by threats and intimidation, forcing her to marry Lee Yong against her will.

Yut Ho was found and brought before the county court. Judge Ygnacio Sepúlveda ordered that she be restored to her real husband, Hing Sing. A fight over Yut Ho erupted in the courtroom, spilling out into the street. The Hong Chow abductors rushed toward the woman and carried her off by force. Some lawmen pursued them and brought her back. Thinking the scandalous episode was over, Hing Sing and his wife made their way home to Calle de los Negros.

That night, however, Yut Ho's new "husband," Lee Yong, obtained another writ of habeas corpus. Policeman Emil Harris and his fellow officers searched for the woman and finally discovered her hidden in one of the apartments along Calle de los Negros. They brought her before District Judge Murray Morrison. According to See Yup members, the police prevented Hing Sing and his friends from entering the courtroom or speaking to the judge. They also claimed that Yut Ho herself had not been asked whether or not she wished to stay with Lee Yong. Her true husband, Hing Sing, sent for his lawyer, who failed to arrive in time. In a surprising reversal, Judge Morrison released Yut Ho to the custody of her abductor, Lee Yong, probably because he held an American marriage certificate. The judge instructed police officers to escort the couple and protect them from a group of angry See Yup members, who followed Lee Yong's carriage through the streets as long as they could keep up with it.[20]

Who was Yut Ho, the demure, coveted young wife at the center of this tug-of-war? Authors of several accounts of this incident have portrayed her as a woman for sale.[21] Actually, her circumstances suggested otherwise. Her husband, Hing Sing, was a moneyed man, so it is unlikely that he would have trolled the cribs of Calle de los Negros looking for some hard-used peasant girl to wed. Instead, he would have sent to China for an unspoiled trophy wife. Yut Ho also had a brother, Ah Guey, who lived in California.[22] Again, it seems improbable that he would have allowed his sister to endure the shame and brutality of brothel life right before his eyes. Rather, the presence of a male relative and protector in the state indicated that Yut Ho did not come to America as chattel to be sold on the auction block but as the intended bride of Hing Sing. Furthermore, the *Star* and the *News*, which seldom missed a chance to disparage the virtue of Chinese women, consistently described Yut Ho as a legitimate wife rather than a prostitute.

The Chinese combatants took their grievances to the press. Sing Lee and six other members of his See Yup Company were the first to tell their side of the story. Claiming to represent the "respectable Chinese residents of this city," they asked the public to "fix the responsibility upon the guilty parties." The See Yup leaders described Lee Yong not as a dashing lover but as one of Yo Hing's "tools." The abduction, they alleged, occurred with the assistance of three unnamed American policemen. They further asserted that Yut Ho had been taken against her will and forced into a marriage ceremony without realizing what was happening. They said that their real adversary was not Lee Yong but Yo Hing, whose "villainous features have appeared at every trial, behind the counsel of the nominal party," and who "perverted the machinery of the law."[23]

Yo Hing did not suffer these insults in silence. Five days later, he responded with a public letter of his own. Rather than denying the charges that Sing Lee had leveled against him or offering an alternative version of the facts, Yo Hing referred vaguely to "evil disposed persons" who were attempting to ruin his good name. Most of his letter consisted of a self-serving testament to his "peaceable, quiet and humble way." "Since I have been here," he wrote, "my business has been principally with the American portion of the population, and to them do I refer for a refutation of the charges made through your columns." He named prominent residents with whom he had been associated: lawyer Andrew J. King, former mayor John G. Nichols, educator William McKee, and the officers of the US Internal Revenue Service.[24]

However, the series of vengeful shenanigans that Hong Chow members had initiated two months earlier belied both Yo Hing's sanctimonious testimonial and the Los Angeles newsmen's far-fetched tales of a scandalous romance. It seems that Yut Ho's kidnapping was the crowning act of retaliation by Yo Hing in connection with the San Bernardino affair. A news article identified her aggrieved husband, Hing Sing, as a suspected informer in Sing Ye's case. The See Yup people claimed that Yo Hing ordered the abduction because he was "filled with baffled rage" that his men's suit against Choo Chee three days before-hand had failed.[25] What remains unknown is whether Yo Hing and the Hong Chow Company intended to hold Yut Ho for ransom, force her into prostitution, sell her, or help Lee Yong keep her as a stolen bride. Regardless, Yut Ho was not a willing participant in a love triangle but a pawn in the protracted fight between the *huiguan*. And in this skirmish, Yo Hing had finally routed his enemies and shown the public of Los Angeles who was Chinatown's boss.

A Counterattack

Some of Yo Hing's victims fought back. In May 1871, Ah Mouie, the wife of San Bernardino laundryman Wong Hing, tried a bold and clever strategy to recover the couple's money that had been attached. She sued Sheriff James F. Burns and Jailor Frank Carpenter, seeking damages for unlawful conversion of her property. In doing so, she became the first Chinese woman known to have filed a lawsuit in a Los Angeles court.

As it turned out, Yo Hing had made a critical error when he took his revenge on the couple in January. His henchman, Lay Yee, had obtained a writ of attachment for Wong Hing's property. However, the evidence in the case showed that $686 of the couple's $694 that was confiscated after their arrest actually belonged to Ah Mouie—her "Chinese God," as she had called it. The writ, as her lawyer argued, did not apply to her separate property. Ah Mouie won her case, and the California Supreme Court affirmed the decision on appeal. However, the court denied Ah Mouie's $1,000 claim for mental suffering caused by having to "inhale the filthy vapors" of the county jail during the half-day she was imprisoned there.

Ah Mouie's claim for payment went full circle. The sheriff and the jailor did not have enough property to satisfy the judgment in her favor, even after the jailor's vacant city lot was sold. Ah Mouie proceeded to recover her money from the two officers' sureties. After they paid the judgment, the sureties sued the three people who had originally executed a bond indemnifying the sheriff for any damages he might sustain by reason of the writ of attachment. One of them was Lay Yee. Thus, the ultimate responsibility for repaying Ah Mouie's losses eventually landed on the Hong Chow Company's doorstep, which must have infuriated Yo Hing. Ah Mouie, in the meantime, neglected to pay her attorneys. They had to sue to recover their fees.[26]

Help from San Francisco

During the summer of 1871, Chinatown remained relatively quiet. The See Yup Company made no further attempts in Los Angeles to recapture the stolen bride Yut Ho, which suggests that her captors had taken her out of town and hidden her. Her case made no news for several months, apart from one minor incident in which two Chinese men obtained a certified copy of her American marriage certificate. The *Los Angeles News* speculated that the document was "doubtless intended to act as a legal bill of sale in some contemplated transfer."[27] Indeed, Yo Hing may have planned to sell Yut Ho and apply the proceeds toward his company's costs in defending the accused torturers of Sing Ye. Or perhaps the two men who obtained the certificate were friends of her husband, Hing Sing, who was preparing to attack the legality of her marriage to Lee Yong. Whatever the case, the war that Yo Hing had launched in Los Angeles's Chinatown was far from finished.

It heated up again that fall. Two Chinese street fights occurred on Calle de los Negros in September 1871.[28] By the fourth week of October, the tension had reached its height. When the steamer *California* arrived at San Pedro harbor from San Francisco, the passengers who turned up in town included several Chinese tong fighters. Most likely, they had been summoned by Sam Yuen and the members of his Nin Yung Company. Sing Lee, the See Yup leader, had left for China during the summer, and the Nin Yung people apparently succeeded the See Yups as the avengers of Yut Ho. The woman's husband, Hing Sing, may have become a member of the Nin Yung association by then. Regardless, Sam Yuen probably welcomed any excuse to go to battle with his longtime nemesis, Yo Hing, and try to check his increasing influence.

The highbinders had come from San Francisco for the express purpose of settling the score against Yo Hing. Their arrival was anticipated in Chinatown. As mentioned earlier, one Los Angeles merchant reported that the local Chinese had purchased between forty and fifty pistols from his store in the days beforehand. The Yut Ho affair was the most obvious cause of the impending battle. However, it is also likely that Yo Hing's adversaries thought he had generally gone too far in persecuting the suspected informers in the San Bernardino case. As one newspaper noted, the Nin Yung people were concerned about "the establishment of a bad precedent" by Yo Hing and his cohorts.

The weather in Los Angeles had turned cool and cloudy that week, the heavy air threatening rain. Around half past nine on the morning of Monday, October 23, 1871, Yo Hing was standing outside the adobe house of a Chinese man known as Charley on the northern end of Calle de los Negros. Two San Francisco gunmen, Ah Choy and Yu Tak, arrived and challenged him in the narrow street. According to Yo Hing, Yu Tak wore some type of body armor that a bullet could not penetrate. A heated argument broke out, resulting in gunfire. Yo Hing ran inside Charley's house. The tong fighters followed him and started shooting. One bullet struck a clock; another hit the wall. According to Yo Hing, a cap got caught in the cylinder of Ah Choy's pistol, which kept the assassin from finishing him off. Nonetheless, another bullet passed through the right side of Yo Hing's coat. He fled the scene.

The police arrived at Charley's house, but the two gunmen had already vanished. They soon apprehended Ah Choy and arrested him. Later, they discovered Yu Tak, the other would-be assassin, lying on a bed in a laundry, complacently smoking an opium pipe. He indignantly denied any involvement in the shooting. Nonetheless, the police hauled him off to jail.

Though imprisoned himself, Ah Choy filed a complaint against Yo Hing, alleging that the Hong Chow leader had fired a pistol at him. Yo Hing was arrested and brought into court. He claimed that his Nin Yung enemies had placed a price of $1,000 on his head. For once he was probably telling the truth. All three defendants were released on bail. Two of Yo Hing's American associates, John G. Nichols and William McKee, served as his sureties.

Sam Yuen offered his Wing Chung firm as surety for the release of the two San Francisco gunmen. However, there was some question as to whether the store could make good on the bail bond. The infinitely patient and conscientious Justice Gray sent the policeman George Gard to find out. Sam Yuen took Gard to his store in Chinatown's Coronel building. He opened a trunk filled with gold and silver coins. Fong Yuen Sing, the firm's bookkeeper, counted the money, which totaled about $3,000. Officer Gard was satisfied, and the bookkeeper put the coins back in the trunk. The policeman then reported in open court that Sam Yuen and his partners had ample cash on hand. By that evening, rumors had spread among the hooligans of Calle de los Negros that the Wing Chung store was harboring a treasure chest.

The three feudists—highbinders Ah Choy and Yu Tak and Hong Chow leader Yo Hing—appeared before Justice Gray at two o'clock the following afternoon, Tuesday, October 24. All of them pleaded not guilty. Their countrymen followed the proceedings closely. Some Chinese who worked on outlying ranches came to town to attend the hearing, siding with their respective *huiguan*. Gray adjourned the cases until the next day. Still fuming, the parties returned to Chinatown.

A little after five o'clock that afternoon, Ah Choy was eating a meal in the back part of a house on the east side of Calle de los Negros. Hearing a commotion in the street, he went to the front door and stepped outside. There he found a party of armed Hong Chow members, which may have included their leader, Yo Hing.[29]

The Hong Chow men had not come to argue or negotiate. With few preliminaries, one of Yo Hing's henchmen raised a pistol and shot Ah Choy in the neck. The tong fighter collapsed into the dust, mortally wounded. His attackers fled.[30] Yo Hing's year-long war in Chinatown, which had started in the courts and then moved to the streets, had finally claimed its first casualty—not a small-time local gangster, but a professional assassin from San Francisco who had been outmatched by his intended victim.

7

The Night of Horrors

The Gunfight

October 24, 1871, 5:30 p.m.

Policeman Jesús Bilderrain was at Christopher Higby's saloon, a block away at the corner of Arcadia and Main Streets, when he heard the gunfire. It did not take him entirely by surprise. Some Chinese informants had already warned him that there was going to be a big fight that afternoon. Bilderrain jumped on his horse. He shouted for a fellow police officer, Esteban Sanchez, to follow him down Arcadia Street to Chinatown.[1] The lawmen rode so fast along the dirt lane that Bilderrain dropped his pistol. He stopped. A farmer from Anaheim named Dan Moody picked it up and handed it to him.

On the southern end of Calle de los Negros, the two policemen found five or six Chinese toughs shooting at each other in the middle of the street. Most likely, the friends of Ah Choy, the fallen San Francisco assassin, were battling Yo Hing's men. Officer Bilderrain charged through them on his horse to break up the fight. In the midst of the shooting, the horse reared. An excited spectator yelled at the mounted officers, "Get off your horses or they'll shoot you!" Just then, a tong fighter with a pistol in each hand fired at Bilderrain.

The officer hopped down. He ordered the feudists not to shoot. They stopped firing and ran off in different directions. He arrested one of the Chinese gunslingers with the help of two bystanders, Ventura Lopez and Juan Espinosa.

Bilderrain turned to see some of the Chinese gunfighters disappearing into the Beaudry adobe. He was about to run after them when he noticed Ah Choy lying on the ground, bleeding. Some Chinese women nearby were weeping for him.

Another local, Adolfo Celis, hurried over to see what was happening. Officer Bilderrain asked him to help take the arrested Chinese gunman to jail. The two of them, along with citizens Lopez and Espinosa, started marching the prisoner west on Arcadia Street. As they passed the door of Sam Yuen's Wing Chung store in the Coronel building, another Chinese man appeared on the gallery, pointing a six-shooter at them. He called out, "Here!" Bilderrain looked up and hollered, "Catch him!" Celis strode toward the brazen gunslinger, who he thought was Sam Yuen, the Nin Yung principal. The man fired a shot over his head.

Officer Bilderrain, leaving his Chinese prisoner with Lopez and Espinosa, jumped up onto the raised, wood-plank gallery of the Coronel building. He ran along it, pursuing the Chinese shooter into the Wing Chung store.[2] The low-ceilinged, windowless adobe room was very dark and, according to Bilderrain, was "plum full of Chinamen," ten to fifteen in all. He did not recognize any of them.

Suddenly, the man he was chasing appeared in front of him. He pressed a pistol against the policeman's chest. Bilderrain grabbed it. The gunman pulled the trigger, but the hammer came down on Bilderrain's thumb, sparing the lawman's life. Bilderrain was about to strike his would-be murderer on the head with his revolver when other Chinese men in the store opened fire on him. Frantically, he tried to escape. The front door was stuck and would not budge.

Wheeling in panic, Bilderrain barreled through the store and ran out the back exit into the corral. There he faced more Chinese feudists and a barrage of gunfire. A bullet struck him in the right shoulder. His arm disabled, he dropped his gun. To escape the volley, Bilderrain dashed back into the store, tumbling over chairs. He believed he was mortally wounded and wanted to die outside. This time, he managed to get the front door open.

Officer Bilderrain staggered outside onto the gallery, minus his hat and his firearm. Clutching a wooden post for support, he exclaimed, "Keep out, Celis, or they will kill you!" An onlooker yelled at him to get down. He stepped off the gallery into Arcadia Street. Mustering all his strength, he blew his whistle to summon his fellow officers. A well-known butcher named Refugio Botello came up to see what was wrong. Bilderrain told Botello he was shot. By then, he was feeling faint and weak from loss of blood.

A few alarmed citizens gathered in the broad, open space on the south side of the Coronel adobe, drawn by the shouting and shooting. The Chinese who were out and about scurried for shelter. Already they sensed the onlookers' hostility. According to one policeman, "By then it would have been unsafe for any Chinaman to come out or to have been seen on the street."

From inside the building, the tong fighters fired indiscriminately through the door of the Wing Chung store at the police, the bystanders, and each other. Apparently, they were trying to keep the law officers at bay until they could escape. Two or three would appear in the doorway, shoot, and then draw back. Random shots were coming from other Chinese tenements as well. One of them struck a teenager, Juan José Mendibles, in the right leg below his knee.

At first, the Angelenos in the street scattered, fleeing the gunfire. Then they quickly regrouped. As one observer recalled, "Almost every man's hand sought the back pocket of his pants, and a pistol was drawn, cocked and discharged at the Chinamen in less time than it takes to tell." The people on the streets of Chinatown aimed to kill. They shot "through doors, windows and every aperture which presented a chance for a Chinaman's life," according to a reporter. Neighboring shop-keepers closed and bolted their iron shutters against the flying bullets.

Special Police Officer Robert Hester heard the shots and hurried to Chinatown. He saw Officer Bilderrain standing in the street, his hand pressed to his shoulder, blood staining his shirt. Three Chinese men stepped out of the Coronel building. One of them fired at Officer Hester with a six-shooter. Hester shot back. The men ducked inside and shut the door.

Officer Hester ran around the corner into the corral behind the Coronel adobe. There he faced about twenty-five Chinese men out back of the building. He commanded them to give themselves up. Instead, the agitated men started firing at him. After returning three shots, Hester retreated to the street.

Meanwhile, another Chinese gunman fired at Police Officer Esteban Sanchez. He chased the man all the way through an apartment in the Coronel adobe on the west side of Calle de los Negros. Close behind him was a longtime resident named Cyrus Lyons. Coming out the back door, they stepped into the corral. Excited Chinese gunmen poured out from the rear of the L-shaped building, shooting furiously at the two men.

Officer Sanchez shot three times. Lyons turned and ran, calling for Sanchez to follow him. They fled from the corral. Then Sanchez ran along the gallery to the south side of the Coronel building.

Bystander Celis rushed up and told Policeman Sanchez that his fellow officer, Jesús Bilderrain, had been hit. A popular rancher and former saloonkeeper named Robert Thompson ran up to them, asking, "What is the matter?"

Celis cried out, "The Chinamen have shot Bilderrain."

Ordering Celis to stand aside, Officer Sanchez cautiously approached the front door of the Wing Chung store. He peered inside. In the doorway of a small interior room, he saw a man whom he thought was Sam Yuen, the proprietor. The man leveled a pistol at the policeman. Sanchez drew his gun, and they fired at each other at the same time. Jumping back, Sanchez took cover on the gallery to the right of the store's main entrance. Robert Thompson stood to the left of it. He had his own pistol drawn.

Then Thompson stepped to the open doorway. He waved his pistol back and forth. Officer Sanchez warned him, "The Chinamen are shooting. Look out, as there are two or three there and they may shoot you." He hurried off into a nearby room to reload his revolver. Ignoring the policeman's warning, Thompson fired a wayward shot into an empty space on the right side of the Wing Chung store.

Adolfo Celis told him, "Don't shoot, Bob. Let's look inside and see where they are."

Celis peered through the doorway. In the small interior room, he saw several Chinese men. Their six-shooters were pointed directly at him. Springing away from the door, he shouted to Thompson, "Don't go there or they'll shoot you."

Thompson replied, "I'll look out for that." He stepped to the doorway. Nothing happened. Then he stuck his arm inside and fired a second random shot. Someone in the small room returned the fire. Thompson drew back, clutching the left side of his chest. He had been hit above the heart. Bravado suddenly dissolved into shocked disbelief. As he staggered into Arcadia Street, Thompson gasped to Celis, "I'm killed."[3]

Revenge

George M. Fall, the twenty-eight-year-old stagecoach agent, heard the gunfire coming from Chinatown. He stepped out of his office. In the street, he saw a group of men carrying Robert Thompson, the wounded volunteer, to Theodore Wollweber's drugstore on Main Street, opposite the intersection of Commercial Street. Another party was escorting injured Officer Bilderrain.

When Fall learned that the shooters of both men were Chinese, he was incensed. He told the superintendent of the stage line, "They shot into my carriage team last year. They killed a horse and shot a Chinaman through the side. It was the same woman that caused the death of Warren, and this thing must be stopped."

Actually, the woman whose multiple arrests had resulted in the city marshal's killing and had also set off the Chinese street fight the previous December was the prostitute Sing Yu, not the abducted bride Yut Ho. All the same, Fall seemed to have carried a grudge against the Chinese ever since. Before arresting Sing Yu, the deputy sheriff of Santa Barbara County had rented a carriage from Fall, and Yo Hing had smashed the front of it during the uproar. A Chinese gunman had also shot one of the stage line's horses, which died outside of town. The stagecoach agent had been waiting for a chance to get even.

A few minutes later, George Fall spotted Yo Hing, the destroyer of his carriage, on the sidewalk outside Alex Rendon's barbershop on Main Street. Fall, who served as a city councilman and was also an organizer of the fire department, immediately forgot his position as a civic leader. Without a word, he picked up a board, went up to Yo Ying, and struck him in the face. Yo Hing had no idea why the stagecoach agent was attacking him, but he was a man with many enemies. He dashed into the Blue Wing Saloon.

Fall followed him inside. He threw a brick at his adversary's head, then followed it with a chair. He hurled these things with so much force that he hurt his own arm. Yo Hing somehow escaped from the saloon without further injury.

Later, Fall ran into Tom Gates, a saloonkeeper and a close friend to Robert Thompson, the fallen rancher. Gates had gone to fetch his rifle. He asked Councilman Fall, "Are you prepared?"

Fall replied, "I am."

"They killed Thompson," Gates announced ominously.[4]

"Bring Them Down"

5:30–6:15 p.m.

City Marshal Frank Baker was at the corner of Los Angeles and Requena Streets when he heard the shots. He ran all the way to Chinatown. By then, everyone was in a panic, both Chinatown's residents and the Angelenos who were starting to flock there. In a sort of chain reaction, they were all shooting wildly, with little concern for who their targets were. When the marshal arrived, he found several Chinese firing randomly from the Wing Chung store. Suddenly, the door slammed shut from the inside.

"Stop shooting," Baker yelled to the crowd that had formed in front of the Coronel building. "We will put a guard around the house."[5]

Sheriff James F. Burns, the county's principal lawman, was soon on the scene as well. He appealed to the men gathered in Arcadia and Los Angeles Streets to remain calm. According to one witness, "no attention was paid to his words."[6] Some people in the crowd clamored to force their way into the Coronel building. They wanted to get their hands on the Chinese who had shot the three wounded Americans. Sheriff Burns tried to assure them that the outlaws would be arrested.

At that critical juncture, Sheriff Burns and City Marshal Baker basically had two choices. They could use their limited forces—nine lawmen in all, including themselves[7]—to clear the streets around the Coronel adobe and disperse the growing horde of armed and agitated locals, a crowd that included many thugs and hotheads. That might protect the innocent Chinese from mob retaliation, even if it enabled the shooters of Bilderrain, Thompson, and the teenager Mendibles to slip away.

Or they could use their officers, together with some volunteers, to cordon the Coronel building, allowing none of the Chinese inside to flee, and wait for things to calm down. Once that happened, they could move in to arrest the tong fighters holed up in the Wing Chung store. It would soon be dark, and they might have to wait until morning to enter the building. Of course, if the belligerent crowd kept increasing, the lawmen might not be able to control it throughout the night.

Without hesitation, the sheriff and the city marshal chose the second course, though they knew that the Coronel block in the heart of Chinatown was home to many blameless Chinese. Burns held the record among Los Angeles lawmen for catching criminals,[8] and he apparently did not want to tarnish it by letting the Chinese tong fighters escape. He issued orders to guard the building until morning. As he later testified, "My orders to those whom I deputized, and to the officers, were that they should prevent anyone from going in or coming out, that if they could not make arrests to bring them down, to prevent escape."[9] Burns sent four or five men to an alley behind the Coronel building. He also put guards on Calle de los Negros to the east and on the plaza to the north. The Chinese were surrounded.

At the intersection of Aliso and Los Angeles Streets, Burns stationed a carpenter named Augustus Cates opposite the southeast corner of the Coronel building. The sheriff told him, "If any persons attempt to leave the block, arrest them."

Cates replied, "The way they are shooting, I would be a fool to run out and arrest anyone."

Burns clarified, "Arrest them. If they won't stop when called upon to do so, shoot them. If they open the door and refuse to shut it, shoot."[10] It scarcely mattered to the sheriff that the fleeing Chinese might not understand English.

Similarly, Marshal Baker ordered Policeman Esteban Sanchez to watch the doors and let no one leave. He also told Deputy Sheriff Sam Bryant not to allow any Chinese to escape. Stationing a grocery employee named S. A. Butler on Sanchez Street at the corner of the Pico House Hotel, he instructed him "to hail any Chinaman attempting to escape and in case he would not stop, shoot him." According to storekeeper Charles Edward Huber, who was deputized and put on guard near the Coronel block, "The marshal told me to stand near the building and if any Chinamen came out to let them have it." When five or six Chinese men darted out of the Beaudry building, "we made them go back."[11]

With these orders, the sheriff and the city marshal sealed the fate of the Chinese trapped inside the Coronel building. What Burns and Baker did not know was that almost all the tong fighters who had taken part in the gun battle, the professional criminals from San Francisco who recognized trouble and knew when to leave, had already escaped from the neighborhood. More critically, the two lawmen either did not realize or were unconcerned that the crowd's mood had turned sinister. To make matters worse, the citizens they enlisted to stand guard around the block included a few of the thieves and brawlers who were regulars on Calle de los Negros and who had probably heard about the treasure chest inside the Wing Chung store. When Marshal Baker deputized a suspected burglar named Louis "Fatty" Mendel, Deputy Sheriff Sam Bryant warned him "that he had placed a very bad man as guard." Baker replied that "it was no matter," as "he had others to watch him."[12]

As evening approached, the patrolmen who were present struggled to manage the restless crowd. Policeman Emil Harris said that he and his partner George Gard tried to stop them from shooting, not so much to protect the Chinese but "for fear they would kill some white person accidentally." He told the people around him, "If you will stop firing, Officer Gard and I will find the guilty parties and bring them out."[13]

But the crowd was only getting more feverish, determined to force the Chinese out into the street. Sheriff Burns overheard impatient cries of "Damn the sheriff! Shoot him! Hang him!" He solicited the help of District Attorney Cameron E. Thom, who stepped up on a box and gave the mob a stern law-and-order talk. Burns also climbed atop a barrel and spoke to the assemblage, calling for them to keep calm. Suddenly, the top of the barrel collapsed, and Burns crashed to the ground. The spectators roared with laughter. The sheriff had lost what little control he still had.[14]

Ah Wing

6:15 p.m.

Huddled inside the dusky adobe apartments, the Chinese residents knew they were in great peril. For the past three years, their countrymen had been tormented on the streets of Los Angeles without cause. Now Angelenos thought they had good reason to come after them. The Chinese also knew what Los Angeles mobs could do. No doubt some of them had seen the vigilantes overpower the local lawmen and hang Michel Lachenais, the accused murderer, ten months earlier. Their friends and relatives in China had told them that the "foreign devils" in America were "wild and fierce and wicked."[15] For the first time, they may have wished they had taken the warnings more seriously.

All of their options were poor. They could make a run for it and try to escape, although it would be nearly impossible to get through the thick herd of armed bystanders unscathed. Or they could remain locked inside throughout the night, in the faint hope that the vengeful throng would not break in and attack them. As one white witness later stated, "Within or without, death was inevitable. The alternative was terrible."[16]

Shortly after six o'clock, as the streets were growing dim and shadowy, one Chinese man decided it was better to act than to wait. His name was Ah Wing,[17] and he worked a block away at the Pico House Hotel. He slipped out of the Beaudry building at the inter-section of Aliso and Los Angeles Streets, cater-cornered from the Coronel adobe. A few people noticed him and quickly seized him. The city marshal, Frank Baker, took Ah Wing from his captors.

From the crowd came a shout, "He is one of them and has a pistol!"

The crowd had no way of knowing whether Ah Wing was guilty of any crime. No one had gotten a good look at the tong fighters. Most of the bystanders had not even been on the block when the gun battle started. But the people on the street were beginning to seize control, and they demanded immediate satisfaction.

Marshal Baker quickly searched Ah Wing and found that he was carrying a four-barreled sharpshooter. Rather than trying to ensure his safety, Baker confiscated the pistol, Ah Wing's best hope of staving off the unpredictable mob, and ordered him back inside the Beaudry building.[18] In doing so, the marshal unwittingly passed a death sentence on Ah Wing.

Desperate, the man made a second try. Armed this time with a hatchet, Ah Wing summoned his courage and charged into the street. He tried to force his way through the clusters of people. A cry went up: "Here is one!" The fleeing man made it a short distance down Los

Angeles Street before someone grabbed him. The onlookers cheered. One of them tried to stab Ah Wing but instead ran the knife through his captor's hand. Others beat Ah Wing on the head with their canes.

Policeman Emil Harris and Constable Richard Kerren ran up and took Ah Wing from his captors. They started hustling him toward the jail with the help of a clerk named Charles H. Avery. A large group of rabble-rousers followed close behind them, clamoring, "Hang him! Shoot him! Take him from Harris!" Officer Harris thought they numbered at least one hundred.

They got as far as the corner of Spring and Temple Streets, a smart business district that boasted several handsome stores and the town's newest bank. Someone grabbed Officer Harris and pinned his arms behind his back. Another hooligan smacked Charles Avery on the ear. He let go of the prisoner. The gang easily overpowered the lawmen, taking hold of Ah Wing.[19]

A carpenter named J. G. Scott rushed out of T. H. Burdick's grocery store with a rope in his hand. He gave it to A. R. Johnston, a shoemaker, who shouted, "Bully, bully!"[20]

The mob dragged Ah Wing northwest along Temple Street and then turned up New High Street. Officer Harris yelled at them not to go that direction; the jail was on Spring Street. Badly outnumbered, he and his helpers apparently made no attempt to reclaim their Chinese charge from the large crowd. Instead, Harris headed back to Chinatown.

At the eastern gate of Tomlinson's corral and lumber yard, a stone's throw from St. Athanasius Episcopal Church, the men dragging Ah Wing halted. A boy scurried up the frame of the wide sliding doors to help fix the rope in place. A. R. Johnston brandished his six-shooter and bellowed, "God damn him, if you don't put the rope around his neck I'll shoot him anyhow."[21] The lynch crew tightened the noose around Ah Wing's throat. When the victim wailed, the crowd around him jeered and laughed.

His killers had not thought to bring a box or chair so that they could drop him. Instead, they hoisted Ah Wing violently off the ground. The rope broke. They tried attaching a stronger one to the trembling, whimpering man. This time they succeeded in lifting him up, snuffing out his life after a short struggle. For some reason, his body did not seem to hang properly. One of his killers climbed the gate and jumped forcefully on his shoulders, shattering both of his collar bones. They left Ah Wing's broken, mutilated corpse dangling from the crosspiece.[22]

Shortly afterward, a wheelwright named Ben McLaughlin passed by Burdick's grocery store. He heard J. G. Scott boast that his bunch had already "hanged one Chinaman."

McLaughlin told him, "It is not right."

"You are a damn Chinaman!" snorted Scott.[23]

Meanwhile, Sheriff Burns was still trying to pacify the throng in Chinatown. He assumed that Ah Wing had been successfully lodged in jail. Then he overheard someone say, "That fellow didn't kick over five seconds."[24] Too late, the sheriff realized what his fellow Angelenos were up to.

"Killing the White Men by Wholesale"

7:00 p.m.

Robert Thompson, the wounded volunteer, died at Wollweber's drugstore shortly before seven o'clock that evening after enduring terrible agony. Just before he expired, he asked his close friend, saloonkeeper Tom Gates, to look after his property for the benefit of his infant daughter, Cecilia. In addition to the little girl, he left behind a wife, Rosario, who was pregnant with twins.[25]

News of Thompson's murder by a Chinese gunman spread quickly. No doubt feelings ran high. Robert Thompson was well liked from his days as an owner of the Blue Wing Saloon. Word that he had died at the hands of a ruthless foreign assassin inflamed the locals even more.

However, the actual fact of Thompson's death was not what pushed the crowd over the edge. From the testimony of several witnesses, it appeared that the mob had already lynched Ah Wing before Thompson died. By then, rumors were out of control. Some people spread a false report that the injured policeman, Jesús Bilderrain, had also been murdered. A man named Norman L. King even heard that the Chinese "were killing the white men by wholesale in Negro Alley."[26] Without a doubt, the slaughter that was about to take place would have happened even if Robert Thompson had survived the night.

The Seige

7:00–8:45 p.m.

As darkness settled in, the crowd surrounding the Coronel building kept swelling. One eyewitness recalled, "Men streamed down from the hills and swarmed from the suburbs."[27] They were armed with pistols, Henry rifles, and shotguns. It was hard to get an accurate count, because people kept milling from one place to another. At its height, the crowd was estimated to have reached five hundred, almost one-tenth of Los Angeles's population. Journalists reported that Chinatown was in a "state of siege." No shots came from the Chinese apartments, which had grown quiet and dark. Though no one outside knew it, practically all the tong fighters had long since fled, abandoning the innocent Chinese occupants to the mob. The law officers on the scene must have thought it was still too risky to enter the Coronel adobe, for they made no attempt to do so.

Aggravated by the standstill, the Angelenos in the streets were impatient for something to happen. It galled them to think that the Chinese might not be punished before nightfall. There were angry cries to "clean the Chinese out of the city." In front of the hay scales on Los Angeles Street, Norman L. King, who worked at the railroad depot, harangued the crowd with an inflammatory stump speech denouncing missionary efforts among the "heathen Chinese." He claimed that the use of Chinese labor caused trouble in the community. King urged his listeners to take matters into their own hands.[28]

Someone else cried out, "All the Chinamen in the country ought to be hung." Refugio Botello, the butcher from Mexico who had been naturalized the previous year, shouted that he "didn't care a damn whether all the Chinamen were killed or not."[29]

Suddenly, the door of the Wing Chung store opened. Two women, Cha Cha and Fan Cho, stood silhouetted in the frame. Deputy Sheriff Sam Bryant, who was standing at the hay scales, called out, "Door's open. Boys, don't fire. They're going to surrender."

A volley of fifteen to twenty shots followed. One man fired his pistol close to Bryant's ear. The deputy sheriff "asked the damned fool what he was doing." It did not help matters that Bryant's fellow lawman, Constable Richard Kerren, had also opened fire.

Finally, depot employee Norman L. King, fresh from delivering his anti-Chinese tirade, hollered, "Don't fire, boys. It's a woman." The men paid attention to him and stopped shooting. But it was too late. The taller woman had been hit and wounded. She and her friend drew back inside.[30]

The lawmen knew they were in danger of losing their ability to restrain the crowd. They made some effort to restore order, but people treated their commands and pleas with disdain. Marshal Baker was afraid that the rabble would make its way up to the plaza. He started getting Chinese men and women out of the buildings on the northern end of Calle de los Negros, where the would-be vigilantes had not yet congregated. The escaping Chinese residents hurried to the jail for safety.

Mayor José Cristobal Aguilar, who had been alerted about the disturbance, made his way to the neighborhood. He rode his horse along Calle de los Negros to see what was going on. Aguilar, a former alcalde and councilman who was serving his third term as mayor, was held in esteem by both Anglos and Latinos. He might have used his considerable influence to calm the mob and warn his fellow citizens that they would be punished if they took the law into their own hands. However, he apparently said nothing to the crowd and remained on the scene only a short time, for no witnesses reported seeing him downtown after that.[31]

The people were getting tired of waiting for the Chinese to come out. The butcher Refugio Botello, armed with a six-shooter, climbed to the flat asphalt roof of the Coronel building. Others followed him, using ladders or simply ascending the adobe wall that enclosed the adjacent corral. Those on the ground passed up axes and pistols. Botello, along with Charles Austin, L. F. "Curly" Crenshaw, Louis "Fatty" Mendel, and several others, ran back and forth on the level roof, looking for any openings in it. Finally, J. C. Cox and Jesús Martinez started chopping into the roof with axes. They made three or four holes. For the Chinese inside, who could not see what was happening, the noises above them must have been terrifying.

As soon as the roof was broken, the men on top started shooting through the openings, trying to drive out the Chinese. They shouted in triumph any time they thought they had hit someone. The gunfire claimed one fatality. A laundryman known as Johnny Burrow was shot through the head and left wrist.

At that point, the Chinese in the Coronel adobe had no way of knowing that Ah Wing, the first escapee from the neighborhood, had been lynched. The wild shooting overhead made them think about following his footsteps and making a run for it. Around eight o'clock, a door opened on Calle de los Negros. Ah Cut, a liquor maker, dashed out into the street.[32] Faced with a horde of armed Angelenos, he quickly turned back and tried to reenter the building through another door. From across the alley, several men did exactly what Marshal Baker and Sheriff Burns had ordered them to do: they started shooting. Charles Edward Huber, one of those who followed police orders and fired, recalled that there seemed to be "five hundred shots at once."[33] The bullets tore up the dirt street around Ah Cut's feet. He fell, struck in the head and abdomen, and did not move.

Some of the deputized bystanders dragged his lifeless body to the porch of the Beaudry building across the alley. Ah Cut's companions inside the Coronel adobe parted a curtain covering a window in his room to see how he had fared. Several people rushed up and blasted through the window with shotguns and pistols. The Chinese returned the fire, then disappeared from view.

Policeman George Gard went up on the roof of the Coronel building to try to stop the random shooting. He peered through one of the holes. Below him, he saw the corpse of Johnny Burrow lying face upward on a top bunk. Blood flowed from a wound in his head. In the commotion, a lamp used for lighting opium pipes set fire to a curtain around Burrow's bunk. Citizen Fatty Mendel used a long stick to retrieve the burning curtain. Officer Gard put out the flame.

That gave the mob a new idea. Repeated cries of "Burn the sons of bitches out!" rang from the street. Other people protested that plan. Charles Edward Huber yelled, "We have enough fire in the United Sates without having any more." The great Chicago blaze had devastated that city only two weeks earlier, and most bystanders feared that things might get out of control if they set the building afire. As a precaution, one group ran to get the fire hose. They attached it to a hydrant on Main Street opposite Arcadia Street.

Despite the warnings, a few people threw fireballs into the open doorways on Calle de los Negros and the holes in the roof of the

Coronel building. The light that briefly shone on their faces allowed bystanders to identify some of the perpetrators in the darkness. One would-be arsonist, J. C. Cox, claimed that he only wanted to see the bodies of the dead Chinese inside. A butcher named Andres Soeur, shirtless and hatless, was seen in the glare clutching a meat cleaver.[34] A Chinese apartment briefly caught fire. Several people cried, "Stop the fire!" They used the fire hose to douse the roof of the tenement and put out the blaze.

Charles Avery, who had tried to help the police protect the first victim, heard someone say, "There is a dead Chinaman in there in a room." Avery went inside with several others and pulled the man out. He had been hit three times but was still alive. The wounded man called for water. Another voice threatened that if anyone showed him that small mercy, "We will shoot you."[35]

The mob next tried using the fire hose to force the Chinese into the street. They shot a powerful stream of water through any open door or window. However, they got no response. The Chinese, by then wounded, drenched, and thoroughly terrorized, still managed to hold the Coronel adobe. For three hours, the crowd had tried unsuccessfully to shoot them out, burn them out, and flush them out. But after seeing their neighbor Ah Cut shot down in the street, they were not going to budge.

The Refuge Breached

8:45 p.m.

The crowd would not wait any longer. And they knew they were far too many for the law officers to stop. Around a quarter to nine, the ring-leaders used a large rock to break down a door of the Coronel building facing Calle de los Negros. A storming party rushed in. They found one Chinese man hiding under a bed and roughly pulled him out. Other rioters tried to enter the next room to the south. Finding the interior door locked, they got a long pole and battered it until it collapsed. The mob poured through the building, demolishing more doors and dragging out all the occupants they could find.

They chased the Chinese into the streets. The men's queues, always a source of pride, became their downfall that night. The long braids made it easy for the crowd to catch them. In the corral out back, four Chinese who were hiding behind some horses were captured.

Policeman Gard hurried into the Coronel building in a hopeless effort to drive out the mob. Under a bunk, he found a petrified survivor—probably Wa Sin Quai, who had lived on Calle de los Negros for five years. The man called him by name. Gard extended his hand and told him to come out from beneath the bed. He discovered that the man was wounded. Just then, several rioters burst into the room and discharged their pistols at once. Wa Sin Quai died from eight gunshot wounds to the abdomen and legs.[36]

Meanwhile, the mob broke into the second apartment of the southern wing of the Coronel building. This was the office and home of Dr. Chee Long "Gene" Tong, the most popular Chinese physician in the city. In his early thirties, he was described as "an inoffensive person" who "attended strictly to his own business." The crowd seized the doctor and his wife, Tong You. They dragged them outside separately. In the street, the couple reunited and clasped each other, terror-stricken. The rioters also grabbed Chang Wan, the doctor's housemate. Dr. Tong, who was well educated and spoke fluent English, pleaded with his captors not to injure him, as he was innocent. They promised they would not.[37]

Policeman Emil Harris was circulating outside the Coronel building, unable to control the mob, which had splintered into many parties. He told the group on Arcadia Street to escort Dr. Tong to jail and not to hurt him. Harris gave the same instructions to other clusters of Angelenos that had hold of Chinese men. Having seen Ah Wing taken from him, however, the police officer could have held only slim hope that they would obey his orders and that their prisoners would not be harmed.

Officer Harris then hurried inside Sam Yuen's Wing Chung store, where he found "a crowd of roughs, entire strangers to me, who tried to fill their pockets with the contents of the store." He chased them out. At that point, Harris, one of the police force's ablest officers, made an astonishing decision. Rather than going back into the street to try to make sure his dubious volunteer "deputies" took their Chinese prisoners to jail, he stayed put in the Wing Chung store "to prevent plundering," as he later testified—even though the store had already been pillaged.[38] For whatever reason, the policeman chose to protect what was left of Sam Yuen's property rather than human life. He guarded the merchandise during the remainder of the riot, while the massacre continued unabated.

Tomlinson's Corral

8:45–9:15 p.m.

No sooner were the captured Chinese outside the Coronel building than their captors were placing ropes around their necks. Though the prisoners could not understand everything the people around them were saying, they knew what the mob had in mind. Some were shaking and moaning. A few begged for their lives. Others remained mute and stoic.

The lynching parties took off in several directions with their Chinese victims, tormenting them along the way. According to an eyewitness, they were "jerked along by as many eager hands as could lay hold of clothing and queue, cuffed and cursed in the meantime by the infuriated multitude."[39] The mob dragged one fallen victim through the streets using the rope fastened to his neck. Some Chinese may have been dead or unconscious before they reached the improvised gallows.

The bodies of those who had been shot earlier were lying on the street and sidewalk. Men stamped on their heads as they passed by. "By God, leave him alone. I've given him Mississippi hell," cried a rioter. An older man with a gray beard thundered as he kicked a wounded Chinese, "I've killed one damn son of a bitch." One Angeleno grabbed a Chinese man by the throat, shook him, and roared, "You son of a bitch, I've been waiting for you."[40]

Joseph Mesmer, the fifteen-year-old son of a German hotelier, watched the events in horrified disbelief. He and some of his teenage friends dashed about wildly from one crime scene to another, "so as not to miss a single thing that happened." Decades later, he was still amazed to recall that

from a state of complete tranquility and repose, a mob of men, in a few minutes, can be transformed into a mob of wild beasts who will stop at nothing if allowed free license to continue in a mad orgy. . . . They were wild-eyed and sweat-grimed. Knives, pistols and sword-canes were in many hands; and some armed themselves with short iron-pipes and clubs. Nearly all hashed about trying to vent their brutality on the unfortunate Chinamen the moment they were within reach.[41]

Near the Blue Wing Saloon, a Los Angeles lawyer, thirty-two-year-old Robert M. Widney, came upon the gang that had hold of laun-dryman Leong Quai and cigar maker Ah Long. Widney was walking north along Main Street from his house to his office and knew nothing about the gun battle in Chinatown. He asked what was going on. Someone in the party said, "We are taking the Chinamen to jail." Widney was suspicious and followed them. Instead of taking Spring Street to the jail, they headed up Temple Street. Widney caught up with them. One member of the group, a heavyset drugstore clerk whom Widney had seen before, finally admitted to him that they were going to hang their captives. Then the man flourished his firearm and tried to justify the mob's plan by saying, "Oh, you damned Chinese, you had a pistol!"

Widney asked a man with a broad face and square-cut whiskers, "Are you a vigilante?"

The man growled, "Damn it, we are all vigilantes." Then he pointedly told the lawyer, "There are a lot of white men here who ought to be hanged also."

Farmer Dan Moody pointed out to Widney, "If you take them to jail, they will take them out and hang them anyhow."[42]

Widney was panic-stricken. He was unarmed and did not know how he could possibly save the two victims from the pack of killers. He could run for help, but by the time he located a lawman or found some citizens to assist him, the hanging would probably be over. As he later explained, his years of experience in the Rocky Mountains and the mining camps of Nevada had convinced him that "words were useless with such rioters."[43]

Widney followed the hanging party along Temple Street, hoping for a chance to intervene. He also tried to find anyone he knew who might have enough influence with the mob members to stop the lynching. The gang hurried their two prisoners to the western gate of Tomlinson's corral, the same portal that the vigilance committee had used to hang Michel Lachenais the previous year. Widney mingled excitedly with the spectators, protesting what the lynch crew was about to do. He asked in vain for a revolver. No one offered to help him confront the hangmen.

While the mob prepared to hang the captives, another distressed witness, Morris Levin, said, "Give them a chance to speak."

Someone in the crowd replied, "The son of a bitch didn't give Bob Thompson a chance to speak."[44] It made no difference to the killers that their victims may not have even known about Thompson's murder. By that point, any Chinese would do. Amid howls of "Boys, hoist him up," Leong Quai and Ah Long were jerked from the ground by their necks.

A few minutes later, the rioters started back down Temple Street toward Chinatown. Widney followed them and eavesdropped, overhearing their plans to kill more Chinese. When they reached the intersection of Temple and Spring Streets, the lawyer saw "a surging mass of excited people" with "many active centers, indicating rioters having Chinese." He then realized that a full massacre was underway.[45]

Shortly afterward, another bunch arrived at Tomlinson's corral with physician Gene Tong and his housemate, Chang Wan. Though the night was overcast, the two captives could see the bodies of their neighbors from Calle de los Negros dangling from the crosspiece of the gate. Dr. Tong once again begged for his life, both in English and Spanish. He reminded them that he was innocent and had taken no part in the gun battle earlier that evening. He even offered his captors his entire savings of several thousand dollars if they would let him go. That only prompted the murderers to rip open his pockets and search for gold coins, stripping him of his trousers in the process. Then someone raised a pistol while he pleaded desperately and shot him through the mouth. The bullet tore off part of his face. Once the mob had finished ransacking the doctor's clothing, they hanged him.

Chang Wan was also hauled up to the beam with great force. The rope broke, and he fell to the ground. Once another rope was attached, he was jerked up against the beam again. His murderers then amused themselves by repeating this action. Teenager Joseph Mesmer, who witnessed this lynching, recalled that "the mob took a special delight in pulling him up and then letting him down, bumping his head forcibly each time against the cross-beam, the blow each time resounding like the breaking of a water-melon." Once they tired of torturing Chang Wan, they left a strong, tall man to guard the gallows. He made sure no one cut down any of the four victims while they might still be alive.[46]

Los Angeles and Commercial Streets

8:45–9:30 p.m.

Another lawyer, twenty-seven-year-old Henry T. Hazard, had been getting a shave at Charley Bowen's barbershop earlier that evening when a young black boy named Pete dashed in and told everyone about the shootout in Calle de los Negros. Breathlessly, he said that Officer Bilderrain was asking for a pistol. Hazard, his face still covered in lather, got up and went to see what was happening. Along the way, he noticed a crowd gathered at Wollweber's drugstore. Hazard stepped inside briefly and learned that Robert Thompson was dying. Then he headed to Chinatown, where he saw the rest of the horrific events unfold.[47]

When the storming party first broke into the Coronel adobe and seized its occupants, Hazard thought the bands of citizens were taking their Chinese prisoners to jail. Then he heard a commotion on Los Angeles Street south of Chinatown. He hurried toward John Goller's wagon shop, where he found a lynch party in action.

This group's three victims had been caught completely unaware. Wan Foo, Tong Won, and Ah Loo were walking home from work when the rioters seized them. Wan Foo and Tong Won were cooks. Tong Won was also a popular musician who had just come to town from San Francisco on the last steamer. Ah Loo, a boy of about fifteen, had arrived from China only a week earlier.

The three domestics had no idea that a gunfight had taken place in Chinatown or that several of their countrymen had been lynched. In all probability, they thought their captors wrongly suspected them of some petty crime and were taking them to jail. One of them said in broken English, "Me no afraid. Me very good China boy. Me no hurt no man."[48] The party placed ropes around their necks and hustled them through the streets.

Henry Hazard followed this bunch as they prepared to hang the three innocent laborers. Standing among the onlookers, he wondered aloud "if something couldn't be done to stop the hanging." A fellow observer told him, "It is more than your life is worth to go into that crowd."[49]

Wagon-maker John Goller, who was famous throughout California for his elaborate carriages, saw the mob with the Chinese captives near his house. He stepped outside and "remonstrated with them for bringing them there, where my little children were." He also told them, "I command you to release those men." A rioter held a rifle to his head, cocked it, and ordered, "You dry up, you son of a bitch." Another ran toward him with a huge carving knife and threatened, "I'll cut your damned heart out if you don't get away."[50]

On the west side of Los Angeles Street near Goller's wagon shop, an awning projected from the buildings over the sidewalk. The mob discovered that there was enough space between the crossbar of the awning and the roof to pass ropes through. As John Goller watched in horror what was taking place, it must have sickened him to realize that the lynch crew was using the very awning he had proudly constructed years earlier.[51]

Wan Foo, Tong Won, and Ah Loo were hanged close together. All three struggled somewhat for their lives. The murders, wrote journalist Ben C. Truman, were "a most barbarous process of slow and unreasoned strangulation." Joseph Mesmer added, "In a legal hanging the trap is sprung, and the fall breaks the victim's neck—being merciful in comparison with the brutal treatment accorded the victims of these human devils."[52] This type of suspension hanging sometimes caused excruciating death by strangulation, which often took several minutes as the victim's weight and struggling caused the noose to tighten.

Tong Won managed to get both hands above his head and grabbed the rope to avoid strangulation. For nearly five minutes, two rioters struck his hands with clubs and pistols. Once they had smashed the bones in both hands and beaten the flesh to a bloody pulp, Tong Won let go and dropped into the noose. Three other mob members discharged their revolvers at him, shattering his head with bullets. He was also stabbed.[53]

A man on a balcony overhead was "dancing a quick step" as he helped pull on the ropes. Someone cried out to him, "Go it, Reilly! Go it, old boy!" After the hanging, he took off his hat and joked, "Here's another soul saved." Then he hollered, "Bring me more Chinamen, boys, patronize home trade." Reilly also complained that he was out of work.[54]

A boy no older than ten also stood on top of the awning. According to one reporter, "He was as active as anyone in doing the hanging. His childish voice sounded strange at that time and place, as he called aloud for more victims; and it was a stranger and sadder sight still to behold him lay his hands to the rope and help to haul them up."[55]

A landlady named Mrs. Grascy loudly congratulated the rioters and urged them to carry on. She kept a boarding house across the street from Goller's wagon shop. When the lynch mob ran out of ropes, she invited one of the men to cut her clothesline. Afterward, she bragged to everyone within earshot that she had provided the makeshift rope.[56]

A few feet away from where Wan Foo, Tong Won, and Ah Loo were hanging, the murderers strung up four more victims. All of them were cooks. Day Kee had come to America from Sydney, and Ah Waa, a native of Hong Kong, had arrived from Yokohama. Ho Hing had landed in Los Angeles only two weeks before. Lo Hey hailed from San Francisco.

Henry Hazard, the young lawyer, was looking for any chance to thwart the mob, which was working with great haste. Around the corner on the south side of Commercial Street, several empty wagons were parked. Another bunch was about to hang more victims from one of them. Hazard climbed up on the wagon next to it and spoke loudly to the crowd. He asked, "Do you know the man you are hanging is guilty?"

Someone yelled, "He's a Chinaman. Hang him."

"You are Christians. He's a heathen," argued Hazard. His remark was bigoted, but he thought he might be able to shame some of the mob members into submission.

A few responded, "You're right."

"You had better dry up and get down or we'll hang you," someone else snapped.

"It isn't right," Hazard shot back.

A voice shouted, "Shut him up!"

Henry Hazard was not easily intimidated. The son of plain country folk, he had driven stagecoaches through Indian country and ridden horseback all the way from Los Angeles to the University of Michigan to attend law school. However, the young lawyer's friends were less audacious. One of them came up and pleaded, "Get down, Hazard, they'll shoot or hurt you." Finally, his companions yanked the bold orator off the wagon just as two or three shots were fired at him.

Then Hazard saw an acquaintance, Ramón Dominguez, and two others leading a Chinese man through the streets. He pressed them, "Will you take the man to be hanged? You would be taking him to be murdered. You will not hang that Chinaman." This time, Hazard's haranguing worked. The trio looked ashamed and let their captive go.[57]

Others were not so lucky. The mob hanged Ah Won, a cook for a family, and Wing Chee, a cook in a Chinese establishment, from the side of one of the wagons on Commercial Street. They robbed Ah Won's body of $200 in coin and a diamond ring, later found in a pawn shop. While Wing Chee was dying, someone shot him in the mouth, "out of which his innocent blood spurted, producing a great spot of clot and spatter upon the ground under which he was hanging but a foot and a few inches," according to journalist Ben C. Truman. Finally, they hanged Wong Chin, a storekeeper, from the tailgate of the wagon.

"That'll do for the son of a bitch," someone growled.[58]

Resistance

9:00–9:30 p.m.

"The cheap labor is done away with now. The sons of bitches are hanged!" The drunken reveler was A. R. Johnston, the shoemaker, at the head of a party leading another Chinese man to be hanged. He was waving his six-shooter, loudly proclaiming that "every damned one" should be "hung by morning," when he finally met resistance. William Widney, the lawyer's younger brother, approached him and asked, "What are you going to do with the Chinaman?"

Johnston blurted out, "Hang him, by God."

The younger Widney stuck his pistol in Johnston's face and ordered him not to do it. At that moment, Samuel C. Foy, who had a saddle and harness shop on Los Angeles Street, grabbed Johnston's gun. Policeman William Sands wrenched it from his hands. Johnston taunted them by saying, "I can get another in two minutes."[59]

When Leon Baldwin arrived at the house where he stayed on Temple Street, he saw a Chinese man hanging from the crosspiece of the gate at Tomlinson's corral. A rioter came to his house and asked for a rope. Outraged, Baldwin requested his brother "to remonstrate with the mob against doing the hanging there, as the house opposite was full of ladies." The brother, John M. Baldwin, was a national guardsman and future deputy sheriff who had tried unsuccessfully to prevent the lynching of Michel Lachenais the previous year. He had just returned from the Bella Union Hotel, where he found many people anxious to put a stop to the massacre but no one to willing to take charge and lead.

John Baldwin went back into the street and addressed the group. Although his brother thought there was as much English as Spanish spoken in the crowd, he decided to speak in Spanish. He rebuked them and told them to stop what they were doing. Several people sneered at his remarks. A hardware dealer named John D. Hicks mockingly misinterpreted his speech in English. Baldwin quickly realized that the crowd's sentiment was very much against him. As he said later, "I might as well have spoken to a cyclone." He went back into his house, sent his family to a neighbor's place for safety, and remained on watch all night.[60]

Several other citizens, with little direction from the sheriff or city marshal, were doing whatever they could to prevent more hangings. All of them were threatened, though no one was actually harmed. When J. D. Connor, the proprietor of a fish market, tried to help a captured Chinese man, someone put a pistol to his face and yelled, "You get away from here, you son of a bitch." One rescuer, resisting a party with another victim, commanded, "There shall be no more hanging unless the Chinamen are taken over my dead body." Someone in the mob replied, "Then we'll hang him over your dead body." After Edward Wright objected to the hangings, a man stuck a pistol to his head and told him, "Dry up. You have nothing to do with it." The lawmen were just as vulnerable. When Sheriff Burns extricated a Chinese man from the mob, a tall fellow named Patrick McDonald drew his pistol and threatened, "Damn you, Burns, we'll hang him anyhow."[61]

Despite the threats against them, the law officers and a few citizens managed to keep the death toll from rising even higher. Deputy Sheriff Sam Bryant protected seven Chinese women by taking them out the back of the Wing Chung store. He had to leave a Chinese man behind, telling him, "I cannot take you as it might endanger the life of the women." Bryant lodged the women in jail for safety. Later, when he was preparing to escort some Chinese men from their hiding places, he stationed Officer Robert Hester near New High Street and instructed him, "Call out when we pass with the Chinamen 'they're all women' to throw off suspicion." The trick worked, and Bryant was able to save a few more potential victims.[62]

Meanwhile, William Widney got into a heated argument with a clothing retailer named Cohen. Widney and his older brother, Robert, had liberated a Chinese man and were trying to take him to safety, while Cohen followed them. The younger Widney wheeled around and asked him, "Mr. Cohen, what are you in favor of?" Cohen shot back, "In favor of hanging every goddamn one of them." Widney snarled, "Get out of our crowd or I will knock you over." Then A. J. Bowman, a passerby who overheard this exchange, grabbed Cohen by the shoulder and flung him into the street.[63]

When Robert Widney and his party got to the corner of Temple and Spring Streets, they saw several groups parading with captured Chinese. Widney and a grocer named John Lazzarovich grabbed one of the Chinese men. William Widney arrived with a pistol, and his brother Robert took it from him. The shoemaker A. R. Johnston, now unarmed, resisted them violently. Robert Widney jerked him back and put the pistol to his face, saying, "You can't do any more hanging. The rest of the Chinamen must go to jail."[64]

Meanwhile, one crew was leading a Chinese woman along the street. Lazzarovich grabbed the man who held her. When the mob members started harassing Lazzarovich, Robert Widney stepped between them and brandished his pistol to chase them off. Another gang was taking a Chinese victim up Temple Street toward Tomlinson's corral. Widney and his companions seized the captive. The crowd made two attempts to grab the man, but the rescuers got him safely to the jail.

Inexplicably, the law officers, unlike some of the volunteer rescuers, did not seem to use their weapons to force the lynchers to release their captives. Nor did they attempt to arrest anyone. Even when Deputy Sheriff Sam Bryant overheard A. R. Johnston say he had hanged four Chinese, he thought the remark was "insufficient to make an arrest upon." One newspaper later charged that the police were "so dazed by the firing that they did nothing more than look on at the wholesale lynching."[65] The lack of arrests was justified in one sense, however: during the time the lawmen would have spent taking a handful of culprits to jail, countless other lynchers could have quickly carried out more hangings unhampered. At that point, it was better for the officers not to leave the scene.[66]

By nine o'clock, nearly all the Chinese who had not escaped early in the evening had either been captured by the mob or found refuge at the jail or in American houses and shops. Their home, the Coronel building, stood in shambles. The looting had started as soon as the residents were driven out. "Help yourselves, boys," someone cried out to the rioters. They did. They broke open the trunk in the Wing Chung store and took all the money. No doubt some of the thieves had heard the rumor the previous afternoon about proprietor Sam Yuen's treasure chest. According to Fong Yuen Sing, the firm's bookkeeper, the mob destroyed or stole about $3,500 worth of merchandise. Then they ransacked the other apartments and tore through chests and drawers. One Chinese merchant who had $4,000 worth of gold coins in his trunk thought about going back inside to retrieve it. His friends stopped him, saving his life. In addition, the thieves carried off hats, caps, boots, shoes, clothing, jewelry, blankets, clocks, cigars, food, and liquor. The total loss was estimated at anywhere between $14,000 and $30,000.[67]

The thieves knew they had to work in haste. One said, "We haven't gone through that end room yet." Another replied, "If we are going, we had better be quick before the Dough-boys come up."[68] He was referring to the soldiers stationed at the army's Drum Barracks in nearby Wilmington. The rioters incorrectly assumed they had been alerted and were on their way.

Other thieves were robbing the Chinese on the streets. Attorney Andrew Glassell's cook, Ah Ku, lost over $400 while he was being taken to jail. A few claimed to have had up to $1,000 stolen. The lynching victims were also robbed of all the cash or jewelry they had on them. Others "had their pockets cut out with knives, which entered into and fearfully lacerated the flesh, the wretches having neither time nor patience to rifle them in the usual way," according to a reporter. One Chinese man, who had worked for a long time at a restaurant in Los

Angeles, had withdrawn his entire savings that morning to send to his elderly father in China. He gave the money to his brother, who was murdered and robbed during the riot.[69]

By 9:20 p.m., most of the mayhem had run its course. Sheriff Burns ascended an embankment at the corner of Spring and Temple Streets and spoke to the crowd once more. He commanded all law-abiding citizens to follow him to Chinatown. This time, he got the help he needed. When he and his volunteers reached the Coronel adobe, the sheriff deputized twenty-five armed men to keep order and guard the neighborhood until morning.

He was much too late, however. Sheriff Burns and his fellow lawmen had squandered their many chances to try to break up the mob during the three hours it held the Coronel adobe under siege. Once the rioters finally invaded the building, there was no way the officers could stop all the multiple bands of lawbreakers. It took them little more than half an hour to hang fourteen Chinese men and destroy their homes.[70]

Celebration

11:00 p.m.

The streets of downtown Los Angeles were quiet and empty by eleven o'clock, as if nothing had happened there. However, the saloons were filled that evening, and "the topic of conversation everywhere was 'the night of horrors.'"[71] Many of the rioters were out celebrating. In their excitement, several of them blurted out admissions they would soon regret.

At J. H. Weldon's saloon on Commercial Street, Edmund Crawford was overheard to say, "I have been doing a dirty job." A middle-aged fellow with blood on his hands and shirt sleeves bragged, "I am satisfied now. I have killed three Chinamen." At Christopher Higby's saloon, shoemaker A. R. Johnston joked that "some of the long-tails" had "gone up." On the corner outside, J. C. Cox boasted that he had fired at a fleeing Chinese man, who "keeled over."[72]

Rioter Andres Soeur, who had been seen carrying a meat cleaver all night, was hungry after taking part in the massacre. He went to have dinner at Eugene Germain's French restaurant across from the Merced Theatre. There he bragged to a Mexican-American man "that he had a hand in hanging five Chinamen."[73]

Some concerned citizens visited the crowded saloons not to socialize but to learn more about what had happened. The saddle and harness merchant Samuel Foy had been hiding some Chinese at his house who were terribly anxious. He went back to town to see if he could find out what had become of their relatives. At Higby's barroom, he overheard shoemaker A. R. Johnston say, "I am not going home while any Chinamen are alive. I have killed five, by God." At around one o'clock in the morning, Johnston's next-door neighbor, Louis Rich, was awakened by the voice of a drunken man outside saying, "This is my shop. I have killed some Chinamen. I have lost my key." After getting in a scuffle with his companions, Johnston broke in.[74]

Another mob member celebrating at Higby's was Samuel C. Carson. Intoxicated, he drew his six-shooter from its holster and boasted, "This never fails." Speaking in Spanish, he implied that his pistol "had got two." Liveryman Mike Madegan, who had helped quell the riot, wanted to examine Carson's gun to see if it had been fired recently. However, Madegan was afraid to approach the confessed killer.[75]

Wagon-maker John Goller, who had remonstrated with the mob when they hanged several Chinese near his house, also went out that night to see what he could learn. While he was at Robert Mulloy's saloon on Main Street, another shoemaker named Patrick Sarsfield (P. S.) Dorney thrust a severed Chinese queue in his face and joked, "If you don't believe this is China, smell it." The bar owner, a brawler with a history of assaults, grabbed Dorney and kicked him out.[76] Fifteen years later, Dorney would write the first eyewitness memoir of the massacre for *The Overland Monthly*, never mentioning his own misdeeds that night.

Sanctuary

Many of the Chinese who had escaped the clutches of the lynch mob fled from the city by all roads, abandoning their belongings to the looters. They took refuge in the vineyards and orange groves on the outskirts of Los Angeles. About forty members of Yo Hing's Hong Chow Company crossed the river and headed eastward. More than one hundred others reportedly went to Wilmington to get on the steamer bound for San Francisco. Sam Yuen and his brother, Cum Yun, were said to have donned aprons, disguising themselves as cooks, and slipped away.[77]

Most of those who stayed in town remained concealed in private houses. About sixty sought sanctuary in an American's residence on Main Street. Some made it to homes in the southern part of the city. William Slaney locked some Chinese workers in his boot and shoe store on the corner of Commercial and Los Angeles Streets and stood guard. Justice of the Peace William H. Gray hid several Chinese men and women in his cellar. For years afterward, he would receive anonymous gifts of Chinese silks, porcelains, and teas in appreciation. Juan and Petra Lanfranco guarded their cook, Sing Ty, for a full week after the massacre.[78] Other Chinese were safely lodged in jail.

After the riot was over, the bodies of fourteen Chinese were still suspended in darkness from the western gate at Tomlinson's corral, the awning on Los Angeles Street, and the wagon on Commercial Street. One eyewitness reported that the "stark, staring corpses hung ghastly in the moonlight," while "others, mutilated, torn and crushed, lay in our streets."[79] The first lynching victim, Ah Wing, had been cut down shortly after he was hanged. His body was carried to the City Cemetery for burial the following day. Late that night, Sheriff Burns gave orders to remove the remaining corpses. Altogether, fifteen Chinese had died by hanging, and three more had been shot to death at the Coronel adobe.[80] Under the direction of County Coroner Joseph Kurtz, the bodies were taken to the jail yard.

Chinatown was desolate and virtually deserted for the rest of the night. A few police officers and deputized citizens stood guard in the dimly lit neighborhood to prevent any more looting of the abandoned tenements. Come morning, the people of Los Angeles would start to sort through the debris and ponder how things had gone so horribly wrong in their city on what the newspapers would soon call "the Black Tuesday."[81]

8

The Aftermath

October 25, 1871, Morning

When the sun rose on Los Angeles the next morning, the first light revealed a "strange and repulsive sight" in the yard of the brick jail-house. Beneath the shadow of the building's north wall, neatly lined up in two rows, lay the mangled bodies of seventeen men. Some still had ropes attached to their necks. Journalists who arrived to look at the disfigured corpses reported that their faces were "ghastly and distorted," "besmeared with blood, and pierced with bullets." Their clothing was in tatters; in some instances, it was stripped off altogether. Two victims, Ah Cut and Wa Sin Quai, were riddled with bullets. Four had their queues cut off. Nearby sat stacks of rough redwood coffins, ready to receive the remains. As noted, the body of one other massacre victim, Ah Wing, had already been taken to the cemetery the night before.

Huddled in a room on the jail's ground floor were more than twenty Chinese survivors. Some of these men and women had fled there on their own; others had been escorted by rescuers. About eleven of them had escaped harm during the riot. Approximately seven were slightly wounded. Another four or five had serious injuries. One of them, a brother of physician Gene Tong, had been shot in the neck. He was stretched out on a blanket thrown over the asphalt floor, moaning pitifully.[1]

Before long, distraught Chinese poured into the white-fenced jail yard to search for missing friends and relatives. Virtually everyone in the small Chinese community was directly affected, as about one out of ten had been murdered. Many survivors had spent the night not knowing whether their loved ones had found refuge or ended up on the gallows. One young fellow told a reporter that when an American gets mad, "he damn fool. He kill good Chinaman all same [as] bad Chinaman." A great many of their countrymen, including the *huiguan* leaders, were still in hiding. Yo Hing was concealed at Alex Rendon's barbershop. Sam Yuen was rumored to be staying in the office of Justice of the Peace William H. Gray. Others claimed he had already left town.[2]

At ten o'clock, the coroner's inquest began. After the jurors had examined the seventeen bodies in the jail yard and determined the causes of death, the silent Chinese bystanders placed them carefully in the coffins. They closed the lids and nailed small slats of wood to the boxes to identify each victim. Then they loaded them into a wagon. Dr. Gene Tong's coffin, draped in black, was carried out first. In solemn procession, the mourners started for the City Cemetery, the nondenominational burial ground four blocks west of the plaza on Fort Hill. Those riding in the makeshift hearse threw tiny pieces of paper along the way, inscribed with Chinese characters. They represented copper coins that the deceased could use to buy safe passage from any vagrant spirits.

The mourners gathered at the southwest corner of the cemetery, where the graves had already been prepared. That section of the city's burial ground was considered "beyond the pale," the final resting place of ne'er-do-wells, paupers, lynching victims, and "Indians who died by violence." A relative or friend of one man opened his coffin just before interment and put a pair of sandals and a shirt inside, things that might be needed in the world beyond. Several coffins were placed in a single grave, for this was just a temporary resting place until the remains could be sent back to China. After the coffins were covered with dirt, some mourners threw rice and burning tapers on the earthen mounds. Others built fires at the foot of the graves and burned Joss sticks. Beside one grave—perhaps Dr. Tong's—a woman knelt and wept. The mass funeral that morning, like the arrest of Sing Yu ten months earlier, had temporarily united the warring Chinese community of Los Angeles. This time, people were brought together by shock and grief.[3]

They also shared unspeakable anger at both the horde of barbarian killers and a handful of their own reckless compatriots. Oddly, the mourners at the cemetery completely ignored the grave of one of the victims. According to a reporter, "None of the Chinese would have anything to do with him. Even after he was interred, they declined to offer to his departed spirit that tribute which it is customary for them to pay." Perhaps they held him partly accountable for what had happened. According to Policeman Emil Harris, who regularly patrolled Chinatown and knew all of the deceased, only one of the eighteen massacre victims had taken part in the gunfight that set off the riot. He was described as a "small, good-looking, well dressed Chinaman," believed to have been a brother of Sing Lee, the See Yup kingpin.[4] The other seventeen had simply been in the wrong place at the wrong time.

Meanwhile, the massacre was practically the only topic of conversation on the streets and in the homes of Los Angeles. The shock weighed heavily on the town that morning, leaving a pall of gloom that contrasted sharply with the revelry in the saloons a few hours earlier. One local recalled, "Men walked with furtive glances at their neighbors as though ashamed of themselves and well they might be." As citizens went quietly about their business, some consciously avoided the sites of the gruesome killings. Others were drawn to them by morbid curiosity. The owner of Tomlinson's corral and lumber yard, tired of both lynch mobs and sightseers, tore down the gates that had been used for the hangings.[5]

Another Funeral

October 25, 1871, Afternoon

Not long after the Chinese burials, another funeral took place from a house on New High Street. A large crowd gathered to pay their respects to Robert Thompson, the only non-Chinese fatality of the previous night. The popular rancher from Arkansas had lived in California for nineteen years and had many friends in Los Angeles. The town's drinking men had gotten to know him during the four years he owned the Blue Wing Saloon. His widow, Rosario de Thompson, was devastated. Only three weeks shy of giving birth to twins, she would be left with three young children to raise by herself.[6]

The Los Angeles dailies praised Thompson as "a well-known and respected citizen" and "a generous hearted, liberal man." The first news reports also heralded his bravery, claiming that Thompson had been "killed while aiding an officer in the discharge of his duty." According to many accounts, Policeman Jesús Bilderrain had asked Thompson to help him subdue the Chinese tong fighters. That was not so. Bilderrain never testified that he asked Thompson to intervene, and another lawman, Esteban Sanchez, even warned him to "go away or he would get shot."[7]

Decades later, Thompson's reputation would be sullied in Horace Bell's retelling of the massacre, published in 1930. Bell relied on a dubious tale related by a single, unidentified Chinese source who insisted that Thompson had gone to Sam Yuen's Wing Chung store just before the riot to steal the proprietors' money and had even fired the first shot.[8] Despite the overwhelming evidence to the contrary, several later writers credited Bell's far-fetched story, vilifying Thompson for his role in the gun battle that precipitated the Chinese massacre.

A more balanced conclusion is that Thompson was an ordinary if excitable citizen who acted recklessly in the heat of a chaotic moment, like countless other Angelenos of his era. Had he realized what was about to unfold in the Chinese quarter, chances are he would have thought better and stepped aside.

A Tour of the Coronel Adobe

October 25, 1871

On any other day, Chinatown would have been a densely packed hub of activity. But the morning after the massacre, the neighborhood was deserted. Hardly a sound was heard on the streets south of the plaza. At daybreak, eight Chinese men and seven women were discovered still hiding in the ravaged Coronel adobe. The few Chinese residents who had not fled the area the night before were packing their belongings and leaving town. During the day, some returned to see how their homes had fared. By sundown, however, the doors and windows of every Chinese house in the city were closed and barred.

At the time the first Chinese residents arrived around 1850, Los Angeles was a compact adobe pueblo of only 1,610 people. This view, looking east, shows the plaza and Our Lady Queen of Angels Church (still standing today) on the left. *Drawing courtesy of the Huntington Library.*

A CHINESE MERCHANT!

— to the —

PUBLIC OF LOS ANGELES!!!

CHUN CHICK

RESPECTFULLY announces to the public of Los Angeles, that he has

OPENED A STORE

On SPRING STREET. opposite the Court House, where he has on hand and for sale, a general assortment of

CHINESE GOODS,

— CONSISTING OF —

TEA, PRESERVES, SUGAR, &c,

including every article of GROCERIES usually imported from China for the American market.

The advertiser requests the public of Los Angeles to call and examine his goods, either to purchase or through curiosity, as he is satisfied he can make it the interest of all citizens to deal with him for his class of merchandise.

He will promptly fill all orders for Chinese goods, with which he may be favored.

July 13, 1861.m CHUN CHICK.

Chun Chick proudly advertised the opening of Los Angeles's first Chinese store in 1861. Like other early Chinese merchants in California, he found it difficult to attract non-Asian customers, and his business did not survive. *Los Angeles Star, July 13, 1861.*

(Continued)

Most of Los Angeles's early Chinese immigrants found jobs as domestics or launderers. Some peddled vegetables, while others worked in the vineyards, orchards, and fields surrounding the town. Chinese men who came to the United States soon stopped wearing the clothing of their homeland and instead embraced American-style attire, including broad-brimmed felt hats. *Peddler photograph courtesy of the California Historical Society; vineyard photograph courtesy of the Huntington Library.*

The *Los Angeles News* complained in 1869 that the town's plaza was "an unsightly affair to everybody," reeking of rotten produce and dead animals. That year, the city planted trees to "hide the ugliness" of the brick water tank on the far right. Our Lady Queen of Angels Church (left) is facing Main Street, and the three streets heading northeast are, left to right, Main, Bath (where several brothels were located), and Vine (present-day Olvera). *Photograph courtesy of the Huntington Library.*

This view of downtown Los Angeles, looking southeast from Fort Hill in 1870, shows, from left to right, the plaza, the Pico House Hotel (the town's first three-storied building), the Masonic Hall (the oldest building still standing south of the plaza), and, in the right background, Calle de los Negros and Chinatown. *Photograph courtesy of the Huntington Library.*

The main building that the Chinese leased in Los Angeles for their homes and businesses was the dilapidated, L-shaped Coronel adobe, photographed by William M. Godfrey around 1870. The third door from the left was the entrance to the Wing Chung store, where citizen Robert Thompson was shot on the evening of the Chinese massacre. Dr. Gene Tong's office and home was behind the second door from the right. The Pico House Hotel (still standing today) is in the left background, and Calle de los Negros is on the right. *Photograph courtesy of the Seaver Center for Western History Research.*

The center of Chinatown was Calle de los Negros or "Negro Alley," renamed Los Angeles Street in 1877. By the time this photograph was taken in the mid-1880s, the Coronel adobe (left) had deteriorated badly and was missing its southern veranda. A fire ravaged the building in 1886. The town's first firehouse, built on the plaza in 1884 and still standing today, is visible in the left background. *Photograph courtesy of the Huntington Library.*

The residents of Los Angeles's first Chinatown tried to make this old Mexican neighborhood feel like home, stringing Chinese banners and lanterns from the galleries. Note the men's long queues. *Photograph courtesy of the Seaver Center for Western History Research.*

Notice.

The public of Los Angeles and vicinity are hereby informed that I have opened a DRUG STORE, on Main street, in the house of Wm. Abbott, No. 25, where medicine will be carefully prepared. A doctor is constantly in attendance. GENETONG, Chinese Physician.

An INTELLIGENCE OFFICE is also connected with the above, and employment will be found f or those desiring it, and those desiring help will do well to call. All sorts of help furnished, farmers, gardeners, cooks, etc. Los Angeles, July 21, 1y

Los Angeles physician Chee Long "Gene" Tong sought to attract non-Asian patients in 1870 and also operated an employment agency for their convenience. The following year, he was brutally murdered during the Chinese massacre. *Los Angeles News, July 23, 1870.*

By the summer of 1870, anti-Chinese sentiment was on the rise in Los Angeles. Two non-Asian laundries proudly advertised the exclusion of Chinese laborers from their establishments, where the work was done by "experienced white women." *Los Angeles News, July 24, 1870.*

REWARD.

$100 REWARD WILL BE PAID BY
the undersigned for the arrest and
delivery to the Sheriff of this county of. a
small Chinese woman named Lon You. Had
\on when last seen a black Chinese coat with
gold buttons, is full faced and about twenty
years old   SING LEE.
Los Angeles, October 16, 1870.   2w

See Yup headman Sing Lee offered a one hundred dollar reward in
1870 for the capture and return of a missing Chinese prostitute,
Sing Yu (identified as "Lon You" in this advertisement). The competition for the reward money resulted in a fatal shootout between
two Los Angeles law officers. *Los Angeles News, Oct. 28, 1870.*

On December 17, 1870, Los Angeles vigilantes stormed the jail, seized the accused murderer Michel Lachenais, and lynched him at the western gate of Tomlinson's corral (approximately the junction of today's Spring and Temple Streets). William M. Godfrey took this photograph immediately afterward. The following year, another episode of mob violence in Los Angeles would result in the murders of eighteen Chinese men, four of whom were hanged from this same transverse. *Photograph courtesy of the Huntington Library.*

Photographer Steven A. Rendall was looking northeast in 1869 when he shot the panoramic view that included the notorious Tomlinson's corral and lumber yard. Buena Vista Street is on the left, and St. Athanasius Episcopal Church (northwest of the present-day City Hall) is on the right. Today, the Hall of Justice stands to the northwest (left) of the site of Tomlinson's corral, and the federal district courthouse property occupies the eastern (right) portion. *Photograph courtesy of the California Historical Society Collection at USC, Title Insurance and Trust/C. C. Pierce Photography Collection.*

(Continued)

This 1869 photograph shows Commercial Street from its T-intersection with Main Street, looking east toward Herman Heinsch's two-storied saddle and harness shop (which was replaced by the present-day Federal Building). Three Chinese were hanged from a wagon parked on the south (right) side of the street. Around the corner to the right, another seven Chinese were hanged from an awning on Los Angeles Street near John Goller's wagon shop, shown in the drawing. Both lynching sites are now occupied by the Los Angeles Mall. *Commercial Street photograph courtesy of the Seaver Center for Western History Research; wagon shop drawing courtesy of the Huntington Library.*

The imposing Temple Block, situated at the three-way intersection of Main Street (left), Spring Street (right), and Temple Street (not visible but veering off on the far right), was only a month away from completion at the time of the Chinese massacre on October 24, 1871. Members of the mob, rather than following police orders to take their Chinese prisoners down Spring Street to the jail, instead turned right on Temple Street and headed to the lynching site at Tomlinson's corral. *Photograph courtesy of the Huntington Library.*

The bodies of seventeen victims of the Chinese massacre lay in the jail yard on the morning of October 25, 1871, until the coroner's inquest was concluded. Some still had ropes attached to their necks, and their faces were "besmeared with blood and pierced with bullets." The remains of one other murdered man had been taken to the City Cemetery the night before. *Photograph courtesy of the Security Pacific National Bank Collection/Los Angeles Public Library.*

The Los Angeles county courthouse, constructed in 1859 between
Main and Spring Streets, was the scene of the closely-followed riot
trials of 1872. *Photograph courtesy of the Huntington Library.*

This section of photographer Steven A. Rendall's panoramic view of Los Angeles in 1869 shows the courthouse on the left and the two-storied brick jail and its enclosed yard on the far right. Much of this area is now occupied by City Hall. *Photograph courtesy of the California Historical Society Collection at USC, Title Insurance and Trust/C. C. Pierce Photography Collection.*

Los Angeles Justice of the Peace William H. Gray was popular among the local Chinese, whom he treated fairly in his court-room. On the night of the massacre, he also saved several potential Chinese victims by hiding them in his cellar. *Photograph courtesy of the California Historical Society Collection at USC, Title Insurance and Trust/C. C. Pierce Photography Collection.*

On the horrific night of October 24, 1871, Robert M. Widney witnessed some of the lynchings and helped rescue Chinese captives from the mob. He later served as presiding judge at the riot trials. *Photograph courtesy of the Huntington Library.*

The area northeast of Sonoratown (now Los Angeles's New China-town) is shown in Carleton Watkins's 1877 photograph from the intersection of Buena Vista Street (left) and Short Street (right). This vantage point is just south of the junction of present-day North Broadway and Cesar E. Chavez Avenue. *Photograph courtesy of the Huntington Library.*

The Chinese community of Los Angeles persevered despite many years of persecution and six decades of the federal exclusion law barring further immigration. This view of a thriving Chinatown shows the intersection of Marchessault and Los Angeles Streets on the northern edge of the plaza around 1880. *Photograph courtesy of the Seaver Center for Western History Research.*

A few lawmen stood silently in the streets, guarding the abandoned Chinese homes and businesses from further looting. They were also stationed there in case of a second assault. Rumors circulated through Los Angeles that the rioters might return that evening, pillaging the stores and houses on the east side of Calle de los Negros. The Coronel building, which had taken the brunt of the mob's fury, was largely uninhabitable. Some Angelenos speculated that it would never be reoccupied and instead would "be a silent reminder of the fearful scenes of violence enacted during the great riot." Ah Yung, a partner in the Wing Chung store, went there the morning after to survey the damage, but the police officers would not let him inside.[9]

However, they allowed a few journalists to wander through the empty tenement. Even those who had witnessed the riot the night before were shocked by what they saw in the daylight. One exterior door had thirty-two bullet holes. The roof was torn open in several places; some of the holes were three or four feet long. Inside, the plaster covering the thick adobe walls was pitted with bullet marks and smeared with blood. The floors were "sprinkled and stained with gore." In the rooms used as brothels, the bedding was torn up and scattered. The mob had ransacked all but two trunks.

The *Star* reporter who toured Sam Yuen's Wing Chung store was astonished by what he found:

Numerous boxes, rattan bags of rice, preserved ginger, casks and trunks lay bursted [*sic*] and cut open by the pillagers. Clothes, Joss sticks, candles, broken chairs and large quantities of sugar were strewn in every direction. Proceeding to the next room a most sickening sight met our gaze. Blood was smeared in all directions on the walls and boxes, and in and under the beds were pools of clotted gore.[10]

In the silence of the Wing Chung partners' vacant dining room, things looked eerily normal, as if the guests had momentarily stepped out for a smoke. The table was set for six. Crossed chopsticks were neatly placed on the right sides of the plates. In the middle of the table sat a huge basin of rice, two bowls of chopped fish, a large dish of greens, and "a variety of Chinese delicacies that we are not familiar with." From the looks of the elaborate feast that had been prepared and served, Sam Yuen and his Nin Yung colleagues must not have been expecting trouble the evening before.

In the kitchen behind the Coronel building, a tin boiler of cold rice sat on the stove. A bullet had passed through it, striking the floor. Attached to the kitchen was the cook's shanty. The linens of his bed were completely saturated with blood. This may have been the room of Wing Chee, identified as a cook in a "China house" who was shot and hanged from the wagon on Commercial Street.

From the awning of the veranda outside Dr. Gene Tong's apartment in the Coronel building, the physician's signboard still swung forlornly in the cool, heavy breeze. Inside the abandoned room, the *Star* reporter was "confronted with the most horrible spectacle of any. Human gore could be traced in all directions." The mob had flown into a frenzy searching for the doctor's reputed stash of gold. "Valises were torn and cut open, clothes with pockets cut out, and shirts severed in twain . . . Drugs were scattered in heaps on the floor." The chairs, table, and bedstead were shattered. As the journalist looked from one hideous sight to another, he discovered one small sign of hope. Beneath the counter, the doctor's trembling poodle was still alive, albeit "with a leg broken and in a half starved condition."[11]

"The Chinese Outrage"

The morning after the massacre, as Angelenos got their first good look at the devastation in Chinatown and saw the chilling traces of human blood and fragments of dangling ropes around town, the *Los Angeles Star* hit the streets with a revolting editorial. Titled "The Chinese Outrage," it began, with no sense of irony:

> The horrible assassinations which were perpetrated in our city last night by the brutal, uncivilized barbarians that infest the country, is an indication of what the consequence would be were their race trans-migrated in large numbers upon this coast. Upon all the earth there does not exist a people who value life so lightly, who practice so many horrors, or who are so unmerciful in their outrages. From their very mode of existence, they have little regard for their own lives and none whatever for the lives of others.[12]

This self-righteous screed had been hastily jotted down at Theodore Wollweber's drugstore prior to the mass killings. Its author was almost certainly reporter Henry M. Mitchell, who later confirmed that he had been at the drugstore that evening. He was also accused of having encouraged the lynch mob. He wrote the column "while listening to the dying groans of the murdered Thompson," the *Star's* editors later explained by way of excuse. However, they chose to print it anyway, knowing that the mob had gone on to murder eighteen random Chinese victims. The *Star* later blamed its terrible judgment on the "lateness of the hour and the excitement of the evening."[13] Whatever the reason, the editorial was uncharacteristic. Unlike the *News*, the *Star* had rarely stirred up anti-Chinese agitation prior to the massacre.

Realizing that they had grossly misread the public's mood, the *Star's* editors quickly retracted their abhorrent opinion—sort of. The following day, they claimed to "emphatically and severely condemn the manifestation of mob rule" that "dealt death to the Chinese, indiscriminately." Nonetheless, they stubbornly reiterated that they had "nothing to say in palliation of the atrocious acts of the Chinese." The editors still maintained, "We are opposed to the Chinese. We condemn them and their conduct in every manner."[14]

The *Los Angeles News,* conveniently forgetting that it had spewed anti-Chinese venom and fomented hatred for nearly three years, delighted in watching its competitor squirm. Its editors insisted that "the *Star* was simply consistent in its first position upon the Chinese mob. It had not then discovered that the drift of popular sentiment was in the other direction . . . Discovering this, it crawfished out of its original position, with the best grace possible."[15]

The hypocritical *News* went on to decry the "wholesale slaughter" of innocents, "Chinamen though they were." Responding to a subsequent accusation that it had misrepresented the *Star's* views on the riot, the *News* let the *Star's* indefensible article speak for itself. It reprinted the original column verbatim, adding: "Can any reader find in the above a single word of condemnation for the murderous doings of the mob? . . . Our contemporary cannot be blamed for desiring to wriggle out of its position, but the disgraceful record must stand." Indeed, the damage was serious. Horace Bell later recalled that the *Star* "never shone brightly after the twenty-fifth of October, 1871. In fact it went out."[16]

Meanwhile, Los Angeles's youngest paper, the *Evening Express*, deferred to its readers' delicate sensibilities by sparing them most of the details about the horrible acts that the lynch mob perpetrated on the Chinese. It determined that the "full particulars" of the massacre were so "sickening and heartrending" that it did "not wish to inflict our readers by publishing them." It did, however, offer veiled criticism of the sheriff and the city marshal for failing to disperse the mob before it got out of control: "A few armed and resolute men could have quelled the riot early in the evening, before the excitement was at its height, by making a determined and resolute charge on the crowd."[17]

"An Unpleasant Prominence"

While Angelenos followed the spat between the *Star* and the *News* with some interest, they were much more anxious to learn how people were reacting elsewhere in California, as well as in distant parts of the country. Los Angeles was enjoying a major real estate boom, and its promoters were deeply worried about the injury to the town's reputation. The *Evening Express* fretted about "the bloody stain upon the fair fame of our city." The *News* even predicted that Los Angeles would become "a reproach throughout the country."[18]

However, the San Francisco press was surprisingly mild in its reprimand, at least initially. The *Alta California* blithely noted, "The olive groves and smiling vineyards of Los Angeles have been brought into an unpleasant prominence by the late tragic occurrences there."[19] The *San Francisco Examiner* was a little harsher. It described the "ruthless slaughter" as "a disgrace to the State," saying there could be no justification for the murders of so many human beings, "although they are Chinese." Nonetheless, it confined its condemnation to the scalawags who frequented Calle de los Negros, asserting that "the bloody work was done by the lower class."[20]

These reactions prompted the *Los Angeles Star* to rejoice: "Contrary to our expectations, the newspapers throughout the State are commenting upon our late riot with marked leniency."[21] However, it spoke too soon. The opinion of the San Francisco press started to shift as more details came to light. Before the week was out, the *Alta California* was already calling the event an "awful massacre" that "must forever remain a foul blot upon the fair fame of Los Angeles." It also opined that the Chinese gunfight was merely "the pretext for the bloody doings of the mob," observing that the rioters would not have engaged in pillage if their sole concern had been avenging the death of Robert Thompson. It concluded, "We do not know of any occurrence lately, even in semi-civilized countries, which equals in atrocity that which has just transpired in an important and heretofore generally admired city of California."[22]

If there remained any doubt which way Californians' opinion of Los Angeles was drifting, it was dispelled by a blistering attack on the city in the *Santa Barbara Press*:

> Los Angeles has a lower stratum in its society, which in diabolical disposition and deeds cannot be surpassed this side of hell. To compare it to the heathen hordes of China or the savage Apaches would be an outrageous insult to the heathen and the savages. Taking all the circumstances into consideration the atrocity is without a parallel in American history. . . . And before these bloody ruffians the city lay powerless. So they would have us believe. . . . The newspapers of Los Angeles are grateful that the press of the State is lenient towards the city. If the press shows leniency, the more shame to it. . . . Los Angeles is not guiltless, because under the smarting of the lash of outraged humanity she makes tearful promises for the future.[23]

The *Press* also took a swipe at anti-Chinese propagandists such as the *Los Angeles News*: "They are responsible directly for this enormous outrage." However, the citizens of Santa Barbara were not unanimous in their opinion. The *Press*'s competitor, the *Santa Barbara Times*, voiced the feelings of at least some of the town's residents when it stated: "This is a most wholesome lesson to these pagans, and will probably learn them to submit their grievances, if they have any, to the law of the land. We do not advocate mob law, but uphold the citizens of Los Angeles" in responding forcefully to the "outrage by the moon-eyed devils."[24]

Few people outside California had even heard of Los Angeles prior to the riot of 1871. The brutal murders placed the town conspicuously on the national map. The *Star* noted that the "terrible outrages" might "be made the subject of investigation by the National Government" and could "affect our relations with a wealthy and powerful nation."[25] Indeed, the concern in New York was not so much the horrible fate of the eighteen murdered people as the potential threat to the lives and property of Americans living in China. The mercantile firm of Olyphant and Company, which was headquartered on Wall Street and was principally engaged in trade with China, asked the New York Chamber of Commerce to draw the federal government's attention to the massacre. Its staff in China feared that "revenge would come on a much better class" of Americans residing there for the "grave injuries" inflicted on Chinese citizens in California.[26]

Editorials across the country soon made it clear what kind of first impression Los Angeles had made on the nation. In fact, the whole state's reputation suffered because of the massacre. The *Philadelphia Inquirer* proclaimed, "California has been disgraced by another . . . wholesale application of Lynch law." The *New York Tribune* lambasted the "debased Mexicans and Caucasians" in the "misnamed 'City of the Angels'" who had demonstrated the "peculiar principles of civilization affected in Southern California." Similarly, the *Albany Evening Journal* pointed out that the town was "singularly misnamed" and concluded that "a great reform is needed in the administration of justice at Los Angeles." An editor in Springfield, Massachusetts, lamented the "sharp and humiliating contrast" between the Los Angeles rioters and the Chinese merchants of San Francisco who generously donated to the victims of the Chicago fire that same month. The *Cincinnati Commercial* blamed "those leaders of public opinion who have encouraged a brutal hatred of the Chinese." A Vermont newspaper decried the "detestable spirit of prejudice and the brutal, inhuman, unchristian hate which has been largely fostered by the leading public men and newspapers" on the West Coast. It even suggested that "certain portions of California" should be "placed under martial law."[27]

Meanwhile, the *New York Herald's* reaction to the massacre was a smug, garbled heap of contempt for Californians, Southerners, Chinese, and Blacks—practically the rest of the country. It inexplicably equated the Los Angeles police force with the Ku Klux Klan, then noted that the law officers were "violently assaulted by a swarming horde of the pigtailed barbarians." However, the Chinese, like "the terrible colored men, who always start the row, got all the casualties." The *Herald's* primary concern was that "mob law proceedings" such as the Los Angeles massacre would eventually lead "John Chinaman" and "his sixty odd thousand pigtailed voters" to the ballot box. The editors were sadly resigned to the day when "John can cast a vote as well as Sambo," and they castigated Angelenos for hastening its arrival.[28]

The Arrests

For several days after the riot, Los Angeles lawmen were busy arresting suspects. The first three taken into custody were Charles Austin, Edmund Crawford, and A. R. Johnston, whose names had surfaced repeatedly during the testimony at the coroner's inquest. Five other suspected murderers had been jailed by the close of the inquest on October 28, 1871. Within a few weeks, at least seven more were apprehended. Some ringleaders were rumored to have left the city.[29]

Meanwhile, all of the wounded Chinese survivors recovered from their injuries except one. San Francisco tong fighter Ah Choy, the first casualty of October 24, died three days afterward from the gunshot wound in the neck inflicted by one of Yo Hing's men. The police searched for his killer, as well as for the Chinese gunmen who had shot citizen Robert Thompson, Policeman Jesús Bilderrain, and teenager Juan José Mendibles.

On the morning of October 26, 1871, a member of Yo Hing's faction told City Marshal Baker that Yu Tak, the tong fighter suspected of having shot Officer Bilderrain, was hiding in a laundry on Main Street. Baker cautiously approached the building. The people inside saw him and quickly shut the windows. The marshal broke through the door. Yu Tak had concealed himself in a large box, ready to kill anyone who tried to arrest him. After a brief standoff, the marshal convinced him to come out and give himself up. He surrendered.

Yu Tak was the first Chinese gunslinger to be jailed. A few days later, Los Angeles lawmen arrested Woo Ging, another Chinese suspected of having instigated the gun battle. Yo Hing told the press, "Yu Tak's company are going to try to get him out because he fights well, and let the other fellow hang because he all the time afraid and no do anything." His reference to Yu Tak's "company" was a rare, candid admission that the *huiguan* of Los Angeles hired tong fighters to settle their members' disputes. Before long, Yo Hing himself was accused of having incited the riot. He was taken into custody at San Juan Capistrano, heading for Arizona. The Hong Chow leader was brought back to Los Angeles, where he shared an increasingly crowded jail with both his Chinese enemies and the suspected lynchers.[30]

Rising from the Ashes

"A good many Chinamen are scared . . . I think many good Chinamen will leave Los Angeles and not come back," Yo Hing told a reporter less than a week after the massacre. By the early part of 1872, the more affluent residents of Chinatown were reported to be finding more "congenial" places to live. They may have simply wanted better living conditions. Or perhaps the night of October 24, 1871, had convinced them that it was too risky to congregate in one neighborhood during an era of increasing anti-Chinese violence. Sam Yuen's partners must have moved their business, because Policeman Emil Harris later testified that he "used to know where the store of the Wing Chung Company was" but no longer knew. When the Chinese of Los Angeles celebrated their New Year in February 1872, the *Alta California* reported that the hospitality was "not as ostentatious as formerly." It concluded grimly, "The number of Chinese has diminished since the riot."[31]

However, these pronouncements of Chinatown's decline were premature. Most of its former residents refused to give up. By the second week of November 1871, there were reports that many who had fled during the rioting had returned. A week later, a Chinese laundryman was preparing to set up business in a portion of the Coronel adobe that had not been severely damaged. The following month, two "half Americanized Chinamen" opened a handsome brick washhouse on Requena Street. The neighborhood was gradually starting to come back to life.[32]

Shortly after the riot, another development signaled that Chinatown was rebounding. Even before the grand jury had convened to consider criminal indictments, the Chinese started making threats of civil lawsuits. Nine days after the massacre, their leaders publicly declared "that the city of Los Angeles will have to make good the losses sustained by them during the late riot." The Chinese of San Bernardino also sent a lawyer to Los Angeles to investigate the riot, and the district associations in San Francisco prepared to lend assistance. The *huiguan* of Los Angeles presented petitions to the city for damages. After the Common Council responded that "the City should not be held liable for any such claims," several Chinese parties filed suit in district court. Meanwhile, the Chinese consul helped the Wing Chung firm obtain the release of its merchandise that Sheriff Burns had confiscated for safekeeping after the riot.[33]

The Chinese leveled criminal charges as well. Nine days after the massacre, Dr. Gene Tong's widow, Tong You, earned the sad distinction of being the first Chinese woman known to have lodged a criminal complaint in Los Angeles. She accused Hong Chow kingpin Yo Hing of "inciting and participating in a mob or riot" that resulted in her husband's murder.[34] As it turned out, six of the innocent massacre victims were members of the smaller Chin Woa and Hop Wo organizations, whose members had played no known role in the Chinatown war of 1870–71. One of them was Dr. Tong, a member of the Chin Woa Company. Tong You's complaint revealed a great deal about what the neutral Chinese of Los Angeles were thinking. They blamed Yo Hing and his Hong Chow cohorts for setting off the chain of events that eventually led to the Black Tuesday. The fact that Tong You did not file charges against any non-Asians suggested that she either was afraid to name any individual perpetrators or was unable to identify the mob members who had seized her husband that night.

Yo Hing, unrepentant after the events of October 24, continued to wage his war against his Nin Yung adversaries in the courts. His associates successfully argued that Sam Yuen and the other partners in the Wing Chung firm owed them around $700 as a consequence of the riot. Since the Wing Chung store had been pillaged, its owners did not have enough property to satisfy the judgment. However, Yo Hing's colleagues somehow were able to attach the merchandise of Sing Kee and Chung Woo. Policemen Emil Harris and Sam Bryant went to the two men's stores and, over their vehement protests, took goods worth nearly $500—yams, vermicelli, dried fish, tea, shark fins, Chinese buckwheat flour, crockery, and so forth. Those two merchants filed suit against Sheriff Burns to recover their goods, and the jury ruled in their favor.[35]

The Chinese were not the only ones filing lawsuits. Antonio Coronel sought to recover $5,000 from the city for the damage done to his adobe tenement. Although the Common Council had flatly denied the claims brought by Chinese businessmen, the city attorney found that Coronel was entitled to damages. The Council agreed to submit the amount to arbitration. Angelenos were outraged. One citizen pointed out that the value of the neglected property on the Los Angeles tax roll was only $300. Another suggested that the city should instead sue Coronel for $100,000 for "perpetrating a nuisance," "a blemish," a "festering ulcer," and a "disgrace to the city." The following year, Coronel was indeed cited for maintaining a public nuisance in the form of "a certain common ill-governed and disorderly house" where men and women "of evil name and fame, and of dishonest conversation," came together for "drinking, tippling, whoring and misbehaving themselves."[36]

The Chinese who came back to Calle de los Negros after the massacre were not too cowed to venture beyond their homes and make their presence known in town. In late November 1871, when an artist was applying gold-leaf lettering to the window of a bank, a group of Chinese gathered and watched him closely to see if "some American was trying to imitate Chinese advertising." The artist decided to have some fun and tried to approximate Chinese characters, but his audience left, displaying scowls "of infinite disgust"—perhaps feeling they were being mocked. In January 1872, two Chinese men visited William M. Godfrey's Sunbeam Photographic Gallery. To the amusement of the other customers, they had a loud, animated conversation about a comical trick portrait featuring a large head superimposed on a small body.[37]

Another event on November 15, 1871, marked a return to normalcy in the Chinese quarter that seemed reassuring—or was it? That afternoon, Ah Sum, the cook at the jail, married Hon Que in Justice Gray's courtroom. The bride was well dressed in a blue silk gown embroidered with flowers and a black sash and ribbons. Once they had exchanged vows, Ah Sum embraced his new wife affectionately. Suddenly, a Chinese man burst into the office, greatly agitated, and started trying to explain that he had some previous arrangement with Hon Que in Sacramento. Justice Gray told him "that there was no use in making an appeal now as the 'bird had flown.'" The man left for Calle de los Negros "in a high state of excitement."[38]

This unnerving incident must have alarmed both the Chinese and the non-Asians of Los Angeles. No one could forget that Yut Ho's contested marriage to Lee Yong was what ultimately provoked the Nin Yung leader, Sam Yuen, to retaliate against his archenemy, Yo Hing. And three weeks earlier, Angelenos had seen all too clearly what could happen when this type of blood feud spilled out of control in a town in which simmering hatred of the Chinese had reached its boiling point.

9

Shouldering the Responsibility

The Coroner's Inquest

October 25–28, 1871

The morning after the Chinatown tragedy, County Coroner Joseph Kurtz impaneled a jury of eleven men to investigate the murders. After spending some time at the jail yard and determining the cause of each victim's death, Dr. Kurtz released the remains for burial. That afternoon, he and the jury met at the city's Common Council chamber to start hearing eyewitness testimony. The room was packed with spectators. The examination of seventy-nine witnesses would take four days. Some sessions lasted until midnight.[1]

The local press claimed that most of the witnesses were hesitant to identify the guilty parties. News articles made snide references to "the apparent forgetfulness as to persons" and "a peculiar ignorance of names." The *Evening Express* chided, "We have reason for believing that there are many respectable citizens holding aloof." Journalists attributed their reluctance to a fear of retaliation. Indeed, J. W. Brooks, a carpenter who had tried to stop the killers, admitted, "I am afraid to betray them, lest they should shoot me." Brooks was later fined twenty dollars for refusing to testify in court. The *New York Herald* suggested that other witnesses were simply unwilling to implicate their cronies.[2]

Even the lawmen who had been on the scene that night could not identify many of the perpetrators. Policeman Emil Harris testified that after the mob stormed the Coronel building, "The excitement was so great I could not recognize any one in particular." The *Los Angeles News* queried whether it was not incredible that the law officers, whose jobs required them to get to know almost everyone in the community, were unable to identify any of the rioters "who were robbing and murdering before their very eyes." The *Los Angeles Star* was already fearful that the difficulty of identification would create a major problem down the road: it might make it impossible for the grand jury to issue any indictments for the murders.[3]

The press's accusations against the witnesses may not have been entirely fair. Most of the murders occurred after dark in parts of Los Angeles that were not well lit. The mob disintegrated into several groups heading in different directions. Moreover, in a town of roughly six thousand people, many of whom were transients or fairly recent arrivals, it was certainly plausible that the witnesses did not know the names of some of the rioters they recognized by face—a clerk who had helped them at a drugstore, a groom they had seen at a stable, a braggart they had overheard in a saloon. Witness S. A. Butler, for instance, did not know the names of the three lynchers he described, although he had previously seen them in buggies "riding through the streets in company with three women of light character."[4] Other witnesses made it clear that they would recognize the culprits if they saw them again and would be willing to point them out.

Several of those who testified were suspected rioters themselves. When questioned, they made all sorts of excuses and denied that they took any part in the lynchings, although they did not hesitate to implicate others. Dan Moody blamed the massacre on "drunken men and Mexicans hallooing." Shoemaker A. R. Johnston said he got so intoxicated that he did not remember what had happened that night. "When I heard there was so many [hangings]," the Irish immigrant remarked, "I was astonished." On further interrogation, he admitted that he was not too drunk "to be able to tell the difference between a pile of lumber and a corral fence"—a reference to his reported presence at Tomlinson's corral and lumber yard, the lynching site on Temple Street. Charles Austin swore that he had tried to keep the peace and quell the uprising.

J. C. Cox even claimed to have rescued a wounded Chinese man and given him water. Norman L. King stated that he had accidentally shot his fingers when his revolver went off and had to leave the scene because of the pain. Edmund Crawford maintained that he had gone home about eight o'clock and stayed put, although numerous witnesses said they saw him later. Andres Soeur swore "positively that I had no cleaver in my hand on Tuesday night." P. S. Dorney, who had waved a dead man's queue at Robert Mulloy's saloon, denied that he had shaved his beard afterward "with the view of disguising myself."[5]

At the conclusion of the coroner's inquest, the jurors drew up a list of people accused of having taken part in the riot. Their verdict also pointed out that the witnesses identified many others "who seemed to have encouraged the mob by their sympathy with them." No names appeared in the version of the verdict released to the press, as the jury did not want "to defeat the ends of justice."[6] However, the identities of most of the suspects had already been revealed in the witness testimony published in the *Star* and the *News*.

Once the coroner's jury had announced its verdict, the responsibility for bringing the wrongdoers to justice fell into the hands of the grand jury and the district attorney. The *Los Angeles Star* acknowledged that there was only one way for the city to redeem itself in the eyes of outsiders: "Let us open the entire affair to the world by a strict, thorough and impartial investigation, and pursue it until the guilt or innocence of every man on the streets that night is established beyond a doubt."[7] Whether or not that would really happen in a town where several brutal crimes had gone unpunished was anyone's guess.

The Suspects

When the testimony of the witnesses at the coroner's inquest was published in the local press, Angelenos had their first chance to decide for themselves who they thought was responsible for the riot and massacre. Newspapers across the country were quick to blame the usual scapegoats—the Mexicans and the Irish. One dissident, the *Santa Barbara Press*, decried this hasty attempt "to shift the responsibility upon Mexicans." Indeed, the coroner's jury concluded that the mob consisted of "people of all nationalities as they live in Los Angeles."[8]

So who were the guilty parties, really? Scholars have mulled over that question for decades. Almost all newspapers initially reported that the lynch mob consisted of "the dregs of society."[9] Of course, the citizens who came up with that whitewashed story were scrambling to salvage the city's soiled reputation. Nonetheless, their claim, condescending and calculated though it was, had considerable merit. A sizable proportion of the accused were undeniably disreputable individuals. Many of those whom eyewitnesses repeatedly identified as rioters and looters were known for having committed other crimes. The examples abound.

Some were drunken louts or had nasty temperaments. Four months before the riot, Patrick McDonald had been fined for assault and battery when he and several companions entered the store of Pierre Adolphe, loudly called for liquor, told the storekeeper's wife that "this is no place for a woman," and pushed her into another room. McDonald admitted "that he was somewhat under the influence of liquor, and may have shoved her more rudely than he intended." As soon as he had paid his fine, he went back to the same store "and was complained of again before night." Francisco Peña, while intoxicated, had started a knife fight with Juan Acuña, described as "a half-witted Mexican, who earns a living by peddling tamales and fruit, and is made the subject of ridicule and practical jokes by a class of men who have little feeling for the misfortunes of their kind." Reporters described another rioter, L. F. "Curly" Crenshaw, as a young drifter who associated with people "of the lowest character." His "favorite resort was the rendezvous of lewd women, pickpockets and cut-throats."[10]

Others had a history of physical violence. Andres Soeur had pled guilty to a charge of assault and battery in 1867. Jesús Martinez, only twenty-two years old, had been charged with assault with a deadly weapon in 1870. In March 1871, Ramón Dominguez had also been fined for assault. Six months before the riot, Esteban Alvarado had been fined for drawing a pistol during a fight. Only a month beforehand, Edmund Crawford had been arrested for beating a boy during a drunken rage.[11]

Several had reputations as thieves. José del Carmen Lugo, a member of one of southern California's largest landowning families that had fallen on hard times, had been sentenced to jail for theft of a horse in 1864. Jesús Martinez had pled guilty to breaking and entering in 1868.

He was said to be a "chum and relative" of the infamous outlaw Tiburcio Vasquez, who was later hanged for murder in San Jose. Edmund Crawford had also been arrested for theft five months before the riot. Around the same time, Louis "Fatty" Mendel had been charged with stealing eighty dollars from a store in San Joaquin, although he was later acquitted. Andres Soeur had been tried for stealing a gold watch and chain only two weeks before the riot. David Thompson, who confessed to taking a silver watch from one of the Chinese victims, was arrested for burglarizing St. Athanasius Episcopal Church a few weeks afterward. He also pilfered some blankets from a hapless old man, "leaving him at the mercy of the inclement weather." Esteban Alvarado was found guilty of stealing a hydrant bend and a cast iron kettle from the city water company. The *Alta California* correctly observed that many of the rioters were driven not so much by "righteous indignation" over the shooting of Robert Thompson as by pillage.[12]

At least a couple of the suspected rioters were believed to have killed on other occasions. The hotheaded Adolfo Celis had nearly been lynched in March 1870 after he pursued and gunned down a man who had stolen two shirts from him, shooting his victim four times. He was convicted of manslaughter and sentenced to one year in the state penitentiary. A German identified as "Dutch Charley" was later sent to prison for murdering an Indian woman. Carmen Sotelo was accused of killing a man in a knife fight.[13]

Journalist Ben C. Truman went so far as to say "the scum of the city, *and only the scum*, were the authors of the infamous deeds recorded."[14] That certainly was not true. A surprisingly large number of those identified as the most active participants were solid, middle-class businessmen, artisans, and regular employees. Refugio Botello was a butcher and cattle buyer whose name had been placed in nomination for the office of county assessor.[15] A. R. Johnston, a shoemaker, had no prior criminal record. Dan W. Moody was a farmer who had clerked in a store at Anaheim. Norman L. King worked at the railroad depot. Samuel C. Carson was a beekeeper. J. G. Scott was a carpenter, a steady job in Los Angeles during that boom period. J. C. Cox was a plasterer, also a sought-after skill. He had even served as a special policeman in 1866. As eyewitness Joseph Mesmer correctly recalled, "[S]ome of our own 'average citizens' took part, mingling with the scum and riffraff from the camps and stables."[16]

Furthermore, the massacre cannot be blamed entirely on rootless drifters or recent arrivals who had no stake in the community. Many of the suspected rioters had lived in Los Angeles for at least a decade. Some were natives. Adolfo Celis, José del Carmen Lugo, and Carmen Sotelo were descendants of distinguished old California families. Nor were all the participants young, single troublemakers. Of the twenty-six suspects whose ages are known, fifteen were over thirty years old. Several were married and had families.

Through the years, many accounts of the massacre have contended that the town's "leading citizens" also played a direct role in the riot. To some extent, the witness testimony substantiated that claim. A clothing retailer identified only as "Mr. Cohen," who had a store in the United States Hotel, reportedly remarked that he was "in favor of hanging every goddamned one" of the Chinese. According to Horace Bell, the prominent hardware merchant John D. Hicks was seen "dealing out rope" to the mob. One eyewitness swore that Councilman George Fall, who confessed to having attacked Yo Hing that evening, later followed the mob and called out "hang them" or "swing them." Fall, in turn, claimed that Prudent Beaudry, a Los Angeles real estate tycoon and future mayor, asked him for the fire hose in order "to wash out the block where the Chinamen were," in direct defiance of the lawmen's orders merely to guard the building. Fall claimed to have piously retorted that he "would not lend assistance to anything of the kind." Henry M. Mitchell, a reporter for the *Los Angeles Star* who had been admitted to the bar seven months earlier and would become sheriff in 1878, allegedly cried "hang him" or "they ought to be hanged." When told that "if they hanged one, they would have to hang fifty," he supposedly replied, "All right." Mitchell denied these remarks, claiming mistaken identity. The *Los Angeles News* quoted one testifier as saying that the renowned silk grower Thomas A. Garey "had helped to hoist up two Chinamen." However, the *Evening Express* asserted that the *News* had misquoted this witness, which was probably the case, as the editors of the *Express* were told by those who attended the coroner's inquest that the published version was not the witness's correct testimony.[17]

Aside from the accusations against these six men, the allegations of upper-class involvement were vague and unverifiable. One reporter claimed that he "saw some of our best people with indignation flashing in their eyes. It is possible that some of them, under this feeling, may have lent encouragement to some sort of demonstration against the Chinese." Robert M. Widney, who had tried to rescue Chinese captives from the mob, cryptically raised the possibility in a subsequent court case that "a majority of the most respectable citizens approved of the acts of the rioters, or assisted therein." In 1883, an article in the *Los Angeles Times* asserted that one riot participant was "a well-known business man a few miles from this city." The same newspaper charged in 1888 that "the man who furnished the first rope is today one of Los Angeles' most exalted citizens." P. S. Dorney, a suspected rioter himself, contended in an 1886 account of the massacre that an unnamed citizen "then and now of standing and influence" was the first to produce a rope. An 1889 history of the city maintained, "There are certain persons in Los Angeles who were helping to murder Chinamen that night who hold their head high today." Horace Bell alleged that many "persons of position and influence . . . boasted of their guilt while the affair was yet hot." Eyewitness Michael M. Rice, who recalled the event in 1934, even claimed that society's "most honorable members were, with few exceptions, importantly connected with the killings."[18]

The charges leveled by Bell and Rice should not be taken at face value. While a few "leading citizens" undoubtedly wanted to avenge the shootings of the three Americans and had no qualms about doing so, it is unlikely that very many members of Los Angeles's ruling class truly resented the presence of the Chinese in their city. In 1870, thirty-seven of the town's wealthier households employed Chinese domestics. Even southern Democrats such as attorneys Andrew J. King and Cameron Thom and jailor Frank Carpenter, whose political party championed white labor, chose to have Chinese cooks in their homes. Several of the county's large-scale orchard and vineyard owners hired Chinese workers, as did the proprietors of the town's major hotels and restaurants. Local lawyers got a fair amount of business from Chinese clients. So did landlords and certain American merchants, especially those who sold boots, hats, and pistols. As seen previously, some affluent residents consulted Chinese physicians.

In short, influential Angelenos were the ones who benefited most from what the Chinese had to offer. More importantly, Los Angeles was enjoying a heady period of growth and prosperity in 1871. The massacre occurred during an era of intense "boosterism," when local business leaders were working hard to attract newcomers to the region. The town's power brokers would have sabotaged their own interests if they had incited a horrifying mass murder that was bound to bring widespread condemnation on Los Angeles. It is also noteworthy that Horace Bell, who was not shy about naming names, could not seem to identify more than a couple of those "persons of position and influence" whom he claimed had "boasted of their guilt."

Rather than speculating about which "leading citizens" may have supplied the ropes or stirred up the crowd, as the traditional narratives of the massacre have done, it may be more instructive to consider the ways in which the town's prominent people helped create an atmosphere in which the mob could carry out its crimes. The community's leadership failed much more through its passivity than its actions, not just on the night of the riot but also during the three years beforehand, when the *Los Angeles News* was spewing anti-Chinese propaganda and the attacks on Chinese residents were on the rise. Journalist Charles Nordhoff once observed, "The respectable classes, though too often silent, are utterly opposed to the cry against the Chinese."[19] For the most part, events in Los Angeles during that period bore out Nordhoff's observation about California's elite—both their disapproval of Chinese persecution and their inaction in the face of it. The verbal and physical assaults on the Chinese from early 1869 until the time of the massacre drew no public reproach from what Nordhoff described as the "respectable classes." On the night of the riot, several men who would later be described as the "city-makers" of modern Los Angeles were undoubtedly guilty of sins of omission, or at least lapses of courage.

Although some of the town's civic leaders, mostly lawyers and merchants, attempted to stop the killings and escort the Chinese to safety, others simply watched the events unfold or fled the scene. Mendel Meyer, a popular shopkeeper, said that he "saw people running away," and "I ran away, too." R. J. Wolf, a future city marshal, helped protect the Chinese near the plaza until he learned that the rioters were lynching their prisoners. At that point, he said "I've got enough of this" and went home. Mayor José Cristobal Aguilar, as seen earlier, made a cameo appearance on Calle de los Negros but did not try to prevent the carnage. That prompted one Angeleno to write, "The Mayor, to do his duty, should read the Riot Act." The highly regarded merchant Harris Newmark hurried to the scene of the massacre but apparently did not attempt to intervene. Witness testimony suggested that County Supervisor James B. Winston, Councilman William Ferguson, former Councilman Elijah Workman, former State Treasurer Antonio Coronel, County Coroner Joseph Kurtz, attorney Andrew J. King, and merchants David Solomon and A. C. Chauvin were downtown that night but declined to get involved. When the sheriff called for a posse to help control the crowd, "the citizens refused to respond." Some "respectable citizens," witnessing the mayhem, merely clucked that "it was a shame, but there were no means to check the mob."[20] Indeed, several esteemed residents may have been "holding aloof" from testifying, as the newspapers charged, because they were ashamed to admit on the record that they had merely stood by and watched.

At the same time, not all of the citizens who risked their own safety trying to rescue Chinese captives were influential people in Los Angeles. J. W. Brooks was a carpenter. A. J. Bowman was a well-borer. Adolph Schwob was an auctioneer. Charles Avery, Walter E. White, and William Widney were store clerks. During the most chaotic, terrifying half-hour of October 24, 1871, when fourteen people were hanged and many other potential victims were rescued, Angelenos made choices that reflected their character, not their social status. As Yo Hing later concluded, "I think there are plenty of good people here and plenty of bad; . . . the good people tried to stop the massacre but couldn't do it."[21]

The *Evening Express* attempted to exonerate Angelenos for their inaction by saying, "Most of our citizens were at their homes and nothing of the kind was expected." Similarly, the *Alta California* pointed out that the murders "commenced at an hour when business men, professional men and all the better classes of our community had retired to their homes." However, Dr. Joseph P. Widney, a brother of rescuers Robert and William, told a different story. He recalled, "The citizens generally knew there was a riot, but a sense of self-preservation kept them away."[22] The editors of the *Santa Barbara Press* also rebuked their fellow journalists who concocted excuses for Los Angeles's elite:

"The hour was one, forsooth, at which the business men had left their stores and were at home—a lame excuse. . . . Will they confess that seventeen [sic] Americans could have been hanged in their streets by a resident mob, before that mob was overpowered? Never. The fact is, human life, if it be but Chinese human life is very cheap."[23]

The lynchings of October 24, 1871, raised the specter of the old vigilance committee, which had not been active in Los Angeles since the hanging of Michel Lachenais in December 1870. Angelenos wondered whether the vigilantes, who had previously lynched prisoners only after deliberating and voting on the matter, had taken an active hand in killing the Chinese. The press put forth wildly inconsistent information. The *Evening Express* maintained that the vigilance committee "had nothing to do with the horrible affair," and Ben Truman also reported that many of its members had taken "scores of inoffensive Chinamen from the possession of squads of the mob." The *Los Angeles Star* was more equivocal: "It is stated, by what authority we know not, that the Vigilance Committee . . . had much to do with the suppression of the riot." The former vigilantes themselves sent a letter to the *Los Angeles News* claiming that they "had nothing to do with the attack on the Chinese." However, the *Alta California* subsequently reported, "It is now stated that the old Vigilantes are the real instigators of the lynching."[24]

The surviving evidence does not suggest that the members of the vigilance committee had anything to do with the Chinese lynchings. That did not completely exonerate them, however. In one editor's opinion, it was immaterial whether or not they were on the scene that night. The vigilantes had already done their damage months earlier, setting examples of flagrant violations of law that the "ignorant perpetrators" emulated during the massacre: "The monstrosity of the thing was in imitation [of] the Vigilance Committee, in hanging those arrested, or who surrendered, instead of allowing the law to take its own course."[25]

The writer had a point. The vigilantes, who included several influential citizens, had helped instill in their fellow Angelenos the idea that justice belonged in the hands of "the people" rather than the courts. And Los Angeles's grand juries had winked at the crimes of the vigilance committee, refusing to indict members of lynch mobs. On the night of

October 24, 1871, the vigilantes got to see what their extralegal actions had finally wrought—not the suppression of violent crime in their city, but rather the random killing of innocent victims by a howling, unstoppable mass of "the people," suddenly conscious of their power to throw off the bonds of law and order if their numbers were great enough.

"Animosity of Race and a Desire for Plunder"

The coroner's inquest revealed a great deal about which individuals may have been responsible for the killings. It shed less light on their motivations. Apologists in the California press suggested that the crowd acted in the heat of passion following the shootings of three Americans. However, the mob's excessive brutality went well beyond mere retribution. More chillingly, many of the rioters were jocular rather than enraged while they carried out the grisly murders. John Hicks mockingly misinterpreted John Baldwin's Spanish remarks to the crowd. The hangman identified as Reilly was "dancing a quick step" on a balcony. At the saloons late that night, rioters joked about hanging the "longtails." Several even took fiendish pleasure in torturing and killing the Chinese. The men who hanged Chang Wan from the gate at Tomlinson's corral entertained the crowd by smashing his head against the beam repeatedly.

In New York, one newspaperman attributed the killings to "the antagonism existing between Chinese labor and the labor of white men" on the West Coast.[26] Some modern historians continue to adhere to that view, placing the massacre squarely within the context of the anti-Chinese labor movement. That fanatical campaign reached its height in the mid-1870s, while the nation was feeling the lingering effects of the economic depression that followed the stock market panic of 1873. During the latter part of that decade, white workers, mostly in northern California but also in other parts of the country, violently protested the continued importation of "cheap Chinese labor," claiming they would be ruined by the competition. Indeed, on the night of the Los Angeles massacre, witnesses heard a few isolated cries of "The cheap labor is done away with now." Agitator Norman L. King made a stump speech denouncing Chinese immigration. The rioter identified as Reilly complained that he was out of work.

On more careful examination, however, the "job competition" ratio-nale does not hold true in this case. While a considerable number of white workers in northern California were unemployed, jobs were plen-tiful in Los Angeles at the time, especially in the construction industry. In fact, Los Angeles reportedly had the lowest unemployment rate of any comparable town on the West Coast at the time of the massacre.[27] The "cheap labor" remark during the riot was attributed to shoemaker A. R. Johnston, who apparently had a secure job. So did depot worker Norman L. King, who made the speech against Chinese labor. More-over, it is doubtful whether the drunks, swindlers, and thieves who frequented Calle de los Negros and reportedly took part in the riot were seeking regular employment. If they were, they faced little competition from the local Chinese. The 1870 census suggested that fewer than half of the town's Chinese (at most, 82 of 179) were employed by non-Asians as cooks, house servants, or unskilled laborers. The rest were either self-employed, primarily as launderers or vegetable peddlers, or worked for Chinese-owned businesses. With a very few possible exceptions, none of the suspected rioters were vying for the same jobs held by their Chinese neighbors. They had no work-related reason to murder peaceable washmen, domestics, and cigar makers—much less a beloved physician.

In Los Angeles of the early 1870s, the outcry against "cheap Chinese labor" was not an expression of a legitimate working-class grievance but rather a thin veil concealing raw hatred of a specific group of immi-grants whose ways were different. The *New York Herald* put forth an explanation for the massacre that may be as good as any: "The mob appears to have been actuated solely from animosity of race and a desire for plunder." The *Santa Barbara Press* agreed, stating that the crowd "rushed into the front of the fray, *not* to avenge the death of Bob Thompson, *not* because their lives were in danger, not to sustain the law, not at all. But because the occasion gave them the opportunity to put into devilish deeds their smouldering hatred for what they were pleased to consider an inferior race." The *Press* also pointed out that the mob, using the Chinese gunfighters' crimes as an excuse, took advan-tage of an opportune moment: "The rascals knew that they could wreak their spite upon this helpless race with comparative immunity from punishment under the prevailing apathy of the public mind." One Los

Angeles editor agreed, adding, "The lawless elements of society have been educated to believe that murder could be indulged in with impunity, provided it was committed by a mob instead of a single individual."[28]

These telling observations are more consistent with the facts than the economic explanations. Perhaps it is most realistic, if most disturbing, to view the massacre as the natural result of a collapse of the communal forces that usually operate to keep the sinister, sadistic side of human nature in check. For nearly three years, Angelenos had ignored or laughed off the escalating attacks on the Chinese, doing little to curb them. Influential pundits such as the editors of the *Los Angeles News* had pronounced the Chinese less than human. Like the white man who, without provocation, had "hit a Chinaman on the head" three months earlier,[29] the rioters of October 24, 1871, apparently tortured and murdered random Chinese victims because they wanted to. They enjoyed it and thought it was fun. And, knowing that their ranks were too large for many to be apprehended, and that Angelenos did not seem concerned about protecting these inconsequential foreigners anyway, they were betting they could get away with it. Some of their stunned fellow citizens feared that they would.

The Grand Jury

November 8–December 2, 1871

Less than two weeks after the coroner's jury announced its findings, Ygnacio Sepúlveda, the twenty-nine-year-old county court judge, called a special grand jury to investigate the riot. Sepúlveda, though young, was able and conscientious. A Los Angeles native and a descendant of an old California family, he had studied in Boston, belonged to the bar for eight years, served in the state legislature, and acted as county judge since 1869. Horace Bell praised him as a "lawyer of rare talent" who discharged his judicial duties "with marked distinction and ability."[30] The fifteen men that Sepúlveda impaneled were not all affluent, powerful Angelenos but instead represented a mix of occupations and income levels—farmers, merchants, carpenters, a blacksmith, a baker, and a drayman.

The foreman was J. J. Warner, who was sixty-four years old and had first arrived in Los Angeles forty years beforehand. He was ideal for the

SHOULDERING THE RESPONSIBILITY 179

job. Warner, who stood very tall and straight, was well known in the region and commanded respect. He was unafraid to express his opinion, no matter how unpopular. The previous year, he had infuriated the citizens of San Bernardino by belittling the white youth who watched the whipping and burning of the prostitute Sing Ye without intervening. He also spoke fluent Spanish, so he could serve as interpreter for Latino witnesses who testified before the grand jury.

Still, Judge Sepúlveda had a very real reason to worry that the grand jurors would not return any indictments. Less than a year earlier, he had implored another grand jury to investigate the vigilance committee that lynched Michel Lachenais. He charged them, "By your speedy, vigorous, and legal action you will impress upon men the belief that their safety and happiness greatly depend in yielding obedience to the laws of the land, and in having due respect for constituted authority; that the violation of law only entails to us injustice, cruelty, dissension, anarchy, and immorality."[31] The grand jurors had ignored Judge Sepúlveda, and the vigilantes went unpunished.

In a town that increasingly viewed Chinese life as cheap, the same thing could happen this time. Even if some rioters were indicted, the *News* raised another concern: "There is an influence at work in the community which aims at shouldering the responsibility upon a few poor devils without money or influential friends."[32] On November 8, 1871, Judge Sepúlveda made an impassioned plea to the grand jurors:

The scenes enacted on the evening of the twenty-fourth of October, when eighteen human beings were mercilessly murdered by a mob, have sent a thrill of horror throughout the State, and a page is marked in the record of Los Angeles forever indelible, making the name of the community a reproach to humanity and civilization. . . . Shall law stand for naught, and immorality and crime have high carnival in our community? . . . Remember, gentlemen, the accountability you owe to society. . . . Set an example of true courage in the performance of your duty; be faithful to your trust. In this way only can you satisfy an offended God, violated law, and outraged humanity.[33]

The grand jurors remained in session for twenty-three days. During that time, they examined 111 witnesses, many of whom reportedly were reluctant to disclose everything they knew about the affair. Meanwhile, a newspaper editor in Vermont, noting that Judge Sepúlveda had asked the grand jury to investigate the murders "fearlessly and without prejudice," sniffed: "It will be interesting to learn whether there are twenty-four [*sic*] men in that locality who can so far overcome their prejudice against the Chinese as to hold their assailants responsible for the outrage recently committed."[34]

That question was answered late in the afternoon of December 2, 1871, when the grand jury announced its findings. It indicted twenty-five men for murder of the Chinese and twelve more for lesser crimes, including rioting, assault with deadly weapons, and assault to commit murder. In addition, it indicted eight Chinese for murder or assault to commit murder in connection with the deaths of tong fighter Ah Choy and citizen Robert Thompson.[35] No list of names of all thirty-seven indicted rioters has survived, although it is possible from the court files and newspaper accounts to identify at least forty-four of the riot suspects who may have been among them.[36]

The accompanying grand jury report, authored by foreman J. J. Warner, focused mainly on the lynch mob, whose crimes "must cause Christianity to weep, civilization to blush, and humanity to mourn." However, the grand jurors also placed some responsibility on the Chinese tong fighters who started the gun battle. They observed that "the great number of shots fired indiscriminately by the Chinese upon the streets . . . created an alarm . . . which opened the way for evil-doers" who wounded, robbed, and murdered "unoffending human beings." Similarly, the *Los Angeles News*, temporarily curbing its usual anti-Chinese rants, offered the more measured observation that "the hostile [Chinese] parties met in the public street and fired at each other, regardless of the laws of the country, or danger to unoffending citizens."[37]

The Chinese spokesmen did not deny the reckless gunfire. In fact, Yo Hing was quick to point out, "The Chinamen think that it was a very bad thing to try to kill the officers, and that the guilty parties should have been punished."[38] Since the tong fighters who shot at the police were apparently recruited by members of the Nin Yung Company, Yo Hing was trying to shift blame from himself to his Chinese enemies, particularly the Nin Yung leader Sam Yuen.

In response, Sam Yuen put forth a poor excuse. He claimed that the men inside his Wing Chung store had fired solely in self-defense, "thinking and believing that Yo Hing and party had come to kill them."[39] Even in the excitement of the moment, it is hardly plausible that the gunmen mistook Jesús Bilderrain, Esteban Sanchez, Robert Thompson, and the other officers and volunteers for Yo Hing's henchmen. As a matter of fact, no one ever determined why the tong fighters had fired randomly and repeatedly into the street that afternoon, other than to try to stave off arrest. Some writers have speculated that Sam Yuen's men were battling Officers Bilderrain and Sanchez because those two policemen had been paid to work for Yo Hing.[40] That is possible, although several bystanders swore that the Chinese gunmen shot "promiscuously," not just at the two lawmen. Furthermore, Officer Bilderrain was Sam Yuen's longtime customer and visited his Wing Chung store frequently, casting even greater doubt on that theory. A more likely explanation is that Sam Yuen and his Nin Yung colleagues got more than they bargained for; they were probably unable to rein in the brash, daring young gunslingers they had imported from San Francisco. In fact, Yo Hing claimed in his statement to the press that the tong assassins would "kill any body who tries to arrest them."[41]

The grand jurors also acknowledged that many Angelenos who witnessed the crimes that night did not participate in them—or try to stop them. They opined that the large majority of the members of the crowd of about five hundred were "unwilling witnesses." Most "would quickly and cheerfully have prevented or put an end to the anarchy, if any resolute and energetic man . . . had placed himself at their head and in a proper manner directed their efforts." However, the grand jurors had no sympathy for the citizen volunteers who obeyed the instructions of the sheriff and the city marshal to shoot any fleeing Chinese: "[T]he orders of an officer are no excuse for the commission of a criminal act."

While the report reprimanded both the Chinese gunslingers and the deputized citizens for shooting at innocent people, the grand jurors were excoriating in their assessment of Los Angeles's law officers. Though they acknowledged that the police made "a feeble, and in most cases ineffectual, effort" to rescue the Chinese victims, the grand jurors also noted that the officers made no attempt "to arrest any of those who in their presence were openly and grossly violating the law, even to the taking of human life." Furthermore, they pointed out that the citizen rescuers, unlike most of the policemen, "were successful, and met with no overpowering resistance. The conviction is forced upon us that had the officers performed their duty, this Grand Jury would not have been called upon to devote weeks to the investigation of this matter, nor would there have been any riotous acts on that night to stain the record of this county or the reputation of Los Angeles city."[42]

The grand jury upbraided the lawmen solely for ineptitude. The public's accusations were much harsher. The *New York Times* reported that the police officers "did absolutely nothing" and even "acted disgracefully in aiding and abetting the rioters." One member of the Common Council, John Osborn, stated not only that "the police force from the Chief down were derelict in their duty" but also that "bribes were offered by some of the police to incite the mob." Similarly, Horace Bell claimed that the police served as "the leaders of the mob." When Policeman George Gard was later examined, he was asked whether he and Officer Emil Harris had promised to pay one of the rioters, Louis Mendel, "if he would make no development with reference to a certain sum of money that was taken from a Chinese house or store that night." Officer Gard denied the accusation of bribery.[43]

Were some of the police officers in fact guilty of having helped start the riot? If so, what was their motive? The local lawmen were not Chinese-haters; on the contrary, they enjoyed a cordial and profitable relationship with the Chinatown businessmen who gave them rewards and gifts. Their only real incentive for encouraging an assault on the Coronel adobe would have been the opportunity for even greater gain, especially by plundering the treasure chest in the Wing Chung store. However, subsequent events made that theory seem less probable. The police did not attempt to protect their alleged co-conspirator, Louis Mendel, but instead promptly arrested him a few days after the riot. More tellingly, the owners of the Wing Chung store apparently did not think Officers George Gard and Emil Harris had stolen their money, because they gave the two policemen presents only three months later.[44]

The allegations of blatant police corruption during the riot seem to have been based more on rumor and innuendo than on any concrete evidence. Still, they showed how badly the lawmen's reputations suffered as a result of their inability to control the mob. Angelenos were angry that the name of their city was being dragged through the mud across the country. They were anxious to assign blame to the police, to the scofflaws of Calle de los Negros, to the Chinese gunfighters—to anyone but themselves, for failing to stem the racial animosity before it got so hopelessly out of hand.

In December 1871, the *New York Times* correctly observed, "It is only right to say of the Grand Jury that it has done its duty most faithfully. The work of bringing the indicted persons to justice devolves upon the District Attorney and the Police." In Los Angeles, the *Evening Express* added, "The citizens of the county owe it to themselves and to the world that the guilty parties be brought to a speedy and exemplary punishment."[45] But how likely was that? Governor Newton Booth, while denouncing mob violence against the Chinese in his inaugural address on December 8, 1871, also brought up the troubling fact that vigilante killings in California usually went unpunished. He voiced concern that the courts were too often controlled by the political influence of the perpetrators. It remained to be seen whether the judiciary of Los Angeles, which had nonchalantly and repeatedly let members of lynch mobs go unpunished and facilitated the trade in enslaved Chinese women, was up to the task at hand. And the whole nation was watching.

10

We May Hope to See at Least
Partial Justice Done

Preparing for Trial

By the second week of December 1871, the Los Angeles county jail was packed with riot suspects. The police had arrested thirteen people as of November 20, and warrants had been issued for fourteen more. When the grand jurors inspected the jail as part of their duties, they found thirty-one prisoners. Their report of December 2 concluded, "Not only the health, but the lives of the inmates, are endangered by the manner in which they are there confined." It pointed out that the prisoners were locked up "day and night within the walls of the jail . . . herded together, in a manner that would not be suffered in the treatment of cattle by any thrifty farmer."[1]

Consequently, District Judge Murray Morrison released ten of the prisoners on bail of $500 each. Seven were non-Asians and three were Chinese. Obviously, they had every incentive to leave Los Angeles before trial. In fact, one of the accused Chinese gunmen, Ah Sing, failed to appear for his arraignment. Nonetheless, District Attorney Cameron Thom did not oppose the prisoners' release "for the reasons that the jail has not the capacity to contain the number of persons now under arrest, and to be arrested." Yo Hing, charged with inciting the riot, had already been set free. Many of the other indicted rioters remained in jail, presumably because they posed the greatest flight risk.[2]

On December 18, 1871, while preparations for the riot trials were underway, Judge Morrison died unexpectedly. Local attorney Robert M. Widney, who had been admitted to the bar six years earlier and had just turned thirty-three, was appointed as his successor.[3] A native of Ohio, Widney had held a variety of jobs since heading west in 1855—fur trapper, woodchopper, mathematics professor, mining engineer, real estate agent, and finally lawyer. However, his previous experience most relevant to the riot trials was that he had witnessed the event. When the defendants appeared in court for their arraignment on February 5, 1872, they must have been mortified to see who was presiding. Some of the accused killers who stood before Robert Widney had nearly come to blows with the new judge on October 24, 1871. That night, as recounted earlier, Widney had protested in vain while the mob hanged Leong Quai and Ah Long at Tomlinson's corral. By his own testimony, he had confronted A. R. Johnston in the street. During the riot, Widney had probably seen some of the other defendants who now declared their innocence before him. They may have even been the men who threatened to kill him if he interfered.

Under the modern law of recusal, a judge ordinarily cannot hear a case if he is biased or has personal knowledge of the facts. That was not so in 1872. Although a California statute disqualified a judge in certain circumstances, prejudice and personal knowledge were not among them. Nor did judicial precedent in California make bias a ground for recusal or a change of venue—even when, as in one San Francisco case from 1861, the presiding county judge belonged to a vigilance committee that had threatened the accused.[4] Thus, Judge Widney had no legal obligation to recuse himself, and the defense lawyers, Edward J. C. Kewen and James G. Howard, had no basis to ask him to step aside or to move the trials to another town.

They came up with a different ground for objection, however. The attorneys argued that prosecutor Cameron Thom's indictment charging the defendants as accessories to Dr. Gene Tong's murder was legally insufficient because it failed to specify that the doctor had actually been killed. This feeble defense was certainly a long shot, but the lawyers thought it was worth a try. The indictment they were attacking stated that the defendants "did feloniously, unlawfully, deliberately, premeditatedly, and of their malice aforethought, stand by, aid, abet, assist, advise, counsel and encourage unknown persons . . . to kill and murder one Gene Tong."[5]

This language was hardly ambiguous. Reduced to its simplest terms, the district attorney's indictment clearly charged the accused men with having helped some unidentified perpetrators murder the doctor. Nonetheless, the novice judge had a dilemma on his hands. Under California law at that time, he could not simply allow the prosecutor to amend the indictment and remove any remote doubts about its validity (by adding, for instance, the phrase "who was in fact murdered" at the end). Instead, he would have to submit the case to the same or a new grand jury. The law allowed Judge Widney to keep the incarcerated suspects in jail if he found it necessary to send the matter back for reconsideration. Nonetheless, the move would be risky. County Judge Sepúlveda had already dismissed the grand jurors who returned the indictments, promising them that they would not have to serve again while he was on the bench.[6] Therefore, the matter would have to come before a different grand jury, and it might decide not to indict anyone. On the other hand, if Judge Widney made the wrong call at this early stage and proceeded under a defective indictment, any subsequent convictions of the accused mob members could be overturned on appeal. What seemed like a dry, insignificant point of law actually had the potential to become a make-or-break issue in the riot cases.

Knowing how much was riding on his decision, Judge Widney approached this procedural challenge very carefully. In his written opinion, he acknowledged that if the indictment had been worded slightly differently, the defense would have a valid legal point, no matter how ludicrous it seemed in light of what had happened on the streets of Los Angeles that terrible night. If it merely alleged that the defendants had "encouraged" or "advised" others to kill the doctor, the indictment would be lacking, because it would not indicate whether or not those other people actually went through with the murder. Likewise, if the indictment had charged that the defendants had "aided" or "assisted" in an *attempt* to kill Dr. Tong, it would not automatically follow that the attempt was successful. However, the language of prosecutor Thom's indictment stated that the defendants "aided" and "assisted" unknown persons in the killing of Dr. Tong. Obviously, the accused men could not have helped others murder the doctor without him ending up dead.

As further support for his decision, Widney pointed out that the law required the words of an indictment to be read "in the usual acceptance in common language." Furthermore, the form of the indictment before him was identical to the one set forth in the governing statute. Finally, he cited a California law providing that a faulty indictment should not be deemed insufficient if the defect did not prejudice the defendants. The judge concluded with confidence, "If the Court had any reasonable doubt as to the sufficiency of the indictment, it would not put the county to the expense of a trial, but would remand the defendants to await the action of a new Grand Jury."[7]

Widney's opinion was legally sound and eminently sensible. It would also be one of the most regrettable decisions of his career.

The First Trial

The Chinese went to trial first. On February 14, 1872, two accused gunmen, Quong Wong and Ah Ying, were tried for the murder of Ah Choy, the San Francisco tong fighter who had been the first casualty of October 24, 1871. Even though the victim in this case was not white, the trial would be an early test of whether Chinese accused of high crimes could get a fair hearing in Los Angeles's district court.

Four policemen and one Latino bystander were examined first. However, prosecutor Cameron Thom's case relied primarily on the testimony of two Chinese, Ah Sing and Charley Ah Chung. It was Judge Widney's practice to allow Chinese witnesses to swear on the severed head of a chicken rather than a Bible. A court interpreter roughly translated the oath they used as follows:

Swear the other of this case, [name] I must speak according the truth evident [sic], if I swear lie, God of heaven punished and binding me like cutting chicken's head, and kill me by the thunder. I swear the truth evident [sic], God protect me and give me good auspicious, [year, month, day, witness's name].[8]

The white attorneys for the Chinese defendants were placed in the awkward position of having to argue that Chinese witnesses were incompetent. They objected to the testimony on the grounds that Ah

Sing did not believe in Christianity and could not understand either the nature of an oath or the responsibilities involved in courts of "civilized nations." Judge Widney overruled these objections. According to one news account, Chinese testimony was "for the first time allowed in evidence in this Court"—a significant development, considering that the district court was only one level below the state's highest court.[9]

That testimony proved to be useless, however. The same witnesses who had spoken freely before the grand jury unexpectedly declared at trial that they knew nothing about the case. District Attorney Cameron Thom was embarrassed and disgusted that the key witnesses for the prosecution had turned on him at the last minute. Announcing that he would proceed no further with the case, he apologized to the jurors "for an apparent trifling with their time." Judge Widney instructed the jury to return a verdict of "not guilty." The *Los Angeles News* huffed, "The trial itself was a complete farce."[10] Quong Wong and Ah Ying were acquitted, and no one was ever punished for the murder of Ah Choy.

Selecting the Jurors

The real drama began two days later. On February 16, 1872, juror selection started in the trial of L. F. "Curly" Crenshaw for the murder of Gene Tong. Crenshaw's case came up first because his name appeared at the top of the indictment. District Attorney Cameron Thom wisely chose to prosecute only Dr. Tong's murder at this stage. He stood to win juror sympathy by focusing on the most renowned victim, a popular Chinese physician who treated non-Asian patients and helped them find Chinese workers. If Thom could get a white jury to convict a white man for helping kill a Chinese who was widely admired among Angelenos, it might be easier to obtain subsequent convictions for the deaths of the lesser-known lynching victims. Moreover, if he failed to get a conviction for Dr. Tong's murder, he could still prosecute Curly Crenshaw, who, along with many fellow defendants, was also under indictment as an accessory to the murders of the other seventeen. As the *Alta California* correctly observed, "The trial may be regarded as a test case for all the others."[11]

Shortly after the massacre, the Los Angeles press had expressed guarded optimism that "we may hope to see at least partial justice done." The "partial" nature of that justice was soon apparent. Cameron Thom announced plans to try only eleven of the thirty-seven indicted rioters. Presumably, he did not think he had enough evidence to convict the other twenty-six or the resources to try that many people. When Curly Crenshaw's trial date finally arrived, the same newspaper pointed out, "The whole country has been looking forward to this event. The progress of the trials, step by step, will evidently be keenly watched by the entire civilized world, and it will no less anxiously await the result."[12]

Aware of the attention the trial would draw, the attorneys proceeded cautiously. They thoroughly questioned potential jurors for bias. One of the first inquiries that came up was, "Have you any prejudice in favor of or against the Chinese race?" Oddly, Judge Widney ruled that this issue was irrelevant. It was not mentioned again.

Another question, seemingly of less relevance, arose repeatedly during the juror screening: "Are you now, or have you ever been, a member of a vigilance committee, or have you ever sympathized with such an organization?" When one potential juror, Louis Duror, admitted that he had once been a vigilante, the queries continued at length:

"Having sympathy with such organization, and still having such sympathy, and having belonged to such organization, viz: a Vigilance Committee, do you think you could impartially try the prisoner at bar?"

Duror said that he thought he could.

"How could you, if the purpose of the organization be to inflict summary punishment on alleged criminals [without] trial by a regular form of law?"

Judge Widney sustained an objection.

Several more questions along these lines were asked, with objections being raised and sustained. The last was, "Do you think your mind is as clear from bias and prejudice against the defendant as if you had never been a member of such organization or sympathized with the same?"

Louis Duror finally confessed, "I do not know."

He was not selected for the jury. Nor were any of the other men who admitted having belonged to a vigilance committee.[13]

It seemed natural that the district attorney would want to know if any potential jurors had been vigilantes, because they might be more sympathetic toward those accused murderers who claimed they were avenging the killing of Robert Thompson. Surprisingly, however, these questions were posed by the defense attorneys, Edward J. C. Kewen and James G. Howard,[14] rather than the prosecutor. Their motives were suggested by a question they asked the potential jurors who admitted having participated in lynch mobs: "Did you then take an oath to punish in a summary manner prisoners accused of crime without due process of law?" Most likely, the defendants' lawyers feared that members of the vigilance committee would be eager to convict anyone associated with a lawless rabble, even on slight evidence, as an example to other would-be hooligans. If that was the reason, the attorneys' concern underscored the arrogant elitism and self-righteousness behind the vigilantes' philosophy that justice belonged in the hands of "the people." What they actually believed was that men of standing were justified in hanging suspects following secret, extralegal deliberations, but the riffraff must be dissuaded from lynching people in the heat of passion without the vigilance committee's approval.

The repeated inquiries about vigilantism were particularly painful for Judge Widney, for a very personal reason. Throughout his life, Widney fought to quell persistent rumors that he had played an active role in the vigilance committee that lynched Michel Lachenais in 1870. Only five days after he became judge, the *Los Angeles News* went public with the rumor. In a savage editorial ridiculing Widney's abilities and experience, the *News* sarcastically proclaimed that Governor Newton Booth had appointed a judge "who has uniformly discountenanced those flagrant outrages of peace and decency, termed 'vigilance committees'; who has never, with them, claimed that law is insufficient to protect; one whose hands are free from human blood; who has never hounded on, much less abetted by his presence, the commission of murder." The *News* suggested that it would be appropriate for the local bar to present Widney with a medal "representing on one side a gallows (improvised from a gateway), with the legend *sus. per coll.* ["*suspendatur per collum*," or "let him be hanged by the neck"], and on the reverse the balances of Justice, with one scale superseded by the effigy of a strangling man and, above it, the motto—'LAW.'"[15] "Gateway" referred to the entrance of Tomlinson's corral, where Lachenais was hanged.

The next day, the *Star* lambasted this editorial as unwarranted.[16] But the damage was done. Moreover, neither Widney nor his friends refuted the *News's* accusations, feeding suspicion that they were true. Not until late in life did Widney publish an indirect denial, claiming in his account of the Chinese massacre that he was president of Los Angeles's "law and order party," a label applied to informal citizens' groups in California that opposed the lawless actions of vigilance committees.[17]

Widney had inadvertently contributed to the rumors when he testified before the coroner's jury shortly after the massacre. At that time, he made a point of stating that none of the old vigilance committee members had taken part in the riot, except in rescuing Chinese from the mob. He said this to clarify his earlier testimony, in which he mentioned that a mob leader had told him, "We are all vigilantes."[18] That man, Widney assured the coroner's jurors, was not a member of the old vigilance committee. His unexpected defense of the vigilantes raised eyebrows. Even if he was just trying to set the record straight, he cast doubt on his own innocence.

He launched his most vigorous defense of his honor in 1877, when he drew a pistol on a trial witness who blurted out in open court that Michel Lachenais had been "hanged by Judge Widney and some others." Widney introduced court minutes to prove that he had been trying a case at the time Lachenais was hanged. Although he thought that would put an end to the talk, the accusations continued to resurface. Horace Bell, who detested Widney for reasons he never disclosed, repeated the rumor in a memoir that was not published until after both men had died. In it, he asserted that Widney was "the prime mover in organizing the hanging party" that lynched Lachenais. Although Widney had shown that he was in court that morning, Bell undermined his alibi, claiming that "at the last moment, after the mob was incited, he dropped out" and let others finish the job.[19] To this day, it remains a mystery whether Robert M. Widney, the man who would preside at the trials of those accused of lynching eighteen people, was a shamefaced former vigilante concealing a dark secret or a blameless man wrongly accused of a terrible crime.

The Trial of Curly Crenshaw

As soon as twelve jurors were selected, Curly Crenshaw's trial as an accessory to the murder of Dr. Gene Tong got underway. The first witness for the prosecution was Henry M. Mitchell, the *Los Angeles Star* reporter. When he took the stand, Mitchell spoke at length but in general terms about seeing the crowd in the street just before the mob stormed the Coronel building. Prosecutor Cameron Thom asked him, "What else did you see there?"

Crenshaw's lawyer objected to any questions about whether a riot had occurred. In response, Judge Widney instructed Mitchell to tell the court only what he knew about the death of Gene Tong or Crenshaw's connection to it. Prosecutor Thom then explained his legal theory to the judge: he intended to show that a mob existed, that it summarily executed Dr. Tong, and that Crenshaw was part of that mob. Widney reconsidered and allowed the prosecutor to ask Mitchell once more, "What did you see?"

Things went downhill from there. Mitchell, to Thom's regret, had seen nothing that was truly relevant. He did not see Crenshaw that night. He did not know Gene Tong, although the doctor's body was pointed out to him the next morning in the jail yard. He did not know where the doctor was hanged. He did see "one Chinaman hanged that night . . . by a party in the crowd . . . on the crossbeam of the gate of the Tomlinson corral." He also saw the bodies of other Chinese men hanging in Los Angeles Street. However, Mitchell did not recognize anyone involved in the lynching.

Prosecutor Thom apparently called Mitchell to the stand because he had seen more of the riot than most witnesses, but his testimony exposed the core problem that the district attorney would wrestle with throughout the riot trials. On the dark, chaotic night of October 24, 1871, fourteen of the hangings had occurred in three separate locations during about half an hour. Many bystanders had seen snippets of the action, watching numerous small bands of rioters hurry past them in different directions with their Chinese prisoners. However, most of those who had actually seen the hangings and were willing to talk did not know who the victims were. More critically, they were rarely close enough to the scene of the crime to identify the perpetrators on that overcast night.

The rest of the testimony that day was no more fruitful. Witness Andrew J. King identified two rioters by name, but Crenshaw was not one of them. All that County Coroner Joseph Kurtz knew of the murder was that Dr. Tong was hanged by a mob, and he did not recognize anyone in the crowd that night. On cross-examination, Kurtz admitted that he had not personally known Dr. Tong.

The first day of trial was disastrous for Thom. Clearly, it was going to be very difficult for the district attorney to link the accused accessory, Curly Crenshaw, to the killing of a particular victim, Gene Tong. Though Thom was trying Crenshaw for aiding and abetting the doctor's murder rather than actually carrying it out, he needed to prove more than the young man's mere presence in a crowd of five hundred that night. No doubt he realized that the subsequent trials would be equally challenging. Angelenos who read the witness testimony in the *Los Angeles News* must have wondered whether any convictions could come out of the riot cases.

The testimony the second day got off to a slightly more encouraging start. Constable Richard Kerren mentioned several rioters by name, particularly A. R. Johnston. However, he did not "know a man sometimes called Curly." Although he had been acquainted with Gene Tong for six or eight months, Kerren had no idea who had helped kill him. Another witness, attorney Henry T. Hazard, could identify where Dr. Tong had his office. But he did not know anything about the doctor or Curly Crenshaw.

The two witnesses that followed were finally able to provide a few relevant specifics. Policeman Emil Harris saw Gene Tong being taken out of his room that night. However, the next time he saw the doctor was when he examined his body the following morning in the jail yard. Furthermore, Harris said he did not recognize any of the people who grabbed Dr. Tong. He saw Crenshaw on the roof of the Coronel adobe but not afterward. Most damagingly, the policeman admitted on cross-examination that he did not see Crenshaw take part in the riot.

Bystander Ben McLaughlin was the prosecution's star witness, but even his testimony was fairly weak. He swore that he saw Crenshaw on the roof of the Coronel building with a pistol but could not say whether he had discharged it. He also heard Crenshaw say "he had killed three Chinamen" and talk "considerably about shooting Chinamen for some time." Unfortunately, he knew nothing specific about Gene Tong's death. This circumstantial evidence was the best Cameron Thom could offer the jury.

Finally, Curly Crenshaw took the stand in his own defense. He was twenty-two years old but looked younger. A drifter, he had left his home in Illinois a year earlier and had gained a "reputation of the worst sort," according to the press. In Crenshaw's version of the events of October 24, Policeman George Gard had asked him to escort a Chinese woman to the jail for safety, which he did. However, he could not remember to whom he delivered her. Afterward, he returned to Billy Rapp's saloon, downed a couple of drinks, and ate his supper. Then he headed home and went to bed. He denied telling Ben McLaughlin that he had killed three Chinese.

Once Crenshaw's testimony concluded, the lawyers made their closing statements. By that point, the district attorney knew full well how thin his case was. After Judge Widney instructed the jurors on the legal issues, they retired to determine Crenshaw's fate. Meanwhile, Curly Crenshaw was not sweating the verdict. According to news reports, he "did not entertain the remotest idea of being convicted, and vowed that as soon as he was once foot loose, he would reform his ways."[20]

Chinese Testimony

Conspicuously absent from Curly Crenshaw's trial were any Chinese witnesses. That was not an oversight on the prosecutor's part. California's statutes flatly prohibited Chinese from testifying in the case. By law, a Chinese person could not give evidence in a criminal matter either in favor of or against any white person—that is, an Anglo or a Latino who was less than half Native American by blood. Similarly, in civil lawsuits, Chinese were barred from giving evidence in any action to which a white person was a party.[21]

Nine years before the state legislature adopted these rules in 1863, the California Supreme Court had already reached the same conclusion. In *People v. Hall*, it applied tortured ethnological and anatomical logic to conclude that Chinese were actually "Indians" under earlier California statutes prohibiting Native Americans or African Americans from testifying against whites. Ever since Columbus landed in America, the court claimed, American Indians and "Mongolians" had been "regarded as the same type of human species." In addition, the state's foremost jurists opined that the Chinese were "a race of people whom nature has marked as inferior." Therefore, it was critical to shield white people from their influence. California's blatantly discriminatory laws limiting Chinese testimony remained in effect until 1873, the year after the Los Angeles riot trials.[22]

Not all white people in California agreed that testimonial exclusion was right. In Los Angeles, the town's humblest jurist had discovered the most effective way to express his disapproval of the unjust law. William H. Gray, the fair-minded justice of the peace, tacitly ignored these statutes whenever possible, letting Chinese testify against whites. In a case in which China Charley accused a white man of assault and battery, Gray noted in his minutes that the injured Chinese relied "altogether upon his own testimony." In a similar case, he rebuffed the idea "that a Chinaman was incompetent to make complaint in this Court against a white man." When a Chinese man named Ah Mow sought civil damages for injuries he received at the hands of a white man, Gray allowed his testimony along with that of his Chinese doctor. As long as he could get away with it, Gray continued to practice his small acts of civil disobedience.[23]

As a practical matter, Chinese testimony would have done little to help prosecutor Cameron Thom prove his case against Curly Crenshaw. The only Chinese who had witnessed Gene Tong's death was his housemate, Chang Wan, who himself was hanged immediately afterward.

The Verdict

The jurors deliberated only twenty minutes, returning to the district courtroom at a quarter past ten on the night of February 17, 1872. The foreman, a well-known banker and rancher named Francis Pliny Fisk Temple, stood to deliver their verdict: "People of the State versus L. F. Crenshaw. The jury in the above entitled cause find the defendant guilty of manslaughter."[24]

The verdict came as a surprise. It was also a huge relief to nearly everyone but Curly Crenshaw, for it meant that Los Angeles would be spared from further denigration in the national press the next day. Cameron Thom had every reason to feel triumphant, though the outcome was less than ideal. Manslaughter was far too benign a description for the heinous crimes that had occurred on October 24,

1871. Voluntary manslaughter typically refers to a killing that occurred in the heat of sudden passion when the perpetrator was understandably provoked. If the bystanders in Chinatown had taken revenge on the particular tong fighter who shot Robert Thompson shortly after it happened, manslaughter would have been an appropriate charge. However, most of the random killings of innocent victims did not take place until more than three hours after Thompson was hit.

At the same time, it was questionable whether the sketchy evidence, which failed to link Curly Crenshaw directly to Gene Tong's death, could sustain an accessory-to-murder conviction. For that matter, it was debatable whether it even satisfied the prosecutor's burden of proof for manslaughter. Nonetheless, eleven of the twelve jurors initially voted in favor of the more serious crime of murder. The *News* explained that one juror held out, and the others compromised by reducing the offense to manslaughter.[25] The verdict may have been the result of jury nullification, that is, a belief among those who determined Crenshaw's fate that the indiscriminate murders of eighteen men cried out for justice, and that it was proper to punish someone who took a leading role in the riot that led to the killings, even if the evidence did not prove that he had actually helped drag Dr. Tong to Tomlinson's corral or affix the noose around his neck. Meanwhile, Curly Crenshaw, unable to fathom what had just happened to him, was taken back to jail to await sentencing.

Nine More Rioters

The lawyers agreed that the cases against the next nine indicted rioters could be heard together, probably because they knew the same witnesses would be called in each case. Like Curly Crenshaw, these defendants would be tried as accessories only to the murder of Gene Tong. Once again, this left the door open for Cameron Thom to try the same men for killing the other seventeen victims if he failed to get convictions in the Tong case. The accused were Esteban A. Alvarado, Charles Austin, Refugio Botello, Adolfo Celis, Louis Mendel, A. R. Johnston, Jesús Martinez, Patrick M. McDonald, and Dan W. Moody. One other indicted rioter, J. G. Scott, was slated to go to trial. However, the case against him was apparently dismissed or postponed.[26]

The questioning of the jury pool began on February 21, 1872. Once more, the potential jurors were asked about their association or sympathy with the vigilance committee. One man readily admitted, "I was a member of the organization who hung Lachenais. . . . I approved of his hanging and do still." The defendants' lawyers, once again the firm of Kewen & Howard,[27] argued before Judge Widney that everyone who participated in the hanging of Michel Lachenais "was a murderer just as much as they who killed these Chinese."[28] Again, it was an odd stance for the defense counsel to take. If anything, it seemed that those who lynched Lachenais, being murderers themselves, might have been more sympathetic toward the indicted men. However, the defense lawyers, undoubtedly shaken by the guilty verdict in Curly Crenshaw's case, apparently feared that the former vigilantes were more eager than anyone to mete out punishment to those responsible for the outbreak of lawlessness in their city.

Thom then raised a question that had been disallowed while selecting Curly Crenshaw's jurors: "Do you entertain any such prejudice against the Chinese as a race as to prevent you from doing justice in a case in which a Chinaman was concerned?" The defense attorneys objected, pointing out that this was not a valid legal ground for disqualifying jurors. However, Judge Widney, without explanation, changed his mind and agreed this time with Thom that the issue of racism was relevant. He allowed the district attorney to proceed.[29]

At the defense attorneys' request, Widney had ordered the sheriff to obtain jurors from the outer areas of Los Angeles County who might be less prejudiced than the townspeople. Inexplicably, all forty-eight men who were called lived in the city. Several of them were excused because they had already formed an opinion. One man stated flatly that "he would not be controlled by the law and the evidence," because "he had seen the affair."[30]

The defense attorneys tried to determine how much each man knew about the events of October 24, 1871. Potential juror William Griffin stated that he subscribed to the *Daily News*, "like a sensible man," and that he had read the paper's accounts of the riot. The questioning continued, with prosecutor Thom objecting frequently:

"Did you read or hear that several Chinamen were killed that night?"
"I did."

"Did you form or express an opinion, unqualified, as to the act itself of the killing of Chinamen?"

"Yes."

"Were you connected with the Vigilance Committee that hanged Lachenais?"

"No."

"Did you sympathize with their acts?"

This time, Judge Widney sustained Thom's objection to the question.[31]

Finding 12 unbiased jurors proved far more difficult than expected. Judge Widney ordered a special venire of 100 men "to be drawn from those who speak and understand English." That was still not enough. He summoned another group. More than three weeks passed and an astounding total of 255 people were questioned before a jury of 12 men was finally impaneled on March 16, 1872.[32]

This second trial would determine whether Curly Crenshaw's conviction had been a fluke. If Los Angeles jurors found one man guilty of contributing to the killing of a Chinese doctor but acquitted the next nine, outsiders would disparage the city once more. Given how hard it had been to find competent jurors, many Angelenos worried that none of the accused would be convicted. The *News* also speculated that the problem of finding unbiased jurors was the reason why the district attorney had announced no plans to try any more indicted men. It even posited that potential jurors in any future riot cases would claim they had already formed an opinion to avoid the possibility of a long stay in the jury box.[33]

The trial began on March 18, 1872. As in Curly Crenshaw's case, it would be nearly impossible to link any of the defendants directly to Dr. Tong's murder. Thom closely examined more than thirty witnesses over the course of seven days, an unusually long time in an era when trial testimony normally took no more than one or two days. The district attorney's thoroughness helped put to rest any speculation that Los Angeles's officials were not really serious about prosecuting the suspected killers.[34] One juror's wife complained that her husband, closely guarded by the sheriff under Judge Widney's orders, was treated like a prisoner during the lengthy trial while some of the accused were free on bail. The defense lawyers examined only a few witnesses, instead relying mostly on procedural and evidentiary challenges. The trial transcript comprised 212 "closely written pages of legal cap," none of which has survived.[35]

During all this, the Chinese showed little interest in the riot trials, possibly because the irreparable damage to their community had already been done. While the testimony was underway, five Chinese women and two children visited the graves of those killed during the massacre. Weeping profusely, they placed sweetmeats, chickens, brandy, tea, and other delicacies on the burial mounds at the City Cemetery. They also burned colored paper and Joss sticks to frighten away evil spirits—which, as they had learned, seemed to abound in Los Angeles.[36]

The attorneys made their closing arguments on March 26. The courthouse was packed with spectators. Judge Widney did not instruct the jury until ten o'clock that night. Speaking nearly an hour, he said in part: "The fact that many citizens or even a majority of the most respectable citizens approved of the acts of the rioters, or assisted therein is no mitigation or justification of the offense. . . . Being engaged in a riot, where the object is the killing of Chinese, every man concerned is just as guilty . . . as if he actually did the fatal act. All are responsible for the acts of each, if done in pursuance and furtherance of the common design."[37]

Judge Widney's reference to "the most respectable citizens" suggested that names such as John D. Hicks, George M. Fall, and Henry M. Mitchell may have surfaced during the trial testimony, as they had at the coroner's inquest. It is also plausible that Widney included that statement because he had seen some of the town's distinguished men watching the mayhem that night, doing nothing to stop the killings and perhaps even encouraging them. Widney's remark raised the possibility that the transcript of the testimony was deliberately misplaced or destroyed after the trial to protect the reputations of some esteemed Angelenos whose judgment had failed them during the riot or whose courage had evaporated when it was most needed. (Granted, it was also true that the bulk of Los Angeles's court records from that period were not well preserved.)

This time, the jurors deliberated for several hours. Many Angelenos believed that they would not be able to agree on a verdict. Indeed, their job was not easy. Undoubtedly, the evidence was more damning for some defendants than others. The jury did not return to the courtroom until two o'clock on the morning of March 27, 1872. George S. Blake, the foreman, read the verdict: "In the District Court of the Seventeenth Judicial District, State of California, in and for the County of Los Angeles, the People of the State of California versus Adolfo Celis and D. W. Moody, we the undersigned jurors find the above named defendants not guilty."

Everyone tensed. The two "not guilty" verdicts signaled that seven other men might be convicted of some offense. But would they be held responsible as murderers? Blake continued: "In the District Court of the Seventeenth Judicial District, State of California, in and for the County of Los Angeles, the People of the State of California versus Louis Mendel, A. R. Johnston, Charles Austin, P. M. McDonald, Jesús Martinez, Refugio Botello, and Esteban A. Alvarado, we the undersigned jurors find the above named defendants guilty of the crime of manslaughter."[38]

Thus, none of the ten men brought to trial would be punished for the crime of murder. The town still saw the verdict as a tremendous victory. Many non-Asian Angelenos, especially those who were actively promoting the region and trying to attract newcomers, were greatly relieved that Cameron Thom had managed to obtain a total of eight convictions. Immediately, the *News* predicted that this verdict would "do much toward appeasing the indignation aroused by the committal of the outrage."[39]

The national press took notice, even though the riot trials drew far less attention than had the massacre. A letter from Los Angeles appeared in the *Cincinnati Gazette*: "The verdict was a surprise because the legal punishment of crime here . . . has been the exception rather than the rule—and especially a surprise in this case because of the obvious generality of guilt among the people, and consequent popular sympathy with the prisoners." Hence, the letter-writer concluded, "the result is a surprise—a happy one to those who care about the reputation of this community. . . . The conviction of these rioters asserts that Chinamen are human beings, and as such are entitled to protection under the laws of California."[40]

Meanwhile, the *Los Angeles Star*, which did not even bother to cover the proceedings, sniffed that the riot trials "elicited very little interest on the part of our citizens."[41] Indeed, many Angelenos had already moved on.

The Sentences

Sentencing took place at ten o'clock on a Saturday morning, March 30, 1872. A crowd assembled in the district courtroom to hear the results. Deputy Sheriff John M. Baldwin, who had remonstrated ineffectively with the lynch mob that night, led in the prisoners. They "looked but little the worse for their confinement in the County Jail, which in the majority of the cases had been continuous since last October."

L. F. "Curly" Crenshaw, the first man tried, was also the first called up for sentencing. When Judge Widney asked the young man if he had any reason why sentence should not be pronounced, Crenshaw maintained that he was innocent. He also said that he had never been charged with a crime and asked for clemency because of his youth. Judge Widney agreed that "bad company had caused his connection with the riot." He held out hope that three years in San Quentin would reform the young man.

Louis Mendel, who had been in trouble before, had nothing to say to the judge. He received a six-year sentence.

Charles Austin told the judge that he was forty-three years old and had never been charged with any crime. He was sentenced to five years.

Patrick M. McDonald pleaded that he "was as innocent as a child," that he was not present at the riot but had been mistakenly identified. He received a five-year sentence.

Esteban A. Alvarado grumbled that he had been convicted as "the result of the machinations of his enemies" and that "if the rope was around his neck he could only declare his innocence." He got five years.

Jesús Martinez, twenty-two, mechanically stated that he was innocent. He was sentenced to four years.

Refugio Botello, the popular butcher and cattle trader, tried to make his case all over again. He claimed that he had assisted the sheriff on the night of the riot. He even recalled finding a Chinese man under a bed and escorting him to jail. Judge Widney sentenced him to two years. Botello was already preparing to appeal his case to the California Supreme Court. Unlike the other seven convicted defendants, he was released on bail of $5,000 until the appeal was concluded.

Shoemaker A. R. Johnston was "exceedingly nervous and much excited" when he was called up. In a rambling speech to the judge, he mentioned his "life of industry." He also said that he was innocent, complaining that "the people were guilty" but "the poor alone suffered." Then he told "a badly mixed story of a dream he had, in which he saw the jury as a rose with green leaves attacked by a bee, which took rose's honey and caused its decay." Finally, the loquacious shoemaker swore that "he felt more for his innocent fellow victims than himself." By "victims," he apparently meant his co-defendants rather than the lynched Chinese men.

Judge Widney was unimpressed by the speech and sentenced Johnston, undoubtedly a ringleader in the riot, to six years. Johnston's attorneys then made a last-ditch effort to keep him out of prison. Having listened to his bizarre rose-and-honeybee story, they tried to convince the judge that their client was insane, arguing this was a new development. Widney agreed to hold a hearing on the insanity defense the following Monday.[42]

Johnston, in his final, desperate attempt to avoid imprisonment or at least get his sentence reduced, shamelessly exploited his military service. Just before the hearing on his sanity, he wrote to Judge Widney:

> Sir: I did not wish to make known my accounts of being slightly deranged in public and in fact never spoke to my attorney in regards to the cause of it but Sir if you will be kind enough to call and see me when you are at leisure I will show you enough to convince you of the truth of my statement on my behalf. As I have been wounded twice in the head and at present there is still a piece of lead a laying on my brain which you can feel with your own hands and it is liable to hurt me at any time. I received my wounds in the 11th Batt. in the late War. Please call and see me. I remain your obedient servant A. R. Johnston.[43]

Judge Widney considered this evidence. No doubt he also recalled scuffling with Johnston over a Chinese captive at the corner of Temple and Spring Streets that unforgettable night. At that time, Johnston had been intoxicated but otherwise seemed possessed of his faculties. The shoemaker's insanity defense failed. Along with six of his cohorts, he boarded the steamer on April 7, 1872, headed for San Quentin. Meanwhile, the only convicted man who was free on bail, Refugio Botello, showed no trace of shame or remorse. Less than six months after being found guilty, he paraded as grand marshal of the city's Mexican Independence Day festival.[44]

Considering that the defendants had originally been charged with murder, the sentences were fairly lenient. California law at that time made manslaughter punishable by imprisonment for up to ten years,[45] but the longest term Judge Widney imposed was six. Apparently, he believed there were mitigating circumstances, most obviously the fact that practically all the evidence was circumstantial and none of the defendants could be directly linked to any of the lynchings. Perhaps, having been a witness to the massacre, Judge Widney was also going out of his way to avoid appearing vindictive. That was hardly necessary. No one would have blamed him for dealing out harsher punishments to those who had shown no mercy on the Black Tuesday.

Arrest of a Fugitive

Those Angelenos who packed the courtroom that morning to watch the sentencing thought they were witnessing the most sensational event in town. Actually, they missed the real excitement. While they were at the courthouse, the city's newest policeman, Frank Hartley, arrested Sam Yuen, the fugitive Nin Yung leader.

The warrant for Sam Yuen's arrest had been outstanding for three months. On November 28, 1871, Officer Jesús Bilderrain had sworn a complaint charging him with being an accessory to the murder of Robert Thompson. Sam Yuen had left town shortly after the riot, reportedly for Sacramento. He had not been spotted in Los Angeles until late March. However, he had made himself scarce and successfully avoided capture. Officer Hartley asked some Chinese informants to help him locate Sam Yuen's hiding place. At the time he was caught, he had a six-shooter up the right sleeve of his coat.[46]

Incidentally, the *Los Angeles News* reported a "suspicious disinclination" on the part of Police Officers Jesús Bilderrain, Emil Harris, and George Gard to arrest Sam Yuen. The newspaper suggested that the three lawmen had privately reached an agreement with the suspect. It also reminded its readers that Policemen Harris and Gard had recently received gifts from Sam Yuen's Wing Chung firm. Bilderrain denied the newspaper's insinuations of graft, saying, "I had a warrant of arrest, but could not find him." He also explained that he initially thought Sam Yuen "was concerned in killing Thompson" but that he no longer believed so.[47]

Sam Yuen was brought before Judge Widney on a writ of habeas corpus. The evidence at the hearing was mixed. Adolfo Celis, who had recently been acquitted in the riot trials, testified that at the beginning of the gun battle, Sam Yuen was the man who had shot above his head from the veranda of the Coronel adobe. He claimed that Sam Yuen had also fired at Officer Bilderrain as he was fleeing from the building. A second witness, Police Officer Esteban Sanchez, identified Sam Yuen as the man who had shot at him while he stood in the door of the Wing Chung store, just before Robert Thompson was hit. Finally, Cyrus Lyons said that he had seen Sam Yuen in the Wing Chung store and in the corral behind the Coronel block five minutes before Thompson's shooting.

On the other hand, bystander Pedro Badillo, who had known the accused for four or five years, said, "Sam Yuen was not one of the three Chinamen I saw on the corridor." Likewise, Officer Bilderrain, the only one who had gone inside the Wing Chung store, testified that he "did not see [Sam Yuen] during the shooting" and "did not know anyone" inside the store. He had also been acquainted with Sam Yuen for four or five years and had even been his customer, going to his store "frequently to get my little night lamp filled with oil."

While Sam Yuen's disappearance from Los Angeles, Bilderrain's shifting story, and his fellow officers' reluctance to arrest the accused all seemed suspicious, it was nonetheless unlikely that the Nin Yung headman had actually opened fire on the policemen or the citizen volunteers that October afternoon. As a rule, well-established Chinese merchants maintained good relationships with the police force and tried not to antagonize the non-Asian population. The first three witnesses, none of whom knew Sam Yuen well, may have simply misidentified the gunslinger they saw. Still, the testimony of Celis, Sanchez, and Lyons was enough to raise questions about Sam Yuen's innocence. Judge Widney concluded that he should be held to answer before the grand jury on a charge of manslaughter. Although he had proven to be a flight risk, Widney decided to release him on bail of $3,000.[48]

The Wing Chung Case

Another riot trial got underway in the district court during the first week of June 1872. However, this one was a civil rather than criminal action. The partners in Chinatown's Wing Chung store sued the city for the destruction and theft of the firm's property on the night of the massacre. This was the most highly publicized civil trial that the Chinese residents of Los Angeles had ever initiated. The suit was based on a California statute that subjected a city to liability whenever a person's property was "destroyed or injured in consequence of any mob or riot."[49] The complaint alleged that the mayor had full knowledge of the riot and that the city government was responsible for failing to control the mob. The Chinese sought to recover $7,000 in damages plus costs of the lawsuit.

The first witness was Ah Yung, one of the firm's partners. A lawyer for the city objected that the testimony of a "Mongolian" was inadmissible against a white person. The counsel for the Chinese merchants responded, quite sensibly, that the City of Los Angeles was not a white person. Judge Widney agreed. Three of the Chinese proprietors of the store, Ah Yung, Fong Yuen Sing, and none other than Sam Yuen, were then examined.[50]

The riot statute prohibited recovery if the property owners "occasioned or in any manner aided" the damage or failed to use "all reasonable diligence to prevent" it. The city's main defense was that the store's owners, "just before the alleged destruction of their property, organized and led on foot a disorderly company of Chinese and armed themselves with deadly weapons." The principal issue was whether or not Sam Yuen had been an instigator of the riot.[51]

Because the testimony was conflicting, it was difficult for the Wing Chung partners to establish their case. The jurors concluded that Sam Yuen "was one of the most prominent actors in the broil which brought on the riot that resulted in the destruction of property for which damages were claimed." On appeal, the lawyers for the Chinese argued that even if the Wing Chung partners had fired on the police officers, their actions did not justify what happened afterward. However, the California Supreme Court upheld the jury's verdict. It concluded from the record that Sam Yuen had "instigated and participated in the riot" and that his partners "were cognizant of the impending conflict between the two companies" but "took no steps to prevent it."[52] Whether or not Sam Yuen had actually fired any shots that afternoon, he had most likely hired the San Francisco tong fighters who escalated the gun battle. Few people believed that his hands were entirely clean.

Sam Yuen's Trial

In November 1872, more than a year after the massacre, Sam Yuen was finally tried for manslaughter in the death of Robert Thompson. The Nin Yung leader's reputation had been tarnished by the riot, but it still seemed somewhat ironic that this generally respectable businessman faced the possibility of going to San Quentin while Chinatown's most notorious troublemaker, Yo Hing, went free. (In fact, nothing ever came of the criminal charge against Yo Hing for inciting the riot.)

The trial testimony in Sam Yuen's case, which took two days, has not survived. However, in his firm's civil suit against the city, Sam Yuen had testified that on the evening of the riot, he left the Wing Chung store around five o'clock and was in his wife's house on the east side of Calle de los Negros.[53] At the conclusion of the case, Judge Widney charged the jurors that if they believed from the evidence that the Chinese were engaged in a fight among themselves, that Sam Yuen participated in the fight, that he and some of the other combatants retreated into his store, and that he was present with the gunman who actually shot Robert Thompson, "then the Jury are justified in finding the defendant guilty as accessory before the fact . . . If you have a reasonable doubt on any of the above points you will acquit the defendant."[54]

By this time, Los Angeles had shown the nation that its jurors were willing to convict white men for killing Chinese. One final question remained: would they be willing to acquit a Chinese accused of helping cause a white man's death if the evidence was lacking?

As it turned out, the jurors agreed on their verdict without any discussion. The *Los Angeles News* explained that the prosecutor failed to connect Sam Yuen directly with Thompson's death. The fact that he may have been present in the store at the time the fatal shot was fired was "not sufficiently clear as to his complicity to deprive the minds of the jury of a reasonable doubt."[55] Sam Yuen was discharged. Like Ah

Choy's murder, the killing of Robert Thompson went unpunished by law—although eighteen Chinese had lost their lives in the aftermath.

The Appeal

By the close of 1872, Angelenos thought it was finally over. Seven of the convicted men were in prison, and the eighth, Refugio Botello, was expected to start serving his sentence once his appeal was finished. The nation seemed to have forgotten the outrage in Los Angeles. The town was prospering, looking to the future.

The news the following spring caught everyone off guard. On May 21, 1873, the California Supreme Court handed down a startling reversal. In *People v. Crenshaw*, the state justices determined that the indictment in all the rioters' cases was fatally defective in that it failed to allege that Dr. Gene Tong was murdered. In a two-paragraph opinion that cited no statutes or judicial precedent, they summarily decided that they were not able to reach the legal conclusion from the language of the indictment that any person was actually murdered.[56] With that cursory dismissal, the convictions of the eight rioters were effectively overturned.

Angelenos were stunned. On June 10, 1873, Judge Widney, who had witnessed the death throes of Leong Quai and Ah Long when they were strung up at Tomlinson's corral, signed an order releasing the convicted killers from San Quentin. It must have been one of the hardest things he ever had to do. The *Los Angeles Star* noted sourly, "To this 'most lame and impotent conclusion' has come the great Chinese riots."[57]

The same newspaper fretted that the Supreme Court's reversal would "bring all that disgraceful business again before the courts."[58] That turned out not to be the case. District Attorney Cameron Thom decided not to try the eight convicted men for the other Chinese murders. Nor did he bring any of the other indicted rioters to trial. He had seen how difficult it was to impanel an impartial jury in the riot cases, since scores of Angelenos had witnessed the event or heard a great deal about it. Furthermore, both locals and outsiders had more or less put the Chinese massacre behind them, so there was very little pressure on Thom to reopen the matter.

Judge Widney came under heavy criticism for having allowed the prosecutor's original indictment to stand. Some blamed him for leaving the rioters' convictions vulnerable to reversal. Horace Bell cruelly remarked that Widney, a "real estate agent" who had been appointed to the bench "by some hook or crook," "had proved to be a very poor judge."[59] Over the decades, many accounts of the Chinese massacre have agreed that the inexperienced district court judge was inept and made a careless mistake.

However, it appears in retrospect that the fault lay not with "a very poor judge" but with a very poor decision by the California Supreme Court. The state's preeminent jurists found it "difficult to see how the indictment here is to be sustained." A more thoughtful, natural reading of the prosecutor's language might have eased their difficulty. In their written opinion, the justices did not even bother to discuss the statutes Judge Widney had cited in his well-reasoned discussion or even say why they thought his rationale was flawed. If the state's highest court had put forth merely a quarter of the effort it had expended in 1854 to show that Chinese were somehow "Indians" and therefore could not testify against whites, it might have been able to conclude that Cameron Thom's indictment adequately indicated that Gene Tong was murdered.

Considering that the Los Angeles riot cases were among the most highly publicized trials California had ever seen, involved one of the worst hate crimes the nation had experienced, and resulted in eight hard-won convictions under difficult circumstances, it is incomprehensible that the justices did not even try to give the appearance of having wrestled with the issue being appealed. Their deliberations may have been compromised by political pressure, for the anti-Chinese labor movement was building steam by 1873. Although they had recently ruled in favor of Chinese litigants in some cases, it is also possible that race influenced the justices' decision. Only a year later, the California Supreme Court, in a much more carefully reasoned opinion, upheld a conviction for the attempted murder of a white man notwithstanding an imperfect indictment.[60] *People v. Crenshaw* is still valid law in California, although the decision has never been cited as authority in any reported appellate case.

Despite this appalling edict from the California Supreme Court, the Los Angeles judiciary could hold its head high following the trials of 1872. The city at large still bore the taint of the shocking Chinese massacre, but its judge, its lawyers, and its jurors had done their jobs better

than anyone had expected. Cameron Thom had evenhandedly prosecuted the riot suspects most strongly implicated by the available evidence, even though at least two of them, Refugio Botello and Adolfo
Celis, were somewhat prominent in the community.[61] The jurors, even
if they harbored prejudice against the Chinese, did not hesitate to indict
and convict members of their own race. At the same time, their acquittal
of two defendants—one Anglo and one Latino—showed that the jurors
were not predisposed to make scapegoats of the ten men who were
tried. Nor did they attempt to avenge Robert Thompson's murder by
making an example out of Sam Yuen. The defense lawyers represented
their clients ably, and Judge Widney's rulings on their objections,
together with the rather lenient sentences he imposed, suggested that he
treated the accused men fairly despite his personal knowledge of what
some of them had done.

Of course, many aspects of the riot trials remained unpalatable. It
was true, as the *Los Angeles News* pointed out, that "the verdict of
manslaughter will not be universally accepted as being exactly the right
one" for the grisly murders committed. Nor were the trials of ten people
a sufficient reckoning when there were many other perpetrators who
escaped punishment.[62] The fact that only seven rioters spent no more
than nineteen months incarcerated was unconscionable. However, the
surviving testimony indicates that the main obstacle in the pursuit of
justice was not simply bigotry or indifference on the part of the Los
Angeles authorities but difficulty of proof. Apparently, the necessary
evidence could not be obtained.

Two years earlier, the vigilance committee that hanged Michel Lachenais had claimed that the lynching was justified by "incompetency or
imbecility in those who have been placed in power" to administer the
law in Los Angeles.[63] The riot trials of 1872 finally proved the vigilantes
wrong. By then, the court system in this booming, rough-edged
Western town, despite its failings in the past, was functioning rea-
sonably well. The vigilantes' power was finally broken, and they would
lynch no more suspects within the city.

More significantly, people with little clout, most notably the Chinese,
had made impressive legal headway in Los Angeles's district court
during 1871–72. As seen earlier, Ah Mouie, the San Bernardino laundryman's wife, won the civil suit she brought in 1871 against a popular

sheriff and jailor, even though the law prohibited her from testifying against the two white men who had confiscated her property. In the murder trial that resulted in the acquittal of Quong Wong and Ah Ying in 1872, Chinese witnesses were sworn for the first time in district court. Although the Wing Chung partners were unable to prevail in their case against the city, they successfully thwarted an attempt to prevent them from testifying and won judicial acknowledgment that the racially diverse City of Los Angeles was not a "white person." Furthermore, Judge Widney ruled that anti-Chinese prejudice was a relevant consideration in selecting jurors. Through all these developments, the local judiciary reminded Angelenos that the Chinese immigrants among them were human beings, not "filthy," "repulsive" "animals" in "dens," as the *Los Angeles News* had portrayed them. More than anything, the trials that came out of the riot and massacre showed people across America that justice could be had in Los Angeles, that explosive California outpost they had just started to notice.

II

It Will Be Forgotten in a Brief Time

Requiem

Eventually, the dead received their due. In August 1872, the traditional Chinese ghost month, the Chinese community of Los Angeles held the first memorial service for the massacre victims, raising around $1,000 to pay for it. Several priests arrived on the steamer from San Francisco. Two reportedly came all the way from China to preside at the ceremonials, which lasted four days. Late into the night, they chanted incantations for the souls of the departed. The Beaudry building, cater-cornered from the Coronel adobe, was transformed into a makeshift temple. On the walls, hand-drawn charts depicted the horrific deaths of the massacre victims. Their killers were portrayed as demons.

On the final day, the Chinese gathered at the temple to begin a long, noisy procession. In wagons and hacks, they made their way through the streets of Los Angeles to the City Cemetery. Men cried out loudly while a band played drums, gongs, and clarinets. The noise was intended to frighten away evil spirits. At the graveyard, some mourners placed small cups of meats, fruits, and tea at the heads of the burial mounds, provisions for the visiting spirits of the murdered men. Others burned incense, candles, and perfumed tapers. A group of Chinese women, said to be professional mourners, wept and threw themselves on the ground, covering their faces. Some of the men stepped outside the cemetery and fired their revolvers into the bright summer sky.

Non-Asian Angelenos who watched the services stood by and laughed. The local press also had a field day. In items with "clever" titles such as "Broken (Hearted) China" and "Slam-Bang-Lamentations," journalists mocked the Chinese rituals. The *Los Angeles Star* complained about "the most hideous music ever heard." The *Los Angeles News* agreed that "the din and confusion contributed by these barbarians have simply been abominable." The *Evening Express*, which had been too squeamish to report the details of how the eighteen victims died at the hands of a howling mob, was the cruelest in deriding their memorial. It described "noises resembling the clanging and banging of all the old tin pans that could be found, with an occasional cat fight thrown in." It even joked about the "unceremonious manner" in which the lynched men had been "transported to that undiscovered country" less than a year earlier. Ridiculing the Chinese ceremony as "a gigantic panorama of *delirium tremens*," it noted that the "feast day of Johnny Soapsuds" was being observed wherever "muchee washee is performed by Celestial suds slingers."[1]

Only a week after the massacre, the *Star* had remarked, "It is likely that no evil of consequence will really befall our city resulting from it, and that . . . it will fall and be forgotten in a brief time." Indeed, the Los Angeles press, barely chastened by the memory, quickly resumed its usual practice of denigrating the Chinese. Four months after the riot, the *Star*, in another outrageous editorial, blamed the "barbarous" foreigners for the "stain upon the name of our fair city," accusing them of "butchering one another as well as those who venture to interpose to preserve the peace." Incredibly, the article did not mention the crimes of the lynchers and looters of October 24, 1871. The *News* had the gracelessness to complain that the Chinese, when visiting the burial sites of the massacre victims, left refuse from firecrackers that "intrudes upon the graves of the whites." In the editors' opinion, "This desecration of the resting place of our dead, for the sake of complying with the heathenish custom of a barbarous race, ought not to be tolerated."[2]

Meanwhile, life as usual resumed in Chinatown. Chinese racketeers continued to abduct and sell women, and American policemen continued to make sure these transactions went smoothly. In February 1872, Sing Hee, a woman of the See Yup Company who escaped from "a life of shame" in "a den of infamy," caused a great uproar when she married Hong Chow member One Za before a justice of the peace in order to obtain legal protection. An abduction was foiled in April 1872 when two men tried to kidnap the woman whom Charley Shew had recently wed. A cook named Ah Sam was murdered by a Chinese storekeeper and his assistant when he tried to steal a woman in 1873.[3]

Modern trade histories often come burdened with overblown subtitles such as "The Race Riot That Changed America," perhaps a testament to our faith that injustices will naturally and spontaneously bring about reform. A more accurate label for this book might be "The Race Riot That Didn't Change a Damned Thing." Although the event is said to have marked the end of mob justice in Los Angeles, that was more likely the result of a gradual decrease in violent crime and improved law administration than collective shame over the lynching of innocent Chinese. In fact, anti-Chinese sentiment increased significantly in Los Angeles during the decade that followed the massacre. This may have been due to the influx of 330 Chinese workers who arrived in the area to dig the San Fernando railroad tunnel in 1875–76. The visiting Austrian archduke Ludwig Louis Salvator noted in 1876 that the Chinese "are not popular and in Los Angeles the anti-Chinese feeling is highly developed." The same year, another writer observed that Los Angeles residents talked about the Chinese "with an unreasoning bitterness." Housewives who hired them to do laundry simultaneously "profess joy at the success which the youngest boys are having of late in hitting Chinamen with stones at unprecedented distances." Missionary pastor Ira M. Condit pointed out, "The feeling against the Chinaman is more bitter and intolerant than that against the Negro."[4]

In 1876, Angelenos organized an Anti-Coolie Club, whose membership included some of the town's most respected citizens. An 1878 amendment to the city charter prohibited the employment of Chinese laborers on public works projects. An increase in the local business license tax in 1879 was aimed directly at Chinese launderers and vegetable peddlers. In 1882, many Angelenos rallied in favor of the Chinese Exclusion Act. This overtly discriminatory federal law, which remained in effect until 1943, marked the first time the US government had banned laborers of a specific nationality from entering the country. (The US Senate finally apologized for it in 2011.)[5] The Chinese community of Los Angeles hung on and weathered the six decades of exclusion. Though its growth was stymied, it persevered.

The After-Stories

After he was acquitted in 1872 for the killing of Robert Thompson, the Nin Yung headman Sam Yuen became far less conspicuous in Los Angeles. In fact, his name virtually disappeared from the local newspapers, leaving his life story incomplete. A legal notice in 1892 mentioned the mercantile firm of Sam Yuen Company on Marchessault Street. However, its namesake was no longer a partner. A well-known theater manager and businessman named Sam Yuen lived in San Francisco in the 1880s and 1890s, although it is doubtful whether he was the same man.[6]

Yut Ho, the young bride at the center of the Chinatown war, vanished from Los Angeles's recorded history after her abduction in March 1871. The local press showed no interest in following her story once the initial excitement was over. The most likely scenario is that her wealthy husband, Hing Sing, paid a fee to redeem her from her Hong Chow captors. Perhaps he then sent her back to China for safety. If so, Yut Ho's time in America was merely a strange interlude in her life, a brief episode of terrifying adventure in a land of barbarians. But this may be wishful speculation. It is also possible that she spent the rest of her days in a California brothel.

Yo Hing's fate, on the other hand, is well documented. On the morning of May 14, 1877, he was walking along Calle de los Negros when a couple of assassins, Wong Chu Shut and Ah Hawk, delivered two blows to his skull with a hatchet. He died four days later. The reason for his murder remains unknown, but considering his knack for making enemies, his violent end came as no surprise. His fame among non-Asians had declined by then. Both the *Los Angeles Star* and the *Evening Express* had to remind their readers that Yo Hing had "figured prominently" in the riot and massacre six years earlier, a fact that "may not be generally known." His funeral drew a large crowd, as he had "made quite an extensive acquaintance" during his years in Los Angeles.[7]

The suspected rioters of October 24, 1871, spent the rest of their lives in obscurity, with one notable exception. P. S. Dorney, who had amused himself and his pals by waving a severed Chinese queue at Robert Mulloy's saloon that night, became a popular stump speaker for white-labor groups. He was also a prolific and inflammatory anti-Chinese journalist. He authored the first memoir of the Los Angeles massacre for *The Overland Monthly* in 1886. It was a schizophrenic article titled "A Prophecy Partly Verified," in which Dorney vacillated between professing horror over the brutality of the slayings and characterizing them as the unavoidable result of introducing Chinese labor into America. Dorney organized a secret white supremacist society known as the Order of Caucasians, which harassed and attacked Chinese farm workers throughout California in 1876–77. He eventually became a staff writer for the *Los Angeles Times*.[8]

The lawyers who had tried to keep order and stop the lynch mob all prospered and became honored citizens in the years to come. Judge Robert M. Widney, after leaving the bench, was a highly successful real estate agent and a founder of the University of Southern California. For all his accomplishments, he seemed to think of his rescue efforts during the Chinese massacre as his life's finest moment. That story got better over time; by the 1920s, he was said to have "stood off the entire mob with his revolver" that night. Attorneys Henry T. Hazard and Cameron Thom, who had made speeches rebuking the mob during the riot, both became mayors of Los Angeles. Some of Hazard's cash-poor clients paid his legal fees in land, and part of that property later became the center of Hollywood. Meanwhile, Ygnacio Sepúlveda, the gentlemanly county judge who championed the rule of law and convened a special grand jury to investigate the massacre, left his increasingly anglicized home-town for Mexico City in 1883, not returning to live in Los Angeles for three decades.[9] And Justice of the Peace William H. Gray, the first local jurist to stand up for the legal rights of Chinese immigrants, was not even mentioned in the numerous biographical records of Los Angeles's distinguished citizens.

Although the town's lawmen took a drubbing for their inability to control the murderous crowd, several of them later enjoyed celebrated careers in Los Angeles. Sheriff James Burns and City Marshal Frank Baker were never formally reprimanded for having ordered the bystanders to shoot any escaping Chinese that night. Years later, Burns was careful not to mention those orders in his brief autobiography.

Instead, he recalled that he had "rushed into the crowd and rescued" a Chinese captive and that order was restored once some citizens triumphantly "placed me on their shoulders and conveyed me to 'Negro Alley.'"[10] Burns and Policemen Emil Harris and George Gard were all eventually appointed chief of police. Gard was also elected sheriff. Even Adolfo Celis, who had been tried but acquitted for Gene Tong's murder, became a deputy sheriff. His boss, Sheriff Henry M. Mitchell, had also been accused of rioting. Amazingly, Refugio Botello, the butcher who had been convicted of helping lynch Dr. Tong but never served any time in prison, was nominated as a candidate for city constable in 1882.[11]

The Chinese massacre of 1871 remained a thorn in the side of Los Angeles's Anglo boosters throughout the remainder of the nineteenth century. As one local recollected, "Society agreed to drop all mention of the incident." An 1876 publication titled *An Historical Sketch of Los Angeles County, California* made no reference to the gruesome event that shocked the nation, though the book's authors—J. J. Warner, Dr. Joseph P. Widney, and Benjamin Hayes—knew quite well what had happened. An outsider named J. Albert Wilson wrote an unexpurgated summary of the race riot for Thompson and West's 1880 *History of Los Angeles County, California*. His publishers felt it necessary to include a defensive caveat: if Angelenos thought the author had "overstated this matter," they noted, "let them turn to the newspaper files of the dates mentioned and judge for themselves." In 1888, the prolific California historian Hubert Howe Bancroft published a florid but mostly accurate account of the lynch mob's monstrous crimes against the Chinese. Dr. Joseph P. Widney, the judge's brother, complained to the local press that Bancroft's version was an unjust reflection on "the moral tone of Los Angeles," because it failed to recount "the efforts of citizens to quell the disturbance." Dr. Widney also assured the public that the event "was simply a race fight" that "had been started by the Chinese themselves." An 1889 history of the city blamed the lynchings on the usual scapegoats— "the lower class of Mexicans and the scum of the foreigners."[12]

The remains of most of the massacre victims were eventually disinterred from the City Cemetery and shipped back to China. In the 1880s, the old graveyard itself fell victim to Los Angeles's real estate boom. Horace Bell complained, "The city allowed promoters to map it, cut it up and sell it off in small building lots." The graves had to be relocated. In 1895, the *huiguan* oversaw the removal of the last Chinese remains.[13] The northern portion of the cemetery site is now occupied by the Ramón C. Cortines School of Visual and Performing Arts. The rest was sacrificed for the freeway in 1949.

Although the Coronel adobe was slated for demolition three months after the massacre, it remained standing for many years in silent defiance of the city's developers. Antonio Coronel never constructed the imposing brick building he had talked about intermittently since 1870. During the early morning hours of October 24, 1886, fifteen years to the day after the Chinese massacre, a fire swept through Chinatown. It started at the plaza and spread down the block, ravaging Coronel's property and destroying about half of the Chinese habitations. The following summer, an arsonist's blaze decimated nearly all of the Chinese-occupied buildings along the east side of the former Calle de los Negros, which had been incorporated into Los Angeles Street in 1877.[14]

Most of what remained of Los Angeles's first Chinatown was obliterated six months later. The city decided to open up Los Angeles Street and extend it to the plaza, which required the demolition of more of the old adobe tenements. As the wrecking crew tore into the roofs and walls on January 10, 1888, the stunned Chinese occupants scurried to remove their belongings, unwilling to believe the threatened destruction was really happening. The city's superintendent of streets, Jacob Kurhts, promised that Chinatown would speedily disappear, adding, "I would like to tear down every vestige of it."[15] Many Chinese residents were forcibly uprooted once again in 1933 to make way for Union Station.

Today, you cannot stand on the site of the old Coronel adobe and contemplate what happened there, because you will get run over. The land was appropriated decades ago for the Hollywood Freeway and a wider Los Angeles Street. If you go to El Pueblo de Los Angeles Historical Monument and look closely at the sidewalk running along the west side of the 400 block of North Los Angeles Street, you will find a handsome plaque that sums up the highlights of the massacre in English and Chinese. It measures eighteen inches in both directions—less than three square feet in a city that now spreads over 469 square miles. No other monument commemorates the race riot of October 24, 1871, arguably the most significant single event in Los Angeles's nineteenth-century statehood history. Ask the Angelenos you meet about the Chinese massacre, and you get blank stares. At least I did.

The Way Forward

Los Angeles forgot about its Black Tuesday long ago, which raises the discomforting question: if Americans of the 1870s learned nothing from the night of horrors, and nothing changed as a result, is there any point in remembering it today?

Certainly, there are lessons to be drawn from this cautionary tale. The main one has to do with the moral crime of remaining silent while propaganda and hate talk go unchallenged. But that is something we should have already learned from other atrocities.

Historians, after interpreting raw information and placing it in context, are expected to make some sense out of the past and explain why people may have made the decisions they did. This writer chooses not to do that with the Chinese massacre. Affixing a tidy, facile economic or political explanation to an outbreak of irrational racial violence would give the erroneous impression that it was understandable or, even worse, inevitable. Also, it would wrongly distance that needless tragedy from us: *no one we know would ever do that, and besides, conditions were different back then. It couldn't happen today.*

Of course it could. Anyone living on the margins of society knows that. In 2008, the *New York Times* reported an alarming increase in unprovoked attacks on homeless people nationwide. In Daytona Beach, a ten-year-old dropped a concrete block on the face of a homeless Army veteran. A camera caught a teenager laughing as he bashed a street person with a baseball bat in Fort Lauderdale. Four teenage thrill-seekers in Los Angeles used their cell phones to record their attacks so they could post them on the Internet. On a Chicago train platform in 2011, a teenager punched a homeless man in the face while his friends laughed and videoed the incident. A young man imprisoned for his role in killing a homeless victim said, "It was just a senseless crime." George Siletti, a former homeless drifter, explained, "People seem to pick on the most vulnerable because they really think that they won't do nothing." Another former street person, David Pirtle, added that "most victims don't feel like there's much of a chance of anyone doing anything about it, even if they do report it."[16]

Other modern hate crimes mirror the attacks on the nineteenth-century Chinese even more closely. Four high school football players in Shenandoah, Pennsylvania, killed an illegal immigrant named Luis Ramirez during a fight in 2008. The same year, seven teenagers in Patchogue, New York, stabbed an Ecuadorean immigrant, Marcelo Lucero, while looking for a random Mexican to thrash. It was a pastime the local youths called "beaner hopping." One of them told the authorities, "I don't go out doing this very often, maybe once a week." When a group of white teenagers beat and kicked Ecuadorean construction worker Carlos Angamarca in 2007, he begged an adult woman passerby to call the police. She laughed and drove off. The mayor of Patchogue warned that illegal immigrants were being portrayed as "animals" who were "expendable." Suffolk County legislator Ricardo Montano remarked, "The constant rhetoric coming from some elected officials has the impact of creating an atmosphere in which a crime like this can occur."[17]

The Los Angeles rioters of 1871 were no more driven by economic insecurity than the killers of Luis Ramirez and Marcelo Lucero were motivated by the recession of 2008. In each case, they did what they did not because they felt threatened or because their families were out of work but because they wanted to. It seemed like fun. They thought they could get away with it because their victims were people who didn't matter. The modern-day crimes occurred in an era of anti-immigrant vitriol spewed by the demagogues of cable television, talk radio, Internet blogs, and chain emails—descendants in spirit of the *Los Angeles News* of 1869, but with a much larger audience.

Meanwhile, some of our elected officials of the twenty-first century have stopped only one step short of harking back to the "degraded heathen" and "idolatrous barbarian" rhetoric of California in the 1860s and 1870s. In 2010, more than 70 percent of Oklahoma's voters approved a constitutional amendment forbidding judges from considering Islamic law in deciding cases—a "manufactured problem" that had "never come up in the state's courts," as one editorial observed. Its main author, State Representative Rex Duncan, warned that Muslims were coming to the United States to take away "liberties and freedom from our children," necessitating a "preemptive strike" in "a war for the survival of America." Shortly afterward, mosques in Oklahoma City and Tulsa were flooded with hate mail. A *Los Angeles Times* columnist rightly charged Oklahoma's lawmakers with appealing "to voters' worst instincts by fanning deep-seated antipathy toward a tiny religious minority." Nonetheless, three other states followed Oklahoma's lead and enacted anti-sharia statutes. Former Speaker of the House Newt Gingrich called for a comparable federal law to counter "stealth jihadis" whom he said were infiltrating America's heartland, seeking "to replace Western civilization with a radical imposition of sharia." Former Alaska governor and vice-presidential candidate Sarah Palin chimed in that if Islamic law is "allowed to govern in our country, it will be the downfall of America." Anti-Muslim sentiment surfaced in Congress in 2011, when US Representative Peter King proclaimed: "There is a real threat to the country from the Muslim community."[18]

That's where things stand today. Recalling the inhuman acts that our fellow human beings inflicted on those eighteen murdered Chinese men in Los Angeles will not prevent the recurrence of racial or ethnic hatred, as these more recent incidents discouragingly prove. Still, forgetting what happened in Chinatown that night would further diminish all of us. The very act of remembrance is one way of restoring our blemished humanity. And if remembering the eighteen victims of the Los Angeles massacre makes us more mindful of the vulnerable, marginalized people around us, as well as those who gang up on them—not only in the streets but also in the news media and the halls of government—so much the better.

Only bits and pieces of their stories remain, but that is enough. Gene Tong and his wife doted on their poodle. Tong Won was a musician, popular at socials. Ah Won sported a flashy diamond ring he had purchased with his savings. Wa Sin Quai had lived on Calle de los Negros for five years. He must have known the inside story about everything that happened there. Ah Long and Ah Cut provided small pleasures—cigars and liquor—to those toiling in a harsh environment. Wing Chee had cooked a sumptuous feast that afternoon, with an abundance of Chinese delicacies, for his company's headmen. He would not live to receive their compliments. Teenager Ah Loo had just arrived from China, eager to scale the heights of Gold Mountain. So many American dreams died on the gallows that night.

The day after the riot of 1871, the *Alta California* remarked that the people of Los Angeles, "sickened with last night's horrors, are determined that no stigma of like character shall ever again rest upon us." It would, of course, in 1943, 1965, and 1992. Did the determination flag somewhere along the way? Or was it just too much to hope for? Rodney King, the Robert Thompson of the 1992 race riot, is remembered for having pleaded with a stunned public while the city burned: "Can't we all just get along?" Actually, he was widely misquoted. What King really asked was, "*Can* we all get along?"[19] That tougher question remains to be answered.

ACKNOWLEDGMENTS

I AM GRATEFUL FOR THE assistance of many knowledgeable librarians and archivists at the Braun Research Library; California Historical Society; California State University, Northridge; Huntington Library; Los Angeles City Archives; Los Angeles County Registrar's Office; Los Angeles Public Library; San Bernardino Public Library; San Francisco Public Library; Seaver Center for Western History Research; Society of California Pioneers; and University of California, Los Angeles and Berkeley. The M. Beven Eckert Memorial Library provided interlibrary loan services.

For encouragement, advice, and help in locating specific sources, I thank Peter Blodgett, John Cahoon, Suellen Cheng, William Deverell, Dixie Dillon, John Mack Faragher, Bill Frank, Tom Jacobson, Eugene W. Moy, Merry Ovnick, Hynda Rudd, Betty Uyeda, Angi Ma Wong, J. W. Wong, and the members of the Chinese Historical Society of Southern California. Rhonda Stoltz gave me the initial idea from which this book grew.

My friend Mary Cook carefully reviewed the manuscript and made many excellent observations that were pivotal in my revisions. Steve Adams, Jenny Cho, Eugene W. Moy, and Paul R. Spitzzeri also read portions of my early drafts and offered valuable suggestions.

I am deeply indebted to those scholars of Chinese Los Angeles and the massacre of 1871 whose pioneering research pointed me in the right direction, especially Paul M. De Falla, William R. Locklear, and Paul R. Spitzzeri.

My agent, Jim Hornfischer, shared his enthusiasm for this project from the outset and worked closely with me to hone it. My editor at Oxford University Press, Tim Bent, guided me through the rewrites with grace, tact, and good humor, and I benefited immensely from his insights. It was also a pleasure to work with his talented and efficient editorial assistant, Keely Latcham. Production editor Leslie Johnson kept the process moving smoothly. Marketing manager Josh Landon and publicist Lana Goldsmith made many helpful suggestions. My gratitude to all of them.

A NOTE ON THE SOURCES

Him Mark Lai, for decades the unofficial dean of Chinese American studies, wrote to a colleague in 1975, "I am concerned there are no 'experts' in the field of Chinese American history, but only people with varying degrees of ignorance, with some perhaps a little less ignorant than others."[1] Although scholarly works in this area have proliferated since then, Lai's comment still resonates. This "ignorance" is not due to a lack of diligence on the part of researchers. Rather, the main obstacle is that very few letters, diaries, memoirs, or other personal documents created by Chinese people living in the American West during the mid-nineteenth century have surfaced. The newspapers they published in the United States have mostly vanished, and the few remaining issues yield only a limited amount of commercial information.

The challenges of writing about the early Chinese of Los Angeles are exacerbated by the fact that surprisingly few non-Asian Angelenos who lived in the city between 1850 and 1880 left memoirs or substantial collections of relevant personal papers detailing that period. Harris Newmark's *Sixty Years in Southern California* is indispensable. Horace Bell's memoirs, though less reliable, are more colorful. The recollections of Jackson A. Graves, Joseph Mesmer, and L. J. Rose, Jr. are also useful. Still, to flesh out this story, it was necessary to incorporate some examples from the Chinese experience in other cities, especially San

Francisco. The nineteenth-century travelogues and magazine articles listed in the Bibliography contain some vivid anecdotes about Chinese immigrants in California.

Given the dearth of more personal material, this book relies extensively on two primary sources: the Los Angeles area court records housed at the Huntington Library and the California newspapers of the era. The dialogue in the narrative scenes was drawn from eyewitness testimony in court cases. The newspaper accounts had to be evaluated critically, since local reporters knew little about Chinese society and often reinforced familiar stereotypes and prejudices. Sometimes journalists concocted entirely fanciful versions of events in Chinatown as entertainment pieces rather than reporting objectively. Even the formal statements that the Chinese merchants of Los Angeles occasionally issued to the press appear to have been crafted by their American lawyers and were usually more self-serving than enlightening.

Historians find it especially challenging to trace the careers of individual Chinese over time, not only because they relocated frequently but also because English transcriptions of their names varied widely from one source to another. Only a few of the Chinese names listed in the early Los Angeles censuses match those that appeared in contemporaneous newspaper stories, judicial documents, and county records. The difficulty of identifying specific Chinese is intensified by the frequent use of the informal prefix "Ah" as a substitute for proper names.

Given these limitations, those of us who choose to write about this aspect of America's history must beg readers' forgiveness for not being able to answer all their questions. One always hopes that the journeys into this part of our past will be worthwhile nonetheless. The main objective is for both reader and writer to end up "less ignorant," in the words of Him Mark Lai. The story of how the early Chinese immigrants adapted to life in the American West, though fragmentary, is too rich to be left unexplored.

ENDNOTES

Chapter 1

1. *Semi-Weekly Southern News* [Los Angeles], June 7, 1861.
2. Strictly speaking, these Gold Rush veterans were not the first people from China to turn up in Los Angeles. Chinese shipbuilders had reportedly visited the pueblo around the time it was founded in 1781. Hubert Howe Bancroft, *The Works of Hubert Howe Bancroft*, vol. 24, *History of California* (San Francisco: History Co., 1890), 335.
3. Harris Newmark, *Sixty Years in Southern California, 1853–1913*, 4th ed. (1916; Los Angeles: Dawson's Book Shop, 1984), 123, 297.
4. *Los Angeles Star*, January 24, 1857.
5. *Los Angeles Star*, March 17, 1860, April 27, 1861, and June 8, 1861. The 1870 federal census of Los Angeles Township listed 178 Chinese nationals and 1 Chinese American, a three-year-old boy born in California. The federal census figures should be viewed as approximations. The census-takers had to rely on information provided by those Chinese who spoke some English, and the censuses may have undercounted the number of migratory Chinese laborers in Los Angeles. In one bizarre episode, a deranged sheepherder conducted his own informal census of Chinatown in 1871 and reported 768 Chinese—"rather an over estimate," the *Los Angeles News* concluded. *Los Angeles News*, February 7, 1871.
6. *Los Angeles News*, February 21, 1871; *Owyhee Daily Avalanche*, July 29, 1875; Joseph Mesmer, "Massacre of Chinese," Joseph Mesmer Papers, UCLA.

7. *Semi-Weekly Southern News* [Los Angeles], June 7, 1861; "The Chinese at Los Angeles, California," *Friends' Review, A Religious, Literary and Miscellaneous Journal* 30 (April 18, 1877): 636; Charles Morley, trans., "The Chinese in California, As Reported by Henryk Sienkiewicz," *California Historical Society Quarterly* 34 (December 1955): 309; Ng Poon Chew, "The Chinaman in America," *Independent* 54 (April 1902): 802.

8. Gunther Barth, *Bitter Strength: A History of the Chinese in the United States, 1850–1870* (Cambridge: Harvard University Press, 1964), 28–29; Stanford M. Lyman, *Chinese Americans* (New York: Random House, 1974), 9, 19–20; A. W. Loomis, "Chinese 'Funeral Baked Meats,'" *Overland Monthly* 3 (July 1869): 28.

9. Chew, "The Chinaman in America," 802; Hamilton Holt, *The Life Stories of Undistinguished Americans as Told by Themselves* (1906; reprint, New York: Routledge, 1990), 185; Ludwig Louis Salvator, *Los Angeles in the Sunny Seventies: A Flower from the Golden Land*, trans. Marguerite Eyer Wilbur (Los Angeles: Bruce McCallister and Jake Zeitlin, 1929), 42.

10. Otis Gibson, *The Chinese in America* (Cincinnati: Hitchcock & Walden, 1877), 397; US House of Representatives, Report No. 4048, 51st Cong., 2d Sess., 536, 539.

11. Salvator, *Los Angeles in the Sunny Seventies*, 124; Ben C. Truman, *Semi-Tropical California* (San Francisco: A. L. Bancroft, 1874), 27–28.

12. Morrow Mayo, *Los Angeles* (New York: Knopf, 1933), 40–41; Henry Winfred Splitter, "Los Angeles as Described by Contemporaries, 1850–90," *Historical Society of Southern California Quarterly* 37 (June 1955): 132; *Los Angeles News*, October 17, 1869.

13. *Los Angeles News*, April 30, 1869; Newmark, *Sixty Years in Southern California*, 388; Salvator, *Los Angeles in the Sunny Seventies*, 125; Albert F. Webster, "Los Angeles," *Appleton's Journal: A Monthly Miscellany of Popular Literature* 1 (September 1876): 211; Charles Loring Brace, *The New West: Or, California in 1867–1868* (New York: G. P. Putnam & Son, 1869), 277.

14. Newmark, *Sixty Years in Southern California*, 28, 34; Splitter, "Los Angeles as Described by Contemporaries," 132; Horace Bell, *Reminiscences of a Ranger; or, Early Times in Southern California* (Los Angeles: Yarnell, Caystile & Mathes, 1881), 22.

15. Bell, *Reminiscences of a Ranger*, 26.

16. Leonard Pitt, "The Midwesternization of a Cowtown," *California History* 60 (Spring 1981): 34, 42.

17. J. J. Warner, Benjamin Hayes, and Joseph P. Widney, *An Historical Sketch of Los Angeles County, California* (1876; reprint, Los Angeles: O. W. Smith, 1936), 5; Lawrence E. Guillow, "Pandemonium in the Plaza: The First Los Angeles Riot, July 22, 1856," *Southern California Quarterly* 77 (Fall 1995): 183–86, 193–94.

18. *Los Angeles News*, September 15, 1869.

19. *Los Angeles Star*, July 16, 1870, and January 19, 1871.

20. The street was also known as "Nigger Alley," although that epithet was used much less frequently, at least in the newspapers. In this author's sampling of articles from the English-language press between 1869 and 1872, "Negro Alley" appeared in seventy items, while "Nigger Alley" was found in eight. The original Spanish name, "Calle de los Negros," showed up only once.

21. Marco R. Newmark, "Calle de los Negros and the Chinese Massacre of 1871," *Historical Society of Southern California Quarterly* 26 (June–September 1944): 98; Horace Bell, *On the Old West Coast*, ed. Lanier Bartlett (New York: Grosset & Dunlap, 1930), 3, 116; Bell, *Reminiscences of a Ranger*, 88.

22. *Los Angeles News*, July 1, 1870; *People v. Wong Chu Shut*, September 27, 1877, 17th Judicial District Court, Richard Courtney Collection, Huntington Library (testimony of A. Carrillo); "Annual Report of Health Officer of Los Angeles City," November 13, 1879, Los Angeles City Archives.

23. *Los Angeles Semi-Weekly News*, February 16, 1866; John Tambolin (groom) and Ah Qu (bride), November 19, 1862, Marriage Records, Los Angeles County Registrar's Office.

24. *Los Angeles Semi-Weekly News*, February 16, 1866.

25. *Los Angeles Star*, June 15, 1861.

26. *People v. John Tambolen* [*sic*] *and Rsone*, Minutes, Justice of the Peace (Shore et al.), February 15, 1868, Los Angeles Area Court Records, Huntington Library (hereafter "LAACR"); *Los Angeles Weekly Republican*, February 22, 1868.

27. *Los Angeles Star*, June 15, 1861, and July 13, 1861.

28. *Tulare Times* [Visalia], August 1, 1868; J. [Joseph] Lamson Diary, unpublished manuscript, California Historical Society, 182; Huie Kin, *Reminiscences* (Peiping, China: San Yu Press, 1932), 25; *Daily California Chronicle* [San Francisco], February 8, 1855. For a biography of Joseph Lamson, see Barbara Lekisch, *Embracing Scenes about Lakes Tahoe and Donner: Painters, Illustrators, and Sketch Artists, 1855–1915* (Lafayette, CA: Great West Books, 2003), 110–12.

29. Newmark, *Sixty Years in Southern California*, 298.

30. Chew, "The Chinaman in America," 802; Holt, *The Life Stories of Undistinguished Americans*, 184.

31. *Los Angeles Star*, March 22, 1872.

32. *People v. Hop Chung*, unnumbered case, July 18, 1877, Los Angeles County Court, Criminal Cases, LAACR; *Joseph Leventhal v. John Doe (a Chinaman)*, Minutes, Justice of the Peace (Gray), March 21, 1874, LAACR.

33. *People v. Henry Brown*, Minutes, Justice of the Peace (Still/Gray), November 21, 1870, LAACR.

34. W. A. Pickering, "Chinese Secret Societies and Their Origin," *Journal of the Straits Branch of the Royal Asiatic Society*, no. 1 (July 1878): 66.

35. *Ah Tim v. Oliver Stearns*, Minutes, Justice of the Peace (Shore et al.), June 29, 1864, LAACR (the court records do not indicate which party prevailed in this case); *Ah Wa v. Larimore & Chester*, Minutes, Justice of the Peace (Still/Gray), November 25, 1869, LAACR; *Ah Mow v. John McDonald*, Minutes, Justice of the Peace (Gray), December 18, 1872, LAACR; *Ah Mow v. John McDonald*, Case No. 75, January 14, 1873, Los Angeles County Justices Court, LAACR.

36. Act of April 20, 1863, ch. 260, §§ 48, 51, [1863] California Statutes 340–41.

37. Bell, *On the Old West Coast*, 176; *Los Angeles News*, September 14, 1871. Some biographical information about William H. Gray and his brother, an early San Francisco real estate magnate named Franklin C. Gray, is found in two published court opinions: *Gray v. Palmer*, 9 California Reports 616 (1858); and *Gray v. Brignardello*, 68 United States Reports 627 (1863).

38. The California statutes did not expressly define the racial category "white." The federal censuses at that time routinely classified both Anglos and Latinos as "white." With respect to mixed-race people, California law prohibited "persons having one half or more of Indian blood" from testifying against a "white person." Act of March 16, 1863, ch. 68, § 1, [1863] California Statutes 60; Act of March 18, 1863, ch. 70, § 1, [1863] California Statutes 69.

39. *Wa Chung v. Samuel Kearney*, Minutes, Justice of the Peace (Still/Gray), July 21, 1869, LAACR; Minutes, Los Angeles County Court, November 10, 1869, LAACR.

40. *People v. Lee Ock*, unnumbered case, January 23, 1877, Los Angeles County Court, Criminal Cases, LAACR.

41. *People v. Ma Chock [China Charley]*, unnumbered case, March 19, 1877, Los Angeles County Court, Criminal Cases, LAACR.

42. *People v. Ah Quang*, Case No. 1031 [originally No. 94], June 14, 1871, Los Angeles County Justices Court, LAACR; *People v. Ah Quang*, Minutes, Los Angeles County Court, July 29, 1871, LAACR.

Chapter 2

1. Robert W. Blew, "Vigilantism in Los Angeles, 1835–1874," *Southern California Quarterly* 54 (Spring 1972): 12; Harris Newmark, *Sixty Years in Southern California, 1853–1913*, 4th ed. (1916; Los Angeles: Dawson's Book Shop, 1984), 115.

2. Charles Dwight Willard, *The Herald's History of Los Angeles City* (Los Angeles: Kingsley-Barnes & Neuner, 1901), 279; Newmark, *Sixty Years in Southern California*, 31; Charles Loring Brace, *The New West: Or, California in 1867–1868* (New York: G. P. Putnam & Son, 1869), 279; Horace Bell, *Reminiscences of a Ranger; or, Early Times in Southern California* (Los Angeles: Yarnell, Caystile & Mathes, 1881), 28–29.

3. Kevin Starr, *California: A History* (New York: Modern Library, 2005), 84–85; Eric Monkkonen, "Western Homicide: The Case of Los Angeles, 1830–1870," *Pacific Historical Review* 74 (November 2005): 609, 615–16; Willard, *The Herald's History of Los Angeles City*, 281–82; Blew, "Vigilantism in Los Angeles," 12; Leonard Pitt, "The Midwesternization of a Cowtown," *California History* 60 (Spring 1981): 31.

4. Monkkonen, "Western Homicide," 611; Robert Easton, "Guns of the American West," in *The Book of the American West*, ed. Jay Monaghan (New York: Julian Messner, 1963), 404; Willard, *The Herald's History of Los Angeles City*, 286; *People v. Ah San*, Minutes, Justice of the Peace (Still/ Gray), August 27, 1869, Los Angeles Area Court Records, Huntington Library (hereafter "LAACR"); *Los Angeles News*, May 20, 1870; Newmark, *Sixty Years in Southern California*, 221.

5. Marco R. Newmark, "Calle de los Negros and the Chinese Massacre of 1871," *Historical Society of Southern California Quarterly* 26 (June–September 1944): 98; Newmark, *Sixty Years in Southern California*, 30–31; Bell, *Reminiscences of a Ranger*, 28; Morrow Mayo, *Los Angeles* (New York: Knopf, 1933): 38; *New York Times*, November 10, 1871; *Los Angeles News*, December 17, 1869, and August 24, 1870.

6. Bell, *Reminiscences of a Ranger*, 28.

7. *Los Angeles Times*, July 2, 1918 (Bell's obituary); Ronald C. Woolsey, "Pioneer Views and Frontier Themes: Benjamin Hayes, Horace Bell, and the Southern California Experience," *Southern California Quarterly* 72 (Fall 1990): 257–58; Horace Bell, *On the Old West Coast*, ed. Lanier Bartlett (New York: Grosset & Dunlap, 1930), xiii; letter, Horace Bell to Lewis C. Granger, March 29, 1887, Horace Bell Papers, Huntington Library.

8. *People v. Horace Bell*, Case No. 793, May 9, 1867, 1st Judicial District Court, Criminal Cases, LAACR; *People v. Horace Bell*, Minutes, Justice of the Peace (Still/Gray), May 13, 1870, LAACR; *Jasper Babcock v. Horace Bell*, Minutes, Justice of the Peace (Gray), January 23, 1872, LAACR; *Los Angeles News*, April 20, 1870, May 14, 1870, and May 15, 1870; *An Illustrated History of Los Angeles County, California* (Chicago: Lewis Publishing, 1889), 249.

9. *Los Angeles News*, May 23, 1871, and May 27, 1871 (Ferguson); *People v. Theodore Wollweber*, Minutes, Justice of the Peace (Still/Gray), December 6, 1869, LAACR; *People v. J. Lazarovich* [*sic*], Minutes, Justice of the Peace (Still/Gray), December 8, 1870, LAACR; *People v. J. J. Bell*, Case No. 968, August 5, 1870, Los Angeles County Court, Criminal Cases, LAACR; *Los Angeles Star*, March 26, 1870 (Beane); Newmark, *Sixty Years in Southern California*, 347–48 (Carlisle and King).

10. *Evening Express* [Los Angeles], August 11, 1877 (Widney); John W. Robinson, "Colonel Edward J. C. Kewen: Los Angeles' Fire-Eating Orator of the Civil War Era," *Historical Society of Southern California Quarterly*

61 (Summer 1979): 170; Newmark, *Sixty Years in Southern California*, 351 (Kewen), 384 (Howard and Nichols).

11. Charles Morley, trans., "The Chinese in California, As Reported by Henryk Sienkiewicz," *California Historical Society Quarterly* 34 (December 1955): 307.

12. *People v. Tue Wy and Pui Wy*, Case No. 577, March 6, 1862, Los Angeles County Justices Court, LAACR; *People v. Ah Lim [John Doe, Chinaman]*, Case No. 81, November 12, 1870, Los Angeles County Justices Court, LAACR; *Los Angeles Star*, April 19, 1862, November 10, 1870, and February 16, 1871.

13. *Los Angeles News*, June 3, 1871, and June 4, 1871; *Los Angeles Star*, July 18, 1871, and August 24, 1871.

14. *Los Angeles Star*, May 13, 1871; *Los Angeles News*, May 14, 1871.

15. *Los Angeles News*, August 28, 1869, and March 3, 1870; *People v. Ah Wo, Ah Sy, Ah Qua and Qua Su*, Minutes, Justice of the Peace (Still/Gray), March 2, 1870, LAACR; *Evening Express* [Los Angeles], April 4, 1871; *Los Angeles Star*, October 9, 1871.

16. *Los Angeles Star*, November 20, 1870, and December 22, 1870; *Alta California* [San Francisco], November 20, 1870; *Los Angeles News*, December 23, 1870, and December 25, 1870.

17. Blew, "Vigilantism in Los Angeles, 1835–1874," 14; Willard, *The Herald's History of Los Angeles City*, 280; Pitt, "The Midwesternization of a Cowtown," 31; Paul R. Spitzzeri, "Judge Lynch in Session: Popular Justice in Los Angeles, 1850–1875," *Southern California Quarterly* 87 (Summer 2005): 85–86, 114; Newmark, *Sixty Years in Southern California*, 140, 209, 324–25.

18. Mildred Wellborn, "The Events Leading to the Chinese Exclusion Acts," *Publications of the Historical Society of Southern California* 9 (1912–1913): 49.

19. Newmark, *Sixty Years in Southern California*, 324.

20. J. A. Graves, *My Seventy Years in California, 1857–1927* (Los Angeles: Times-Mirror Press, 1927), 410.

21. *People v. Michael Lachenais*, Case No. 741, February 26, 1866, 1st Judicial District Court, Criminal Cases, LAACR; *People v. Michael Lachenais*, Case No. 775, November 14, 1866, 1st Judicial District Court, Criminal Cases, LAACR; *Los Angeles Star*, December 15, 1870, December 16, 1870, and December 18, 1870; *Los Angeles News*, December 15, 1870, December 16, 1870, and December 18, 1870; *Alta California* [San Francisco], December 16, 1870, and December 18, 1870; *Evening Express* [Los Angeles], August 13, 1877; Joseph Mesmer, "Cold-Blooded Slaying," Joseph Mesmer Papers, UCLA; Newmark, *Sixty Years in Southern California*, 303–4, 419–20; Bell, *On the Old West Coast*, 177–80.

22. *Los Angeles Star*, December 23, 1870, and December 24, 1870; *Los Angeles News*, December 23, 1870, and December 24, 1870.

Chapter 3

1. *People v. Ah Wo, Ah Sy, Ah Qua and Qua Su*, Minutes, Justice of the Peace (Still/Gray), March 2, 1870, Los Angeles Area Court Records, Huntington Library (hereafter "LAACR"); *Los Angeles News*, March 3, 1870.

2. *People v. Long Jim, a Chinaman*, Case No. 942, April 16, 1870, Los Angeles County Justices Court, LAACR; *People v. Ti Peo, Deck Chowa and Ah Gou*, Minutes, Justice of the Peace (Still/Gray), April 21, 1870, LAACR; *Los Angeles Star*, April 23, 1870; *Los Angeles News*, April 23, 1870.

3. Fong Kum Ngon, "The Chinese Six Companies," *Overland Monthly*, 2nd ser., 23 (May 1894): 526.

4. *Semi-Weekly Southern News* [Los Angeles], December 11, 1861; Mary Roberts Coolidge, *Chinese Immigration* (New York: Henry Holt, 1909), 402; US House of Representatives, Report No. 4048, 51st Cong., 2d Sess., 227.

5. Ngon, "The Chinese Six Companies," 523.

6. Letter, Him Mark Lai to Eve Armentrout, November 17, 1975, Him Mark Lai Papers, Ethnic Studies Library, UC Berkeley; Stewart Culin, "Customs of the Chinese in America," *Journal of American Folk-Lore* 3 (July–September 1890): 192.

7. *People v. Wong Chu Shut*, September 27, 1877, 17th Judicial District Court, Richard Courtney Collection, Huntington Library.

8. *Los Angeles News*, November 23, 1870, and July 19, 1871.

9. *People v. Sing Lee*, Minutes, Justice of the Peace (Shore et al.), September 5, 1864, LAACR; *People v. Sing Lee*, Minutes, Justice of the Peace (Shore et al.), September 8, 1866, LAACR; *People v. Ah Shang*, Minutes, Justice of the Peace (Still/Gray), November 9, 1867, LAACR.

10. *People v. James Ganahan*, Minutes, Justice of the Peace (Gray), November 7, 1870, LAACR.

11. *Los Angeles Star*, November 23, 1870, November 25, 1870, and November 30, 1870; *Los Angeles News*, November 23, 1870; *People v. Lee Fat, John Doe and Richard Roe* (names unknown), Minutes, Justice of the Peace (Gray), November 25, 1870, LAACR.

12. *Los Angeles Star*, July 19, 1871; *Los Angeles News*, July 19, 1871.

13. *Los Angeles News*, July 19, 1871.

14. Stewart Culin, "The I Hing or 'Patriotic Rising,' a Secret Society Among the Chinese in America," *Proceedings of the Numismatic and Antiquarian Society of Philadelphia* 3 (November 1887): 57.

15. *California Chronicle* [San Francisco], January 30, 1854; *San Francisco Herald*, February 6, 1855.

16. *San Francisco Herald*, February 6, 1855; *San Francisco Chronicle*, August 5, 1873.

17. *San Francisco Herald*, February 5, 1855, February 6, 1855, February 7, 1855, February 8, 1855, and February 10, 1855; *California Chronicle* [San Francisco], February 7, 1855; *San Francisco Daily Town Talk*, February 9, 1855, and February 12, 1855.

18. Culin, "The I Hing or 'Patriotic Rising,'" 53.

19. *San Francisco Chronicle*, July 31, 1873; *Evening Bulletin* [San Francisco], July 30, 1873.

20. Coolidge, *Chinese Immigration*, 408 n.12; *Alta California* [San Francisco], May 27, 1876; US House of Representatives, Report No. 4048, 51st Cong., 2d Sess., 230.

21. Hart H. North, "Chinese Highbinder Societies in California," *California Historical Society Quarterly* 27 (March 1948): 25; Charles Nordhoff, "Northern California, Oregon, and the Sandwich Islands," in *Nordhoff's West Coast: California, Oregon and Hawaii* (1875; reprint, London: KPI, 1987), 148.

22. North, "Chinese Highbinder Societies in California," 22; *Evening Bulletin* [San Francisco], February 25, 1869.

23. *Los Angeles Star*, October 30, 1871.

24. Culin, "The I Hing or 'Patriotic Rising,'" 52; *San Francisco Chronicle*, August 5, 1873; Coolidge, *Chinese Immigration*, 407; *Alta California* [San Francisco], January 5, 1854; *Evening Bulletin* [San Francisco], August 22, 1873.

25. Culin, "The I Hing or 'Patriotic Rising,'" 57; North, "Chinese Highbinder Societies in California," 22; *San Francisco Herald*, February 6, 1855.

26. *Evening Bulletin* [San Francisco], July 30, 1873, August 4, 1873, August 9, 1873, and August 22, 1873; *San Francisco Chronicle*, July 31, 1873; *New York Times*, July 31, 1873.

27. *San Francisco Chronicle*, August 12, 1873.

28. *Wing Chung Co. v. Los Angeles City*, Case No. 1941, June 22, 1872, 17th Judicial District Court, Civil Cases, LAACR.

29. *Wing Chung Co. v. Los Angeles City*, Case No. 1941, June 22, 1872, 17th Judicial District Court, Civil Cases, LAACR (testimony of Jesús Bilderrain).

30. Coolidge, *Chinese Immigration*, 408; US House of Representatives, Report No. 4048, 51st Cong., 2d Sess., 227; Hamilton Holt, *The Life Stories of Undistinguished Americans as Told by Themselves* (1906; reprint, New York: Routledge, 1990), 182.

31. US House of Representatives, Report No. 4048, 51st Cong., 2d Sess., 309–10, 340–41, 524.

32. *San Francisco Chronicle*, August 5, 1873; *Evening Bulletin* [San Francisco], April 27, 1864, and May 18, 1868; Judy Yung, Gordon H. Chang, and Him Mark Lai, eds., *Chinese American Voices: From the Gold Rush to the Present* (Berkeley: University of California Press, 2006), 21, 24.

33. *San Francisco Chronicle*, April 21, 1876; *Evening Bulletin* [San Francisco], February 25, 1869; US Senate, Report No. 689, 44th Cong., 2d Sess., 94.

34. *Wing Chung Co. v. Los Angeles City*, Case No. 1941, June 22, 1872, 17th Judicial District Court, Civil Cases, LAACR.

35. *People v. Sing Lee, Sam Yung, Sou Go and Yo Hing*, Minutes, Justice of the Peace (Shore et al.), September 8, 1866, LAACR; *Los Angeles News*, July 19, 1871; *Los Angeles Star*, March 10, 1871.

36. W. A. Pickering, "Chinese Secret Societies and Their Origin," *Journal of the Straits Branch of the Royal Asiatic Society*, no. 1 (July 1878): 66.

37. *People v. Ah Song*, Minutes, Justice of the Peace (Still/Gray), March 26, 1869, LAACR; *People v. Choo Chee and Gi On*, Minutes, Justice of the Peace (Gray), March 4, 1871, LAACR; *People v. Fong Ching*, Minutes, Justice of the Peace (Gray), June [18 or 19], 1872, LAACR; *People v. Ah Ten, Ah King and Ah Ching*, Minutes, Justice of the Peace (Gray), August 5, 1872, LAACR; *Los Angeles Star*, June 15, 1861, November 30, 1870, and March 10, 1871; *Los Angeles News*, November 29, 1870, and March 12, 1871.

38. *Los Angeles Star*, October 24, 1871; *People v. Lom Lin*, unnumbered case, August 9, 1877, Los Angeles County Court, Criminal Cases, LAACR.

39. *Los Angeles News*, March 5, 1871; Eng Ying Gong and Bruce Grant, *Tong War!* (New York: Nicholas L. Brown, 1930), 26; *Evening Express* [Los Angeles], April 1, 1873; R. David Arkush and Leo O. Lee, trans. and eds., *Land Without Ghosts: Chinese Impressions of America From the Mid-Nineteenth Century to the Present* (Berkeley: University of California Press, 1989), 48; Otis Gibson, *The Chinese in America* (Cincinnati: Hitchcock & Walden, 1877), 363.

40. Prentice Mulford, "Glimpses of John Chinaman," *Lippincott's Magazine of Popular Literature and Science* 11 (February 1873): 222; *San Francisco Chronicle*, July 31, 1873; *Los Angeles Star*, April 9, 1864.

41. Yung, Chang, and Lai, *Chinese American Voices*, 21; *San Francisco Chronicle*, April 21, 1876; Gibson, *The Chinese in America*, 137.

42. Common Council Records, October 26, 1871, January 18, 1872, November 14, 1872, and May 21, 1874, Los Angeles City Archives; L. J. Rose, Jr., *L. J. Rose of Sunny Slope, 1827–1899: California Pioneer, Fruit Grower, Wine Maker, Horse Breeder* (San Marino, CA: Huntington Library, 1959), 88. In addition to these complaints, a neighbor of Officer Jesús Bilderrain accused him of stealing chickens. However, Justice of the Peace William H. Gray dismissed the case, noting that the prosecution "was without sufficient foundation and was wholly malicious." *People v. J. A. Bilderain* [*sic*], Minutes, Justice of the Peace (Gray), January 4, 1872, LAACR; *Los Angeles News*, January 5, 1872, and January 24, 1872.

43. Minutes, Justice of the Peace (Trafford), June 11, 1873, LAACR; *Los Angeles Star*, July 30, 1873; *Evening Express* [Los Angeles], July 30, 1873.

44. *Los Angeles Star*, November 2, 1870; *Los Angeles Tri-Weekly News*, May 30, 1865, and June 13, 1865; Common Council Records, May 7, 1866, Los Angeles City Archives.

45. *People v. William C. Warren*, Case No. 787, February 28, 1867, Los Angeles County Justices Court, LAACR.

46. *Los Angeles Semi-Weekly News*, October 22, 1862; *Daily Republican* [Los Angeles], July 19, 1877.

47. *Los Angeles Star*, April 25, 1871.

48. *Los Angeles News*, March 9, 1871; *Los Angeles Star*, March 10, 1871.

49. *Los Angeles Star*, January 31, 1872; *Los Angeles News*, March 30, 1872.

Chapter 4

1. *Los Angeles Star*, October 22, 1859, and November 26, 1859.
2. US House of Representatives, Report No. 4048, 51st Cong., 2d Sess., 83, 213.
3. R. David Arkush and Leo O. Lee, trans. and eds., *Land Without Ghosts: Chinese Impressions of America From the Mid-Nineteenth Century to the Present* (Berkeley: University of California Press, 1989), 44.
4. *California Chronicle* [San Francisco], February 8, 1855; Judy Yung, Gordon H. Chang, and Him Mark Lai, eds., *Chinese American Voices: From the Gold Rush to the Present* (Berkeley: University of California Press, 2006), 20–21.
5. Otis Gibson, *The Chinese in America* (Cincinnati: Hitchcock & Walden, 1877), 31, 134; Sui Seen Far [Edith Maude Eaton], "The Chinese Woman in America," *Land of Sunshine* 6 (January 1897): 60, 62.
6. A. W. Loomis, "Chinese Women in California," *Overland Monthly* 2 (April 1869): 348.
7. Loomis, "Chinese Women in California," 349; *Los Angeles Star*, November 16, 1871.
8. *Los Angeles News,* January 8, 1871, August 4, 1871, and October 10, 1871; *Los Angeles Star*, August 3, 1871.
9. *Wilmington Journal*, July 14, 1866.
10. *Los Angeles News*, February 23, 1872; *Evening Bulletin* [San Francisco], July 20, 1869; *San Francisco Chronicle*, April 18, 1876.
11. *Wing Chung Co. v. Los Angeles City*, Case No. 1941, June 22, 1872, 17th Judicial District Court, Civil Cases, Los Angeles Area Court Records, Huntington Library (hereafter "LAACR"); *Los Angeles Star*, March 10, 1871, and October 9, 1871; *Los Angeles News*, February 18, 1872, February 27, 1872, and April 7, 1872; *Harper's New Monthly Magazine* 50 (January 1875): 302.
12. *Evening Express* [Los Angeles], February 8, 1873; *People v. Ah Son, Wah Hing and Ah Shoah*, Case No. 136, February 8, 1873, Los Angeles County Justices Court, LAACR.
13. *Los Angeles Star*, April 27, 1861, and June 8, 1861.
14. Case Nos. 610, 611, 614, 615, 616, and 646, November 8, 1862, Court of Sessions, Los Angeles Criminal Cases, LAACR; *Los Angeles Star*, November 22, 1862; Harris Newmark, *Sixty Years in Southern California, 1853–1913*, 4th ed. (1916; Los Angeles: Dawson's Book Shop, 1984), 335 (discussing Main and San Pedro Streets in the 1860s).
15. *People v. Yow*, *People v. A. Keep*, *People v. Arline*, and *People v. Lewis*, Minutes, Justice of the Peace (Shore et al.), March 12, 1864, LAACR; *People v. Sing Lee, Sam Yung, Sou Go and Yo Hing*, Minutes, Justice of the Peace (Shore et al.), September 8, 1866; *Los Angeles Tri-Weekly News*, February 1, 1864.
16. *Los Angeles Star*, September 6, 1870.
17. Common Council Records, May 21, 1874, Los Angeles City Archives.
18. Common Council Records, September 1, 1870, and September 8, 1870, Los Angeles City Archives; *Los Angeles News*, September 9, 1870, and September 11, 1870.

19. *People v. Pierre Basange*, Minutes, Justice of the Peace (Still/Gray), September 22, 1870; *Los Angeles News*, September 11, 1870, September 23, 1870, and September 24, 1870.

20. Prentice Mulford, "Glimpses of John Chinaman," *Lippincott's Magazine of Popular Literature and Science* 11 (February 1873): 225; Albert F. Webster, "Los Angeles," *Appleton's Journal: A Monthly Miscellany of Popular Literature* 1 (September 1876): 211; Albert S. Evans, *À la California: Sketches of Life in the Golden State* (San Francisco: A. L. Bancroft, 1873), 284–85.

21. *People v. Ah Sing Quay and Ah Sing Foy*, Minutes, Justice of the Peace (Still/Gray), March 26, 1869, LAACR; *Los Angeles News*, October 11, 1871; *Santa Barbara Post*, October 31, 1868.

22. J. [Joseph] Lamson Diary, unpublished manuscript, California Historical Society, 184.

23. Evans, *À la California*, 284.

24. Hamilton Holt, ed., *The Life Stories of Undistinguished Americans as Told by Themselves* (1906; reprint, New York: Routledge, 1990), 183; Yong Chen, *Chinese San Francisco, 1850–1943: A Trans-Pacific Community* (Stanford: Stanford University Press, 2000), 77.

25. Gibson, *The Chinese in America*, 156, 356–57; *San Francisco Chronicle*, April 21, 1876.

26. *People v. Ah Hoo, Ah Choy and Ah Lee*, Case No. 201, May 5, 1876, Los Angeles County Justices Court, LAACR.

27. *People v. Mary Jane and Sarah Jane, Chinawomen*, Case No. 214½, April 9, 1879, Los Angeles County Justices Court, LAACR.

28. Loomis, "Chinese Women in California," 346; Yung, Chang, and Lai, *Chinese American Voices*, 23.

29. US Senate, Report No. 689, 44th Cong., 2d Sess., 96, 145–46; Gibson, *The Chinese in America*, 139–40; Lucie Cheng Hirata, "Free, Indentured, Enslaved: Chinese Prostitutes in Nineteenth-Century America," *Signs: Journal of Women in Culture and Society* 5 (Autumn 1979): 17; Hart H. North, "Chinese Highbinder Societies in California," *California Historical Society Quarterly* 27 (March 1948): 25.

30. Horace Bell, *Reminiscences of a Ranger; or, Early Times in Southern California* (Los Angeles: Yarnell, Caystile & Mathes, 1881), 48–49; J. M. Guinn, *A History of California and an Extended History of Los Angeles and Environs* (Los Angeles: Historic Record, 1915), 1:272; George Harwood Phillips, "Indians in Los Angeles, 1781–1875: Economic Integration, Social Disintegration," *Pacific Historical Review* 49 (August 1980): 446; Charles Dwight Willard, *The Herald's History of Los Angeles City* (Los Angeles: Kingsley-Barnes & Neuner, 1901), 283.

31. *People v. Ah Luce*, Minutes, Justice of the Peace (Shore et al.), August 1863, LAACR; *Evening Express* [Los Angeles], May 9, 1871; *Los Angeles Star*, July 19, 1871, and August 16, 1871; *Los Angeles News*, July 19, 1871, and August 16, 1871; *San Francisco Chronicle*, July 29, 1873; Yung, Chang, and Lai, *Chinese American Voices*, 16.

32. *Los Angeles Star*, February 25, 1871, and February 26, 1871.

33. *San Francisco Chronicle*, August 14, 1873; Gibson, *The Chinese in America*, 135–36; Holt, *The Life Stories of Undistinguished Americans*, 177.

34. Evans, *À la California*, 285.

35. *Los Angeles News*, December 24, 1870.

36. *Los Angeles News*, June 6, 1871.

37. *Los Angeles News*, August 26, 1870.

38. Minutes, Justice of the Peace (Gray), August 25, 1870, August 27, 1870, and August 30, 1870, LAACR; *Los Angeles Star*, August 26, 1870, and August 28, 1870; *Los Angeles News*, August 26, 1870, and August 28, 1870.

39. *Los Angeles News*, October 16, 1870.

40. *People v. Joseph F. Dye*, Case No. 1006, February 23, 1871, 17th Judicial District Court, Criminal Cases, LAACR; Joseph Mesmer, "Feud Between Officers," Joseph Mesmer Papers, UCLA; *Los Angeles Star*, November 1, 1870, November 2, 1870, November 3, 1870, and February 28, 1871; *Los Angeles News*, November 1, 1870, November 2, 1870, November 3, 1870, and November 6, 1870.

41. *Los Angeles News*, August 28, 1870.

42. *People v. Sing Yee*, Minutes, Justice of the Peace (Trafford), July 7, 1873, LAACR; *Daily World* [San Diego], May 18, 1873, July 13, 1873, July 15, 1873, and July 16, 1873; *Los Angeles Star*, July 15, 1873; *Evening Express* [Los Angeles], July 14, 1873; George P. Marston and Harriett Marston, "'My Dear Lilla': Marston Family Letters from 1870s San Diego," ed. Gregg R. Hennessey, *Journal of San Diego History* 43 (Summer 1997): 197.

43. *Los Angeles Star*, November 16, 1871; *Los Angeles News*, October 21, 1871, November 16, 1871, and February 23, 1872.

44. George B. Morris, "The Chinaman As He Is," unpublished manuscript, Bancroft Library, 83.

45. *People v. Yo Hing*, Minutes, Justice of the Peace (Gray), February 23, 1872, LAACR; *Los Angeles Star*, January 31, 1872, February 24, 1872, and February 27, 1872; *Los Angeles News*, February 23, 1872, and February 25, 1872; *Evening Express* [Los Angeles], February 23, 1872; *Alta California* [San Francisco], February 26, 1872, and February 29, 1872.

46. *Ah Chu v. Fong Chong*, Minutes, Minutes, Justice of the Peace (Gray), October 9, 1872, LAACR.

47. *Los Angeles Star*, June 2, 1875.

Chapter 5

1. *People v. Yow, People v. A. Keep, People v. Arline*, and *People v. Lewis*, Minutes, Justice of the Peace (Shore et al.), March 12, 1864, Los Angeles Area Court Records, Huntington Library (hereafter "LAACR").

2. *Los Angeles Star*, March 6, 1864.

3. Ludwig Louis Salvator, *Los Angeles in the Sunny Seventies: A Flower from the Golden Land*, trans. Marguerite Eyer Wilbur (Los Angeles: Bruce McCallister and Jake Zeitlin, 1929), 29, 129.

4. Mildred Wellborn, "The Events Leading to the Chinese Exclusion Acts," *Publications of the Historical Society of Southern California* 9 (1912–1913): 49; J. M. Guinn, *A History of California and an Extended History of Its Southern Coast Counties* (Los Angeles: Historic Record, 1907), 1:230; *Los Angeles Star*, January 24, 1871; Salvator, *Los Angeles in the Sunny Seventies*, 43.

5. Charles Nordhoff, "California for Health, Pleasure and Residence," in *Nordhoff's West Coast: California, Oregon and Hawaii* (1874; reprint, London: KPI, 1987), 90; Charles Loring Brace, *The New West: Or, California in 1867–1868* (New York: G. P. Putnam & Son, 1869), 208; L. J. Rose, Jr., *L. J. Rose of Sunny Slope, 1827–1899: California Pioneer, Fruit Grower, Wine Maker, Horse Breeder* (San Marino, CA: Huntington Library, 1959), 81.

6. Rose, *L. J. Rose of Sunny Slope*, 81; *Los Angeles Star*, September 17, 1871.

7. *Los Angeles News*, July 23, 1870; *Los Angeles Star*, October 9, 1872.

8. William M. Tisdale, "Chinese Physicians in California," *Lippincott's Monthly Magazine* 63 (March 1899): 412–13, 416; US House of Representatives, Report No. 4048, 51st Cong., 2d Sess., 593.

9. Sidney Andrews, "Wo Lee, and His Kinsfolk," *Atlantic Monthly* 25 (February 1870): 224.

10. *People v. G. Moreno and A. Bareles*, unnumbered case, November 29, 1873, Los Angeles County Court, Criminal Cases, LAACR.

11. Ezra Gregg to "Distant Brother and Sister," letter, May 9, 1863, Ezra Gregg Letters, Bancroft Library.

12. Elizabeth Fitzgerald B. Knowlton Memoirs and Diary, unpublished manuscript, California Historical Society, 2:112–13.

13. Albert S. Evans, *À la California: Sketches of Life in the Golden State* (San Francisco: A. L. Bancroft, 1873), 246; Otis Gibson, *The Chinese in America* (Cincinnati: Hitchcock & Walden, 1877), 77.

14. Gibson, *The Chinese in America*, 75, 77, 118; "The Chinese in California," *Lippincott's Magazine of Literature, Science and Education* 2 (July 1868): 38.

15. William Perkins, "El Campo de los Sonoraenses or: Three Years Residence in California," unpublished manuscript, Bancroft Library, 217–18; J. [Joseph] Lamson Diary, unpublished manuscript, California Historical Society, 183; Prentice Mulford, "Glimpses of John Chinaman," *Lippincott's Magazine of Popular Literature and Science* 11 (February 1873): 222; "The Chinese in California," 38; Stewart Culin, "Customs of the Chinese in America," *Journal of American Folk-Lore* 3 (July–September 1890): 198; Brace, *The New West*, 209.

16. *Los Angeles Semi-Weekly News*, February 16, 1866; *Kern County Weekly Courier* [Bakersfield], February 18, 1871; Samuel Bowles, *Our New West: Records of Travel between the Mississippi River and the Pacific Ocean* (Hartford: Hartford Publishing, 1869), 407.

17. Culin, "Customs of the Chinese in America," 192; "The Chinese at Los Angeles, California," *Friends' Review, A Religious, Literary and Miscellaneous Journal* 30 (April 18, 1877): 636; Gibson, *The Chinese in America*, 391.

18. Andrews, "Wo Lee, and His Kinsfolk," 228, 230; Bowles, *Our New West*, 399; Sui Seen Far [Edith Maude Eaton], "The Chinese Woman in America," *Land of Sunshine* 6 (January 1897): 59.

19. Hubert Howe Bancroft, *The Works of Hubert Howe Bancroft*, vol. 24, *History of California* (San Francisco: History Co., 1890), 336; Guinn, *A History of California*, 1:232; Bowles, *Our New West*, 404.

20. Judy Yung, Gordon H. Chang, and Him Mark Lai, eds., *Chinese American Voices: From the Gold Rush to the Present* (Berkeley: University of California Press, 2006), 10; Hamilton Holt, ed., *The Life Stories of Undistinguished Americans as Told by Themselves* (1906; reprint, New York: Routledge, 1990), 177.

21. On the question of the Chinese immigrants' level of education, American observers differed. Journalist Charles Nordhoff reported that "scarcely a Chinaman comes to California who does not know how to read and write in his own language." Nordhoff, "California for Health, Pleasure and Residence," 92. Other writers agreed that education was "all but universal in the old Empire at home" and that "[e]very Chinaman reads and writes." Andrews, "Wo Lee, and His Kinsfolk," 230; "The Chinese in California," 37. However, Methodist missionary Otis Gibson contradicted these accounts, estimating that "not one-fifth of the population have what may be called a common-school education." He believed that most of the immigrants could only read the Chinese characters pertaining to food and clothing. Gibson, *The Chinese in America*, 27.

22. Quelp, trans., "Chinese Letters," *The Pioneer; or, California Monthly Magazine* 3 (March 1855): 165.

23. R. David Arkush and Leo O. Lee, trans. and eds., *Land Without Ghosts: Chinese Impressions of America From the Mid-Nineteenth Century to the Present* (Berkeley: University of California Press, 1989), 32, 34, 38; Holt, *The Life Stories of Undistinguished Americans*, 183–84.

24. Bowles, *Our New West*, 403–04; Ng Poon Chew, "The Chinaman in America," *Independent* 54 (April 1902): 802; Holt, *The Life Stories of Undistinguished Americans*, 185.

25. Yung, Chang, and Lai, *Chinese American Voices*, 11; *California Chronicle* [San Francisco], February 8, 1855; Arkush and Lee, *Land Without Ghosts*, 91.

26. Huie Kin, *Reminiscences* (Peiping, China: San Yu Press, 1932), 26–28; *Los Angeles News*, July 19, 1871.

27. Harris Newmark, *Sixty Years in Southern California, 1853–1913*, 4th ed. (1916; Los Angeles: Dawson's Book Shop, 1984), 380; *Los Angeles Star*, August 17, 1861; *Los Angeles Semi-Weekly News*, March 22, 1867, and June 21, 1867.

28. *Los Angeles News*, May 21, 1869, May 28, 1869, May 2, 1870, and July 9, 1870.

29. *Los Angeles Daily News*, April 28, 1869, May 21, 1869, and November 17, 1870; *People v. Hall*, 4 California Reports 399 (1854).

30. US Senate, Report No. 689, 44th Cong., 2d Sess., 308.

31. *Los Angeles News*, September 15, 1869, and October 12, 1869.

32. *Los Angeles News*, April 28, 1869, October 6, 1869, and January 8, 1871; Remi Nadeau, *City-Makers: The Story of Southern California's First Boom, 1868–76* (Los Angeles: Trans-Anglo Books, 1965), 37.

33. *Kern County Weekly Courier* [Bakersfield], February 18, 1871; *Los Angeles Star*, July 21, 1870; *Santa Barbara Press*, October 28, 1871.

34. Holt, *The Life Stories of Undistinguished Americans*, 184; Ng Poon Chew, "The Chinese in Los Angeles," *Land of Sunshine* 1 (October 1894): 102; Nordhoff, "California for Health, Pleasure and Residence," 90, 139, 148; Bancroft, *History of California*, 349.

35. Iris Chang, *The Chinese in America: A Narrative History* (New York: Viking, 2003), 118; Richard Steven Street, *Beasts of the Field: A Narrative History of California Farmworkers, 1769–1913* (Stanford: Stanford University Press, 2004), 272; Rose, *L. J. Rose of Sunny Slope*, 107; Nadeau, *City-Makers*, 142.

36. Nordhoff, "California for Health, Pleasure and Residence," 90; Gibson, *The Chinese in America*, 107; US House of Representatives, Report No. 4048, 51st Cong., 2d Sess., 537.

37. *Los Angeles News*, April 1, 1869, July 27, 1869, July 9, 1870, November 17, 1870, December 24, 1870, and February 9, 1871.

38. Bancroft, *History of California*, 342.

39. *People v. George Inkhardt*, Minutes, Justice of the Peace (Still/Gray), May 18, 1869, LAACR; *People v. John Doe*, Minutes, Justice of the Peace (Still/Gray), August 31, 1869, LAACR; *Los Angeles News*, July 29, 1869.

40. *Los Angeles News*, May 1, 1870, July 27, 1870, July 28, 1870, August 26, 1870, and August 27, 1870; *Los Angeles Star*, October 8, 1870.

41. *People v. Santiago Aguella* [*sic*], Minutes, Justice of the Peace (Still/Gray), October 21, 1870, LAACR; *People v. Daniel Nickson and William Jackson*, Minutes, Justice of the Peace (Still/Gray), December 5, 1870, LAACR; *Los Angeles News*, September 24, 1870, October 4, 1870, October 22, 1870, and December 14, 1870; *Los Angeles Star*, December 15, 1870.

42. *People v. P. H. Gleason*, Minutes, Justice of the Peace (Gray), May 27, 1871, LAACR; *Los Angeles News*, March 5, 1871, May 2, 1871, May 28, 1871, June 16, 1871, August 15, 1871, August 25, 1871, September 19, 1871, and October 8, 1871; *Los Angeles Star*, March 5, 1871, May 28, 1871, June 16, 1871, June 17, 1871, and July 25, 1871; *People v. Andy Sharkey*, Minutes, Justice of the Peace (Gray), December 5, 1871, LAACR.

43. *Los Angeles Star*, April 27, 1871, and July 24, 1870; *Los Angeles News*, July 24, 1870, July 29, 1870, and August 3, 1871.

44. *Santa Barbara Post*, July 18, 1868; *Guardian* [San Bernardino], January 29, 1870.

45. Charles Dwight Willard, *The Herald's History of Los Angeles City* (Los Angeles: Kingsley-Barnes & Neuner, 1901), 286; Kin, *Reminiscences*, 26–27.

46. *Los Angeles News*, June 22, 1871, and July 20, 1871.

47. *Los Angeles Weekly Republican*, September 14, 1867.
48. Nordhoff, "California for Health, Pleasure and Residence," 139; Guinn, *A History of California*, 1:231.
49. *Evening Express* [Los Angeles], November 17, 1871; *Los Angeles News*, November 19, 1871.
50. Arnold Shankman, "Black on Yellow: Afro-Americans View Chinese-Americans, 1850–1935," *Phylon: The Atlanta University Review of Race and Culture* 39 (Spring 1978): 6; *Pacific Appeal* [San Francisco], February 28, 1880.
51. *Los Angeles News*, February 15, 1869, February 12, 1870, July 1, 1870, October 4, 1870, October 7, 1870, December 8, 1870, and February 9, 1871; *Los Angeles Star*, February 7, 1871, and April 23, 1871.
52. *People v. John Doe, a Chinaman*, Minutes, Justice of the Peace (Gray), October 19, 1871, LAACR; *Los Angeles News*, October 18, 1871; *Los Angeles Star*, October 21, 1871.
53. *People v. Lee Woo*, Minutes, Justice of the Peace (Gray), December 8, 1870, LAACR; *Los Angeles Star*, December 23, 1870, December 24, 1870, and October 27, 1871 (testimony of George Fall); *Los Angeles News*, December 11, 1870, December 23, 1870, December 24, 1870, and October 27, 1871 (testimony of George Fall).
54. *Alta California* [San Francisco], July 31, 1870.

Chapter 6

1. *Guardian* [San Bernardino], November 5, 1870, November 26, 1870, and December 3, 1870; *Los Angeles Star*, November 16, 1870, November 29, 1870, December 13, 1870, December 14, 1870, December 17, 1870, December 24, 1870, and March 10, 1871; *Los Angeles News*, November 10, 1870, and November 26, 1870; *Alta California*, November 12, 1870; *Evening Bulletin* [San Francisco], November 12, 1870; *New York Times*, November 13, 1870; *Ex parte Ah Cha*, 40 California Reports 426 (1870).
2. J. A. Graves, *My Seventy Years in California, 1857–1927* (Los Angeles: Times-Mirror Press, 1927), 275; US House of Representatives, Report No. 4048, 51st Cong., 2d Sess., 593; *People v. Ma Chock*, unnumbered case, March 19, 1877, Los Angeles County Court, Criminal Cases, Los Angeles Area Court Records, Huntington Library (hereafter "LAACR").
3. *Los Angeles Star*, March 15, 1871, and October 30, 1871; *People v. Sing Lee, Sam Yung, Sou Go and Yo Hing*, Minutes, Justice of the Peace (Shore et al.), September 8, 1866, LAACR. Sam Yuen was sometimes referred to as "Sam Yung."
4. Emma Woo Louie, *Chinese American Names: Tradition and Transition* (Jefferson, NC: McFarland, 1998), 126; *Evening Express* [Los Angeles], October 23, 1871; *Los Angeles Star*, October 30, 1871; Horace Bell, *On the Old West Coast*, ed. Lanier Bartlett (New York: Grosset & Dunlap, 1930), 170, 177; C. P. Dorland, "Chinese Massacre at Los Angeles in 1871,"

Annual Publication of the Historical Society of Southern California 3 (1894):
22; *Harper's New Monthly Magazine* 50 (January 1875): 302.

5. *People v. Ah Soi, Ah Han, Ah Yee, Yo Hing, Ah Yung and Sam Yung,* and
People v. Sam Yung, Minutes, Justice of the Peace (Still/Gray), May 4,
1868, and May 7, 1868, LAACR; *Los Angeles Star,* October 31, 1871 (Sam
Yuen's statement).

6. *Los Angeles News,* May 28, 1870, June 7, 1870, June 21, 1870, and July
14, 1870; *Los Angeles Star,* October 30, 1871 (Yo Hing's statement). The
See Yup Company's continued separate existence was confirmed by a
news account of another quarrel over a Chinese women, which stated:
"We are assured . . . that the late disturbance was not caused by the old
feud existing between the Wing Choung [Nin Yung] and the Yo Hing
[Hong Chow] Companies . . . and that the See Yup Company . . . had
nothing whatever to do with the riot of the 24th of October." *Los Angeles
Star,* February 24, 1872. The following year, the See Yup Company was
again mentioned in the local press as a distinct entity. *Los Angeles Star,*
September 6, 1873.

7. Fong Kum Ngon, "The Chinese Six Companies," *Overland Monthly,* 2nd
ser., 23 (May 1894): 523; A. W. Loomis, "The Six Chinese Companies,"
Overland Monthly 1 (September 1868): 225.

8. *Los Angeles Star,* March 10, 1871.

9. *Los Angeles News,* May 6, 1871, October 26, 1871, and February 25, 1872.

10. *Los Angeles Star,* October 30, 1871; *Wing Chung Co. v. Los Angeles City,*
Case No. 1941, June 22, 1872, 17th Judicial District Court, Civil Cases,
LAACR (testimony of Ah Yung).

11. *Los Angeles News,* August 24, 1870, October 15, 1870, and May 4, 1871.

12. *Los Angeles Star,* October 30, 1871. Although this story came from Yo
Hing's biased statement, Sam Yuen's colleagues, in their response, did not
deny that the events had occurred. *Los Angeles Star,* October 31, 1871.

13. *Los Angeles Star,* November 10, 1870, November 13, 1870, November 15,
1870, November 30, 1870, and March 10, 1871; *Los Angeles News,* November 10, 1870, November 13, 1870, November 29, 1870, and November 30,
1870.

14. *Lay Yee v. Wong Hin* [*sic*], Case No. 1765, January 23, 1871, 17th Judicial
District Court, Civil Cases, LAACR; *Ah Mouie v. James F. Burns and
Frank J. Carpenter,* Case No. 1814, May 18, 1871, 17th Judicial District
Court, Civil Cases, LAACR; *Los Angeles Star,* January 24, 1871, January
26, 1871, and March 10, 1871; *Alta California* [San Francisco], March 11,
1871.

15. *Los Angeles Star,* January 31, 1871.

16. *People v. Choo Chee and Gi On,* Minutes, Justice of the Peace (Gray),
March 4, 1871, LAACR; *Los Angeles Star,* March 5, 1871, March 8, 1871,
and March 10, 1871; *Los Angeles News,* March 5, 1871.

17. *People v. Lae Yu,* Minutes, Justice of the Peace (Gray), March 9, 1871,
LAACR; *Los Angeles Star,* March 11, 1871; *Alta California* [San Francisco],

March 11, 1871; *Yo Hing v. Sam Gut Gee*, Minutes, Justice of the Peace (Gray), March 11, 1871, LAACR; *Los Angeles News*, March 12, 1871.

18. C. P. Dorland mistakenly identified this woman as "Ya Hit," a name that has been repeated in several secondary accounts of the Chinese massacre. Dorland, "Chinese Massacre at Los Angeles in 1871," 22.

19. Lee Yong (groom) and Yut Ho (bride), March 3, 1871, Marriage Records, Los Angeles County Registrar's Office; *Los Angeles Star*, March 8, 1871; *Los Angeles News*, March 8, 1871.

20. *In the Matter of Ute How* [*sic*], Minutes, Los Angeles County Court, March 7, 1871, LAACR; *People v. Yo Hing et al.*, Minutes, Justice of the Peace (Gray), March 8, 1871, LAACR; *Los Angeles Star*, March 8, 1871, March 9, 1871, and March 10, 1871; *Los Angeles News*, March 9, 1871.

21. Some accounts of the Chinese massacre have confused Yut Ho with the Los Angeles prostitute Sing Yu, whose possession "often changed from one company to that of another" and whose arrest by a deputy sheriff from Santa Barbara County set off the Chinese street row on December 22, 1870. *Los Angeles News*, December 24, 1870.

22. *Los Angeles Star*, October 31, 1871. The Nin Yung Company's statement identified Yut Ho's brother as Ah Guey, although some American accounts stated that she was a sister to Ah Choy, a San Francisco tong fighter. *Los Angeles Star*, October 24, 1871; Dorland, "Chinese Massacre at Los Angeles in 1871," 23.

23. *Los Angeles Star*, March 10, 1871.

24. *Los Angeles Star*, March 15, 1871.

25. *Alta California* [San Francisco], March 11, 1871; *Los Angeles Star*, March 10, 1871.

26. *Ah Mouie v. James F. Burns and Frank J. Carpenter*, Case No. 1814, May 18, 1871, 17th Judicial District Court, Civil Cases, LAACR; *Ah Mouie v. Samuel B. Caswell and Phineas Banning*, Case No. 2219, April 25, 1873, 17th Judicial District Court, Civil Cases, LAACR; *Samuel B. Caswell and Phineas Banning v. John G. Nichols, John Wilson and Lay Yee*, Case No. 2271, July 30, 1873, 17th Judicial District Court, Civil Cases, LAACR; *Thom & Ross v. Wong Hing and Ah Mouie*, Minutes, Justice of the Peace (Trafford), July 11, 1873, LAACR.

27. *Los Angeles News*, April 21, 1871.

28. *Los Angeles News*, September 21, 1871; *Los Angeles Star*, September 22, 1871.

29. According to Sam Yuen, Ah Choy said that Yo Hing was with the party that shot him. *Los Angeles Star*, October 31, 1871. Yo Hing claimed that he was at Alex Rendon's barbershop at the time. *Los Angeles Star*, October 30, 1871. Rendon corroborated that story: "Yo Hing was in my shop from 4 o'clock p.m. [on the 24th], until Thursday, the 26th, and he never left the shop until all the trouble was over." *Los Angeles Star*, November 1, 1871. However, witness George Fall claimed that he saw Yo Hing on the street in front of Rendon's barbershop sometime after the gunfire started. *Los Angeles Star*, October 27, 1871.

30. *People v. Ah Choy and four other Chinamen,* Minutes, Justice of the Peace (Gray), October 23, 1871, LAACR; *People v. Yo Hing,* Minutes, Justice of the Peace (Gray), October 23, 1871, LAACR; *Wing Chung Co. v. Los Angeles City,* Case No. 1941, June 22, 1872, 17th Judicial District Court, Civil Cases, LAACR; *Los Angeles Star,* October 24, 1871, October 30, 1871, October 31, 1871, and November 1, 1871; *Los Angeles News,* October 24, 1871; *Evening Express* [Los Angeles], October 23, 1871.

Chapter 7

1. Several accounts of the Chinese massacre contend that Officers Bilderrain and Sanchez were drinking on the job that afternoon, but this is mere conjecture. Officer Bilderrain testified, "I was at Higby's saloon [on the] corner of Arcadia and Main streets; I was stationed there because I had been informed by some Chinamen that there was going to be a row among the Chinese that afternoon." He also mentioned that he was talking to Officer Sanchez "at the corner of Higby's." *Los Angeles News,* February 15, 1872. In a later proceeding, he testified that he was "in a saloon . . . talking with a man." *Los Angeles News,* April 2, 1872. From these slightly differing statements, it is not entirely clear whether Bilderrain was inside or outside the saloon. Even if he was inside, it is certainly plausible that a policeman in a tough neighborhood would have gone to a saloon to question potential informants.

2. The only casualty of the Chinese gunfight, Ah Choy, was a Nin Yung man. Some writers have questioned why Officer Bilderrain pursued another Nin Yung member into the Wing Chung store rather than trying to apprehend Yo Hing's henchman who had shot Ah Choy, suggesting that Bilderrain worked for Yo Hing and sided with him in the feud. That may be reading too much into the facts. Ah Choy had just arrived in Los Angeles a few days beforehand, according to the *Los Angeles Star,* October 24, 1871, so it is doubtful whether Bilderrain knew who he was or which faction he was affiliated with. Instead, it appears from the testimony of several eyewitnesses, cited below, that the policemen simply tried to arrest the feudists who were shooting at the time they arrived.

3. The foregoing account of the gun battle was derived entirely from eyewitness testimony. *Wing Chung Co. v. Los Angeles City,* Case No. 1941, June 22, 1872, 17th Judicial District Court, Civil Cases, Los Angeles Area Court Records, Huntington Library (hereafter "LAACR") (testimony of George Gard, Jesús Bilderrain, and Esteban Sanchez); *Los Angeles News,* February 15, 1872 (testimony of Jesús Bilderrain, Esteban Sanchez, Emil Harris, George Gard, Ventura Lopez, and Ah Ling), March 31, 1872 (testimony of Adolfo Celis), April 2, 1872 (testimony of Esteban Sanchez and Jesús Bilderrain), and April 3, 1872 (testimony of Jesús Bilderrain and Pedro Badillo). The reconstruction of the events in the remainder of this chapter was drawn from the following primary sources, listed in what the author believes to be the order of their reliability. First is the testimony

246 NOTES TO PAGES 126–128

given in the criminal and civil cases that came out of the riot. The eyewitnesses who were examined included Chinese businessmen, law officers, and impartial bystanders. Their accounts are generally consistent but differ in some particulars. *Wing Chung Co. v. Los Angeles City*, Case No. 1941, June 22, 1872, 17th Judicial District Court, Civil Cases, LAACR; *People v. Richard Kerren*, Case No. 1101, January 5, 1872, Los Angeles County Court, Criminal Cases, LAACR; *Los Angeles News*, February 17, 1872, and February 18, 1872. Second are the news accounts written by reporters who either witnessed the riot or interviewed eyewitnesses. *Los Angeles Star*, October 25, 1871, and October 26, 1871; *Los Angeles News*, October 25, 1871; *Alta California*, October 25, 1871, and October 26, 1871; *San Francisco Chronicle*, October 26, 1871; *San Diego Bulletin*, November 4, 1871 (article by Ben C. Truman, who arrived in Los Angeles a few days after the riot); and *New York Times*, November 10, 1871 (correspondence from the *San Francisco Bulletin*). Third is the testimony of seventy-nine eyewitnesses taken at the coroner's inquest, which the *Los Angeles Star* and *Los Angeles News* published in their editions of October 26 through 29, 1871. Much of the dialogue in this chapter was taken from these accounts. However, the depositions must be read carefully, as some of those who testified were suspected rioters. Fourth are the statements that Yo Hing and Sam Yuen gave to the press, which, though heavily biased against each other, contain some valuable uncontroverted information. *Los Angeles Star*, October 30, 1871, and October 31, 1871. Fifth are eyewitness recollections recorded many years after the fact. P. S. Dorney, "A Prophecy Partly Verified," *Overland Monthly*, 2nd ser., 7 (March 1886): 230–34; Harris Newmark, *Sixty Years in Southern California, 1853–1913*, 4th ed. (1916; Los Angeles: Dawson's Book Shop, 1984), 434–35; R. M. Widney, "Chinese Riot and Massacre in Los Angeles," *Grizzly Bear*, January 1921, 3–4, 22 (also published in *Los Angeles Examiner*, September 7, 1924); Michael M. Rice, "I Saw the Wild West Tamed!," *Los Angeles Times*, May 13, 1934; James Franklin Burns, "James Franklin Burns, Pioneer," *Historical Society of Southern California Quarterly* 32 (March 1950): 64–65; and Joseph Mesmer, "Massacre of Chinamen in 1871" and "Massacre of Chinese," Joseph Mesmer Papers, UCLA.

4. *Los Angeles Star*, October 27, 1871 (testimony of George Fall); *Los Angeles News*, October 28, 1871 (testimony of Emiliano Acevedo).

5. *Los Angeles Star*, October 26, 1871 (testimony of Frank Baker).

6. *Los Angeles News*, October 27, 1871 (testimony of Charles Avery).

7. In addition to the city marshal and the sheriff, the other seven lawmen on the scene that night were Police Officers George Gard, Emil Harris, Esteban Sanchez, and William Sands, Special Police Officer Robert Hester, Constable Richard Kerren, and Deputy Sheriff Sam Bryant.

8. *An Illustrated History of Los Angeles County, California* (Chicago: Lewis Publishing, 1889), 714; Los Angeles County Pioneer Society, *Historical Record and Souvenir* (Los Angeles: Times-Mirror Press, 1923), 75.

9. *People v. Richard Kerren*, Case No. 1101, January 5, 1872, Los Angeles County Court, Criminal Cases, LAACR; *Los Angeles News*, October 29, 1871 (testimony of James Burns).

10. *Los Angeles Star*, October 27, 1871 (testimony of Augustus Cates).

11. *Los Angeles News*, October 27, 1871 (testimony of S. A. Butler), October 29, 1871 (testimony of Sam Bryant), and April 2, 1872 (testimony of Esteban Sanchez); *Los Angeles Star*, October 27, 1871 (testimony of Charles Huber).

12. *Los Angeles News*, October 29, 1871 (testimony of Sam Bryant).

13. *Los Angeles Star*, October 26, 1871 (testimony of Emil Harris).

14. Burns, "James Franklin Burns, Pioneer," 65; Newmark, *Sixty Years in Southern California*, 434–35.

15. Hamilton Holt, ed., *The Life Stories of Undistinguished Americans as Told by Themselves* (1906; reprint, New York: Routledge, 1990), 177.

16. Dorney, "A Prophecy Partly Verified," 233.

17. This first victim was not identified by name at the coroner's inquest. A news article stated that the body taken to the cemetery that night (the first man hanged) was "said to be that of Ah Wing," the name used in this chapter. *Los Angeles Star*, October 26, 1871. Ben C. Truman identified the man as "Wong Chin," although he used the same name for the storekeeper who was later hanged from a wagon. *San Diego Bulletin*, November 4, 1871. The indictments against the rioters appeared to identify this victim as "Ah Choy," the same name used by the San Francisco tong fighter who was shot by Yo Hing's men. *People v. Ambrosio Ruiz et al.*, Case No. 1068, December 2, 1871, 17th Judicial District Court, Criminal Cases, LAACR. Historian Paul De Falla, who wrote the earliest comprehensive account of the riot, referred to the first victim of the lynch mob as "Wong Tuck." The source of that name is unknown, although it has been repeated in many subsequent accounts of the massacre. Paul M. De Falla, "Lantern in the Western Sky," pt. 1, *Historical Society of Southern California Quarterly* 42 (March 1960): 74. The names of the seventeen other victims, which were recorded with much greater consistency, were derived from: the reports of the coroner's inquest that appeared in the *Los Angeles Star* and the *Los Angeles News* on October 26, 1871; Ben C. Truman's account of the riot and massacre in the *San Diego Bulletin*, November 4, 1871, specifying which victims were hanged at each location; and the subsequent criminal indictments, Case Numbers 1067 through 1084, 17th Judicial District Court, Criminal Cases, LAACR.

18. *Los Angeles Star*, October 26, 1871 (testimony of Frank Baker).

19. *Los Angeles News*, October 25, 1871, and October 27, 1871 (testimony of Charles Avery); *Los Angeles Star*, October 26, 1871 (testimony of Emil Harris).

20. *Los Angeles News*, October 27, 1871 (testimony of William W. Widney). While the news accounts consistently identified the shoemaker as "Johnson," he spelled his name with a "t" in a handwritten letter. Letter,

A. R. Johnston to R. M. Widney, April 1, 1872, in *People v. Mendel*, Case No. 1089, December 2, 1871, 17th Judicial District Court, Criminal Cases, LAACR.

21. *Los Angeles Star*, October 27, 1871 (testimony of J. W. Brooks).

22. *Los Angeles Star*, October 25, 1871; *San Diego Bulletin*, November 4, 1871.

23. *Los Angeles News*, October 28, 1871 (testimony of Ben McLaughlin).

24. *Los Angeles News*, October 29, 1871 (testimony of James Burns).

25. *Los Angeles Star*, October 25, 1871; *In the Matter of the Estate of Robert Thompson*, Minutes, Los Angeles County Probate Court, November 20, 1871, LAACR.

26. *Los Angeles Star*, October 27, 1871 (testimony of Norman L. King).

27. Dorney, "A Prophecy Partly Verified," 232.

28. *Los Angeles News*, October 29, 1871 (testimony of Frederick Weaver).

29. *Los Angeles News*, October 27, 1871 (testimony of Mike Madegan), and February 17, 1872 (testimony of Henry M. Mitchell).

30. *Los Angeles News*, October 29, 1871 (testimony of Sam Bryant).

31. *Los Angeles Star*, October 28, 1871 (testimony of Mike Madegan).

32. Eyewitness C. F. N. Dennuke identified Ah Cut as the man shot on Calle de los Negros. *Los Angeles News*, October 29, 1871.

33. *Los Angeles Star*, October 27, 1871 (testimony of Charles Huber).

34. Dorney, "A Prophecy Partly Verified," 233. Dorney identified this man as "Jacques, a Frenchman." However, Police Officer Emil Harris said that Andres Soeur was the man carrying the cleaver. *Los Angeles News*, October 29, 1871. No one named Jacques was implicated by the testimony at the coroner's inquest.

35. *Los Angeles Star*, October 27, 1871 (testimony of Charles Avery).

36. *Los Angeles News*, October 26, 1871 (information about Wa Sin Quai), and October 28, 1871 (testimony of George Gard).

37. Mesmer, "Massacre of Chinese"; *Los Angeles News*, February 18, 1872 (testimony of Emil Harris).

38. *Los Angeles Star*, October 26, 1871 (testimony of Emil Harris).

39. Dorney, "A Prophecy Partly Verified," 233.

40. *Los Angeles News*, October 28, 1871 (testimony of Charles Anthony), and October 29, 1871 (testimony of C. F. N. Dennuke and H. Schlotterbeck).

41. Mesmer, "Massacre of Chinese."

42. *Los Angeles News*, October 27, 1871 (testimony of Robert M. Widney and William W. Widney).

43. Widney, "Chinese Riot and Massacre in Los Angeles," 4.

44. *Los Angeles Star*, October 27, 1871 (testimony of Morris Levin).

45. Widney, "Chinese Riot and Massacre in Los Angeles," 4.

46. *San Diego Bulletin*, November 4, 1871; Mesmer, "Massacre of Chinese"; *Los Angeles News*, October 27, 1871 (testimony of Leon Baldwin).

47. *Los Angeles Star*, October 26, 1871 (testimony of Henry T. Hazard); *Los Angeles News*, October 26, 1871 (testimony of Henry T. Hazard).

48. *Los Angeles Star*, October 26, 1871; *San Diego Bulletin*, November 4, 1871.
49. *Los Angeles News*, February 18, 1872 (testimony of Henry T. Hazard).
50. *Los Angeles News*, October 29, 1871 (testimony of John Goller); *San Diego Bulletin*, November 4, 1871.
51. Newmark, *Sixty Years in Southern California*, 82–83.
52. *San Diego Bulletin*, November 4, 1871; Mesmer, "Massacre of Chinamen in 1871."
53. *San Diego Bulletin*, November 4, 1871.
54. *Los Angeles Star*, October 27, 1871 (testimony of Adolph Schwob and S. A. Butler).
55. *New York Times*, November 10, 1871.
56. *Los Angeles News*, October 29, 1871 (testimony of John Kress); *New York Times*, November 10, 1871.
57. *Los Angeles News*, October 26, 1871, and February 18, 1872 (testimony of Henry T. Hazard); Henry Thomas Hazard biographical file, Los Angeles Public Library.
58. *Los Angeles News*, October 26, 1871 (testimony of Charles A. Hoffman), and October 27, 1871 (pawn shop reference); *San Diego Bulletin*, November 4, 1871.
59. *Los Angeles Star*, October 27, 1871 (testimony of Samuel C. Foy and C. E. White); *Los Angeles News*, October 27, 1871 (testimony of William W. Widney), and October 29, 1871 (testimony of Sam Bryant).
60. *Los Angeles News*, October 27, 1871 (testimony of Leon Baldwin); *Los Angeles Star*, October 27, 1871 (testimony of Leon Baldwin and John M. Baldwin); Horace Bell, *On the Old West Coast*, ed. Lanier Bartlett (New York: Grosset & Dunlap, 1930), 174.
61. *Los Angeles News*, October 27, 1871 (testimony of Samuel C. Foy), and October 29, 1871 (testimony of J. D. Connor and James Burns); *Los Angeles Star*, October 26, 1871 (testimony of Edward Wright).
62. *Los Angeles News*, October 29, 1871 (testimony of Sam Bryant).
63. *Los Angeles Star*, October 27, 1871 (testimony of A. J. Bowman), and October 28, 1871 (testimony of William W. Widney); *Los Angeles News*, October 27, 1871 (testimony of William W. Widney).
64. *Los Angeles Star*, October 28, 1871 (testimony of Robert M. Widney).
65. *Los Angeles News*, October 29, 1871 (testimony of Sam Bryant); *New York Times*, December 15, 1871. Historian Paul De Falla posited that the police thought it would be futile to arrest any mob members, since California law prohibited Chinese from testifying against whites: "No testimony available from [Chinese] witnesses or victims, no arrests." Paul M. De Falla, "Lantern in the Western Sky," pt. 2, *Historical Society of Southern California Quarterly* 42 (June 1960): 170–71. However, Los Angeles policemen had arrested several Anglos and Latinos for assaulting Chinese during the years preceding the massacre, as discussed in Chapter 5. This author believes that the police did not attempt to take any non-Asians

into custody during the massacre because they knew, as Officer Emil Harris had seen with Ah Wing, that the mob was in control and would forcibly prevent any arrests.

66. The law officers did not account for their whereabouts at all times during the evening, which later caused speculation that some of them, including the sheriff and the city marshal, had abandoned their duties and left the scene while the riot was still in progress. However, neither the eyewitness testimony at the coroner's inquest nor the grand jury's report (which excoriated the lawmen for their poor performance) supports that conclusion. For instance, even though Officer Emil Harris indicated that Sheriff Burns left Chinatown during the siege of the Coronel adobe, witness Jacob A. M. Harned recalled seeing the sheriff around the time rioter A. R. Johnston's pistol was confiscated at the corner of Spring and Temple Streets. Another witness, Morris Levin, "met Sheriff Burns and Mr. [Henry C.] Austin with a Chinaman on their way to jail." Also, Deputy Sheriff Sam Bryant saw Burns at the Coronel adobe after it had been invaded. *Los Angeles Star*, October 26, 1871 (testimony of Emil Harris), and October 27, 1871 (testimony of Jacob A. M. Harned and Morris Levin); *Los Angeles News*, October 29, 1871 (testimony of Sam Bryant). Thus, it appears that the sheriff was circulating throughout downtown during the evening, albeit ineffectually.

67. *Wing Chung Co. v. Los Angeles City*, Case No. 1941, June 22, 1872, 17th Judicial District Court, Civil Cases, LAACR; *Los Angeles Star*, October 26, 1871; *Los Angeles News*, October 26, 1871; *Alta California* [San Francisco], October 27, 1871.

68. *Los Angeles Star*, October 28, 1871 (testimony of Mike Madegan).

69. *Los Angeles News*, October 26, 1871; *Los Angeles Star*, October 26, 1871; *New York Times*, November 10, 1871.

70. Although the exact times of the critical events cannot be pinpointed, it is evident that the massacre happened quickly once it finally got underway. The *Star* indicated that the "storming party" entered the Coronel adobe around 8:45 p.m. and that order was restored when the sheriff made his speech at 9:20 p.m. *Los Angeles Star*, October 25, 1871. The *Alta California*'s correspondent reported that the Coronel building was still under guard when he sent a dispatch at 9:00 p.m. and that eight Chinese had been hanged by 9:15 p.m. By the time of his next dispatch at 9:30 p.m., the number of hanging victims had reached its total of fifteen, and the correspondent reported that "the crowd is dispersing." *Alta California* [San Francisco], October 25, 1871.

71. *Los Angeles Star*, October 25, 1871.

72. *Los Angeles Star*, October 27, 1871 (testimony of M. D. King, J. W. Brooks, and Morris Levin); *Los Angeles News*, October 27, 1871 (testimony of J. H. Weldon).

73. *Los Angeles News*, October 29, 1871 (testimony of Eugene Germain).

74. *Los Angeles Star*, October 27, 1871 (testimony of Samuel C. Foy and Louis Rich); *Los Angeles News*, October 27, 1871 (testimony of Samuel C. Foy).

75. *Los Angeles News*, October 27, 1871 (testimony of Mike Madegan); *Los Angeles Star*, October 28, 1871 (testimony of Mike Madegan).

76. *Los Angeles News*, October 29, 1871 (testimony of John Goller, P. S. Dorney, and Robert Mulloy).

77. *Los Angeles News*, October 25, 1871; *Los Angeles Star*, October 26, 1871, and October 30, 1871.

78. *Los Angeles Star*, October 26, 1871; Boyle Workman, *The City That Grew* (Los Angeles: Southland Publishing, 1936), 146; Bell, *On the Old West Coast*, 323 n.3; Newmark, *Sixty Years in Southern California*, 433.

79. *Alta California* [San Francisco], October 26, 1871.

80. The total number of massacre victims has been reported inconsistently. This author believes the correct count is eighteen. Paul De Falla identified a nineteenth victim, Fun Yu, whom the *Los Angeles Star* reported was shot on the evening of the riot but did not die until October 27. *Los Angeles Star*, October 28, 1871; De Falla, "Lantern in the Western Sky," pt. 2, 162. However, another news account described this man as "[o]ne of the Chinamen who came down from San Francisco, as is alleged, for the purpose of killing Yo Hing." *Los Angeles News*, October 28, 1871. Thus, it appears that the man the *Los Angeles Star* identified as "Fun Yu" was actually Ah Choy, the tong fighter who was mortally wounded by his Chinese enemies prior to the riot. County Judge Ygnacio Sepúlveda, in his charge to the grand jury two weeks after the massacre, confirmed that the mob had killed a total of eighteen Chinese. *Los Angeles Star*, November 9, 1871. Sepúlveda was in a position to know the facts, and his statement is the best evidence.

81. *Los Angeles News*, November 16, 1871.

Chapter 8

1. *Los Angeles Star*, September 17, 1871 (description of the county jail); *Los Angeles News*, October 26, 1871, and October 31, 1871; *Alta California* [San Francisco], October 27, 1871.

2. *Los Angeles News*, October 26, 1871 (quote), and April 2, 1872 (testimony of Jesús Bilderrain responding to a question about whether Sam Yuen had been concealed at Justice Gray's office); *Los Angeles Star*, October 30, 1871 (Yo Hing's statement asserting that Sam Yuen and his brother had left town), and November 1, 1871 (Alex Rendon's letter).

3. *Los Angeles Star*, January 18, 1871 (description of the City Cemetery), and October 26, 1871; A. W. Loomis, "Chinese 'Funeral Baked Meats,'" *Overland Monthly* 3 (July 1869): 25.

4. *Los Angeles News*, October 31, 1871; *Los Angeles Star*, October 26, 1871 (testimony of Emil Harris).

5. *Los Angeles Star*, October 27, 1871; Michael M. Rice, "I Saw the Wild West Tamed!," *Los Angeles Times*, May 13, 1934.

6. *Los Angeles Star*, October 26, 1871; *In the Matter of the Estate of Robert Thompson*, Minutes, Los Angeles County Probate Court, November 20, 1871, Los Angeles Area Court Records, Huntington Library (hereafter "LAACR").

7. *Wing Chung Co. v. Los Angeles City*, Case No. 1941, June 22, 1872, 17th Judicial District Court, Civil Cases, LAACR; *Los Angeles News*, October 25, 1871, October 26, 1871, and April 2, 1872; *Los Angeles Star*, October 26, 1871.

8. Horace Bell, *On the Old West Coast*, ed. Lanier Bartlett (New York: Grosset & Dunlap, 1930), 171–72, 176. In order to accept Horace Bell's uncorroborated tale, one would have to assume that all eight eyewitnesses who testified in detail about the gun battle during three separate legal proceedings not only lied but somehow managed to coordinate their stories.

9. *Wing Chung Co. v. Los Angeles City*, Case No. 1941, June 22, 1872, 17th Judicial District Court, Civil Cases, LAACR (testimony of Ah Yung); *Los Angeles News*, October 26, 1871; *San Francisco Chronicle*, October 26, 1871; *Alta California* [San Francisco], October 27, 1871.

10. *Los Angeles Star*, October 27, 1871.

11. *Los Angeles Star*, October 26, 1871, and October 27, 1871; *Los Angeles News*, October 26, 1871, and November 7, 1871; *Alta California* [San Francisco], October 31, 1871, and November 11, 1871.

12. *Los Angeles Star*, October 25, 1871.

13. *Los Angeles Star*, November 10, 1871; *Los Angeles News*, October 29, 1871 (testimony of Frederick Weaver accusing Mitchell), and February 17, 1872 (testimony of Henry M. Mitchell).

14. *Los Angeles Star*, October 26, 1871.

15. *Los Angeles News*, November 7, 1871.

16. *Los Angeles News*, October 26, 1871, and November 9, 1871; Bell, *On the Old West Coast*, 175.

17. *Evening Express* [Los Angeles], October 25, 1871, and October 26, 1871.

18. *Evening Express* [Los Angeles], October 28, 1871; *Los Angeles News*, October 27, 1871.

19. *Alta California* [San Francisco], October 26, 1871.

20. *Examiner* [San Francisco], October 26, 1871.

21. *Los Angeles Star*, October 30, 1871.

22. *Alta California* [San Francisco], October 27, 1871.

23. *Santa Barbara Press*, October 28, 1871, and November 4, 1871.

24. *Santa Barbara Times*, October 28, 1871.

25. *Los Angeles Star*, October 28, 1871.

26. *New York Herald*, December 8, 1871; *Alta California* [San Francisco], December 16, 1871; *New York Times*, December 9, 1878 (history of Olyphant and Company). Several accounts of the Chinese massacre say that the United States paid a large indemnity to China, although no one has substantiated that claim.

27. *Philadelphia Inquirer*, October 26, 1871; *New York Tribune*, October 26, 1871; *Albany Evening Journal*, October 28, 1871; *Springfield Weekly Republican*, November 3, 1871; *Cincinnati Commercial*, October 27, 1871; *St. Albans Messenger*, November 7, 1871.

28. *New York Herald*, October 26, 1871.

29. *Los Angeles News*, October 27, 1871 (first three men arrested), October 29, 1871, and November 14, 1871 (José del Carmen Lugo); *Alta California* [San Francisco], October 27, 1871, and December 10, 1871 (Jesús Martinez, Louis Mendel, Dan W. Moody, Patrick McDonald, and Andres Soeur).

30. *Los Angeles Star*, October 27, 1871, October 28, 1871, October 30, 1871, November 1, 1871, and November 6, 1871; *Los Angeles News*, October 28, 1871; *Evening Express* [Los Angeles], October 26, 1871; *Alta California* [San Francisco], November 4, 1871.

31. *Los Angeles Star*, October 30, 1871, and January 17, 1872; *Chung Woo v. J. F. Burns*, Case No. 454, December 8, 1871, Los Angeles County Court, LAACR; *Alta California* [San Francisco], February 10, 1872.

32. *Alta California* [San Francisco], November 10, 1871; *Los Angeles Star*, November 20, 1871, and December 9, 1871.

33. *Los Angeles Star*, November 3, 1871, and November 11, 1871; *Alta California* [San Francisco], November 1, 1871; *New York Times*, November 5, 1871; Common Council Records, January 4, 1872, February 1, 1872, February 15, 1872, and February 29, 1872, Los Angeles City Archives.

34. *People v. Yo Hing*, November 2, 1871, Minutes, Justice of the Peace (Gray), LAACR; *Los Angeles Star*, November 4, 1871.

35. *Chung Woo v. J. F. Burns*, Minutes, Justice of the Peace (Gray), December 8, 1871, LAACR; *Chung Woo v. J. F. Burns*, Case No. 454, December 8, 1871, Los Angeles County Court, LAACR; *Evening Express* [Los Angeles], December 28, 1871.

36. Common Council Records, November 16, 1871, November 23, 1871, December 2, 1871, and December 7, 1871, Los Angeles City Archives; *Los Angeles Star*, November 18, 1871, November 20, 1871, and November 22, 1871; *People v. A. F. Coronel*, Case No. 1168, December 10, 1872, Los Angeles County Court, Criminal Cases, LAACR.

37. *Alta California* [San Francisco], November 10, 1871; *Los Angeles Star*, November 20, 1871, November 30, 1871, December 9, 1871, and January 22, 1872.

38. *Los Angeles Star*, November 16, 1871; *Los Angeles News*, November 16, 1871.

Chapter 9

1. *Los Angeles Star*, October 26, 1871; *Los Angeles News*, October 26, 1871, October 27, 1871, October 28, 1871, and October 29, 1871.

2. *Los Angeles News*, October 27, 1871; *Alta California* [San Francisco], October 27, 1871; *Los Angeles Star*, October 28, 1871, and March 26, 1872 (Brooks fined); *Evening Express* [Los Angeles], October 28, 1871; *New York Herald*, October 28, 1871.

3. *Los Angeles News*, October 27, 1871, and February 18, 1872 (testimony of Emil Harris); *Los Angeles Star*, October 28, 1871.
4. *Los Angeles News*, October 27, 1871 (testimony of S. A. Butler).
5. *Los Angeles Star*, October 27, 1871, and October 28, 1871; *Los Angeles News*, October 27, 1871, and October 29, 1871.
6. *Los Angeles News*, October 29, 1871.
7. *Los Angeles Star*, October 28, 1871.
8. *Santa Barbara Press*, October 28, 1871; *Los Angeles News*, October 29, 1871. The jurors may have meant the word "nationalities" to include race and ethnicity as well as citizenship. If so, their statement was probably overbroad: no African Americans or Native Americans were known to have taken part in the riot.
9. *San Francisco Chronicle*, October 26, 1871; *New York Herald*, October 26, 1871.
10. *People v. Patrick McDonald*, Minutes, Justice of the Peace (Gray), June 26, 1871, Los Angeles Area Court Records, Huntington Library (hereafter "LAACR"); *Los Angeles News*, June 28, 1871 (McDonald), and February 20, 1872 (Crenshaw); *Evening Express* [Los Angeles], January 20, 1872 (Peña); *Alta California* [San Francisco], February 19, 1872 (Crenshaw).
11. *People v. Andres Saur* [*sic*], Minutes, Justice of the Peace (Still/Gray), November 13, 1867, LAACR; *People v. Jesús Martinez*, Minutes, Justice of the Peace (Still/Gray), April 19, 1870, LAACR; *People v. Esteban Alvarado and Juan Gonzales*, Minutes, Justice of the Peace (Gray), April 11, 1871, LAACR; *Los Angeles Star*, April 12, 1871 (Alvarado); *Los Angeles News*, March 11, 1871 (Dominguez), April 12, 1871 (Alvarado), and September 13, 1871 (Crawford).
12. *People v. José del Carmen Lugo*, Minutes, Los Angeles County Court, September 21 and 24, 1864; *People v. Jesús Martinez*, Minutes, Justice of the Peace (Still/Gray), January 6, 1868, LAACR; *People v. Lewis Mendell* [*sic*], Case No. 90, May 20, 1871, Los Angeles County Justices Court, LAACR; *People v. Lewis Mendel*, Case No. 1048, September 23, 1871, Los Angeles County Court, Criminal Cases, LAACR; *People v. Esteben* [*sic*] *Antonio Alvarado*, Minutes, Justice of the Peace (Gray), February 12, 1872, LAACR; *Los Angeles Star*, May 18, 1871 (Crawford), September 24, 1871 (Mendel), October 6, 1871 (Soeur), October 9, 1871 (Soeur), December 18, 1871 (Thompson), and December 20, 1871 (Thompson); *Los Angeles News*, May 19, 1871 (Crawford); P. S. Dorney, "A Prophecy Partly Verified," *Overland Monthly*, 2nd ser., 7 (March 1886): 232 (Martinez); *Alta California* [San Francisco], October 27, 1871.
13. *People v. Adolfo Celis*, Case No. 946, May 11, 1870, 17th Judicial District Court, Criminal Cases, LAACR; *People v. Carmen Sotello* [*sic*], Minutes, Justice of the Peace (Gray), August 12, 1872, LAACR; *Los Angeles News*, March 13, 1870 (Celis); *San Francisco Bulletin*, May 16, 1870 (conviction of Celis); Dorney, "A Prophecy Partly Verified," 232 (Dutch Charley).

14. *San Diego Bulletin*, November 4, 1871.

15. *Los Angeles Star*, July 30, 1871.

16. Joseph Mesmer, "Massacre of Chinese," Joseph Mesmer Papers, UCLA.

17. *Los Angeles News*, October 27, 1871 (testimony of A. J. Bowman and W. W. Widney), October 28, 1871 (testimony of Edward Wright), and October 29, 1871 (testimony of Frederick Weaver); *Los Angeles Star*, October 27, 1871 (testimony of George Fall), and October 30, 1871. Horace Bell quoted John M. Baldwin as saying that John D. Hicks was "dealing out rope." Horace Bell, *On the Old West Coast*, ed. Lanier Bartlett (New York: Grosset & Dunlap, 1930), 174. However, Baldwin did not make that accusation against Hicks when he testified at the coroner's inquest. *Los Angeles Star*, October 27, 1871; *Los Angeles News*, October 27, 1871. With respect to Thomas A. Garey, the *News* quoted witness Edward Wright as testifying that he "saw one of the men who participated in the hanging of Chinamen on the street yesterday; . . . a warrant was issued for his arrest, but when drawn out, the man had disappeared; . . . saw a Mr. Geary [*sic*], a silk grower, since on the stand last; said he had helped to hoist up two Chinamen." *Los Angeles News*, October 28, 1871. However, the *Evening Express* maintained that the *News* omitted some critical lines and that Wright actually said that Garey had helped him try to find the unidentified man who bragged about taking part in the two hangings. *Evening Express* [Los Angeles], October 28, 1871 (editorial defending Thomas A. Garey), and October 30, 1871 (Garey's letter of thanks). Notably, both Thomas A. Garey and Prudent Beaudry (owner of one of the Chinese tenements) employed Chinese cooks, so they could not have been altogether anti-Chinese.

18. *Los Angeles Star*, October 27, 1871; *People v. L. M. Mendel*, Case No. 1084, December 2, 1871, 17th Judicial District Court, Criminal Cases, LAACR (Widney's jury instructions); *Los Angeles Times*, October 27, 1883, and January 12, 1888; Dorney, "A Prophecy Partly Verified," 232; *An Illustrated History of Los Angeles County, California* (Chicago: Lewis Publishing, 1889), 250; Bell, *On the Old West Coast*, 175; Michael M. Rice, "I Saw the Wild West Tamed!," *Los Angeles Times*, May 13, 1934.

19. Charles Nordhoff, "Northern California, Oregon, and the Sandwich Islands," in *Nordhoff's West Coast: California, Oregon and Hawaii* (1875; reprint, London: KPI, 1987), 139.

20. *Los Angeles Star*, October 26, 1871 (testimony of Henry T. Hazard, Mendel Meyer, and David Solomon), October 27, 1871 (testimony of George Fall and M. D. King), and October 28, 1871 (testimony of R. J. Wolf and Mike Madegan); *Los Angeles News*, February 17, 1872 (testimony of Andrew J. King and Joseph Kurtz); Harris Newmark, *Sixty Years in Southern California, 1853–1913*, 4th ed. (1916; Los Angeles: Dawson's Book Shop, 1984), 434.

21. *Los Angeles Star*, October 30, 1871.

22. *Evening Express* [Los Angeles], October 28, 1871; *Alta California* [San Francisco], October 26, 1871; *Los Angeles Times*, July 23, 1888.

23. *Santa Barbara Press*, October 28, 1871.

24. *Evening Express* [Los Angeles], October 25, 1871; *San Diego Bulletin*, November 4, 1871; *Los Angeles Star*, October 26, 1871; *Los Angeles News*, October 26, 1871; *Alta California* [San Francisco], October 27, 1871.

25. *Los Angeles News*, October 28, 1871.

26. *New York Herald*, December 8, 1871.

27. William R. Locklear, "The Celestials and the Angels: A Study of the Anti-Chinese Movement in Los Angeles to 1882," *Historical Society of Southern California Quarterly* 42 (March 1960): 244.

28. *New York Herald*, October 28, 1871; *Santa Barbara Press*, October 28, 1871; *Los Angeles News*, October 27, 1871.

29. *Los Angeles Star*, July 25, 1871.

30. Horace Bell, *Reminiscences of a Ranger; or, Early Times in Southern California* (Los Angeles: Yarnell, Caystile & Mathes, 1881), 294.

31. *Los Angeles Star*, November 9, 1871.

32. *Los Angeles News*, November 16, 1871.

33. *Los Angeles Star*, November 9, 1871.

34. *Los Angeles News*, December 3, 1871; *St. Albans Messenger*, November 13, 1871.

35. *Los Angeles News*, December 3, 1871; *Alta California* [San Francisco], December 3, 1871; *Los Angeles Star*, December 4, 1871.

36. Esteban A. Alvarado, Charles Austin, Refugio Botello, Samuel C. Carson, Adolfo Celis, J. C. Cox, Edmund Crawford, L. F. Crenshaw, [first name unknown] Doland, Ramón Dominguez, A. R. Johnston, Victor Kelley, Jesús Martinez, Patrick M. McDonald, Louis Mendel, Dan W. Moody, Ambrosio Ruiz, and J. G. Scott were indicted for murder. Case Nos. 1067 through 1085, December 2, 1871, 17th Judicial District Court, Criminal Cases, LAACR. Indictments for riot were returned against [first name unknown] Keller, Norman L. King, Francisco Peña, and Andres Soeur. *People v. Mendel*, Case No. 1115, 1872, 17th Judicial District Court, Criminal Cases, LAACR. Constable Richard Kerren was indicted for assault with a deadly weapon on two Chinese women. *People v. Richard Kerren*, Case No. 1101, January 5, 1872, Los Angeles County Court, Criminal Cases, LAACR; *Los Angeles News*, February 18, 1872 (testimony of Richard Kerren). In addition, complaints were sworn against José del Carmen Lugo, Bautisto Moreno, and William Patterson. Minutes, Justice of the Peace (Gray), November 13–17, 1871, LAACR. According to news accounts, Carmen Sotelo and David Thompson were also arrested in connection with the riot. *Los Angeles Star*, November 13, 1871, and December 20, 1871. Finally, testimony at the coroner's inquest implicated Prudent Beaudry, [first name unknown] Cohen, P. S. Dorney, George M. Fall, [first name unknown] Foster, Thomas A. Garey (probably not actually

accused, as discussed above), [first name unknown] Grascy [*sic*; probably Grasky] (the landlady who provided the clothesline and the only known female suspect), Enoch Griffin, John D. Hicks, Charles Edward Huber (who fired on the officers' orders), Patrick Maguire, [first name unknown] McLaughlin, Henry M. Mitchell, [first name unknown] Reilly, Antoine Silva, and [first name unknown] Ybarra.

37. *Los Angeles News,* October 28, 1871, and December 3, 1871.

38. *Los Angeles Star,* October 30, 1871.

39. *Los Angeles Star,* October 31, 1871.

40. The first article to propose this theory was Paul M. De Falla, "Lantern in the Western Sky," pt. 2, *Historical Society of Southern California Quarterly* 42 (June 1960): 164–69.

41. *Los Angeles News,* April 2, 1872 (testimony of Jesús Bilderrain); *Los Angeles Star,* October 30, 1871.

42. *Los Angeles News,* December 3, 1871.

43. *New York Times,* October 28, 1871, and December 15, 1871; Common Council Records, October 26, 1871, Los Angeles City Archives; Bell, *On the Old West Coast,* 172; *Los Angeles News,* February 18, 1872.

44. *Los Angeles News,* October 29, 1871 (arrest of Louis Mendel); *Los Angeles Star,* January 31, 1872.

45. *New York Times,* December 15, 1871; *Evening Express* [Los Angeles], October 28, 1871.

Chapter 10

1. *Alta California* [San Francisco], November 21, 1871; *Los Angeles News,* December 3, 1871.

2. Minutes, 17th Judicial District Court, December 9, 1871, December 11, 1871, and February 5, 1872, Los Angeles Area Court Records, Huntington Library (hereafter "LAACR"); *Alta California* [San Francisco], December 6, 1871, and December 10, 1871. The men released were Adolfo Celis, Ramón Dominguez, J. G. Scott, J. C. Cox, Lee Sing (a.k.a. Ah Sing), Wong Ying (a.k.a. Ah Ying), Quong Wong, Jesús Martinez, Juan Alvarado [*sic*; probably Esteban Alvarado], and Victor Kelley. According to a news account, Louis Mendel, Dan Moody, Charles Austin, A. R. Johnston, Edmund Crawford, and L. F. Crenshaw remained in jail. *Los Angeles Star,* February 17, 1872. In addition, there is no record that four other men who were arraigned were ever admitted to bail: Patrick McDonald, Norman L. King, Ambrosio Ruiz, and Samuel Carson.

3. Robert M. Widney was admitted to the bar in San Francisco in 1865 by District Judge Samuel H. Dwinelle and started practicing law in Los Angeles in 1868. *Evening Express* [Los Angeles], December 30, 1871; Robert Maclay Widney biographical file, Los Angeles Public Library. At that time, California's lower tribunals (i.e., the district and county courts) could admit attorneys to practice solely before courts of that level, which

was apparently what happened in Widney's case. Act of March 5, 1861, ch. 49, § 2, [1861] California Statutes 40. The law was later changed so that only the California Supreme Court could license attorneys, who were then permitted to practice in any of the state's courts. California Code of Civil Procedure § 277 (1872). The rules also required that candidates for admission personally appear in court. *Ex parte Snelling*, 44 California Reports 553 (1872). Widney did not sit for his examination before the California Supreme Court and obtain a broader license to practice in all California courts until 1876. J. A. Graves, *My Seventy Years in California, 1857–1927* (Los Angeles: The Times-Mirror Press, 1927), 269; Marco R. Newmark, "Two Community Builders of Los Angeles," *Historical Society of Southern California Quarterly* 33 (June 1951): 136. Consequently, many writers have incorrectly stated that Widney was not a member of the bar or even an attorney at the time he was appointed district court judge in 1871, wrongly implying that the riot trials were conducted by an unqualified jurist.

4. Act of April 20, 1863, ch. 260, § 66, [1863] California Statutes 343; *People v. Mahoney*, 18 California Reports 180 (1861); *People v. Williams*, 24 California Reports 31 (1864).

5. *Los Angeles News*, February 9, 1872.

6. Act of May 1, 1851, ch. 29, §§ 284, 293, 295, [1851] California Statutes 243–44; *Los Angeles News*, December 3, 1871 (Sepúlveda's promise to the grand jurors).

7. Act of May 1, 1851, ch. 29, §§ 238, 244, 247, [1851] California Statutes 238–39; *Los Angeles News*, February 9, 1872.

8. Robert Maclay Widney, "Scrapbook and Folder of Miscellaneous Items," Huntington Library, 12; Boyle Workman, *The City That Grew* (Los Angeles: Southland Publishing, 1936), 148.

9. *Alta California* [San Francisco], February 16, 1872.

10. Minutes, 17th Judicial District Court, February 14, 1872, LAACR; *Alta California* [San Francisco], February 16, 1872; *Los Angeles News*, February 15, 1872.

11. *Alta California* [San Francisco], February 19, 1872.

12. *Los Angeles News*, October 27, 1871, and February 17, 1872.

13. *Los Angeles News*, February 17, 1872.

14. Although Judge Widney initially appointed the law firm of Chipley & Wilson to represent Crenshaw, Kewen & Howard were substituted as his attorneys prior to trial. Minutes, 17th Judicial District Court, February 5, 1872, LAACR.

15. *Los Angeles News*, January 3, 1872.

16. *Los Angeles Star*, January 4, 1872.

17. R. M. Widney, "Chinese Riot and Massacre in Los Angeles," *Grizzly Bear*, January 1921, 3 (also published in *Los Angeles Examiner*, September 7, 1924). For information on "law and order" groups, see Josiah Royce,

California: A Study of American Character from the Conquest in 1846 to the Second Vigilance Committee in San Francisco (1886; reprint, Berkeley: Heyday Books, 2002), 351–52, and Hubert Howe Bancroft, *The Works of Hubert Howe Bancroft*, vol. 37, *Popular Tribunals* (San Francisco: History Co., 1887), 141–42.

18. *Los Angeles News*, October 27, 1871; *Los Angeles Star*, October 28, 1871.

19. *Evening Express* [Los Angeles], August 11, 1877; *Los Angeles Star*, August 14, 1877; Hubert Howe Bancroft, *The Works of Hubert Howe Bancroft*, vol. 35, *California Inter Pocula* (San Francisco: History Co., 1888), 639; Horace Bell, *On the Old West Coast*, ed. Lanier Bartlett (New York: Grosset & Dunlap, 1930), 179–80.

20. *Los Angeles News*, February 17, 1872, February 18, 1872, and February 20, 1872; *Alta California* [San Francisco], February 19, 1872.

21. Act of March 16, 1863, ch. 68, § 1, [1863] California Statutes 60; Act of March 18, 1863, ch. 70, § 1, [1863] California Statutes 69.

22. *People v. Hall*, 4 California Reports 399 (1854); *People v. McGuire*, 45 California Reports 56 (1872) (discussing the abrogation of the statute); J. A. C. Grant, "Testimonial Exclusion Because of Race: A Chapter in the History of Intolerance in California," *UCLA Law Review* 17 (November 1969): 192–201.

23. *People v. Henry Brown*, Minutes, Justice of the Peace (Still/Gray), November 21, 1870, LAACR; *People v. J. O'Riley*, Minutes, Justice of the Peace (Gray), August 8, 1872, LAACR; *Ah Mow v. John McDonald*, Minutes, Justice of the Peace (Gray), December 18, 1872, LAACR.

24. Minutes, 17th Judicial District Court, February 17, 1872, LAACR.

25. *Los Angeles News*, February 20, 1872.

26. *Alta California* [San Francisco], February 21, 1872; *Los Angeles Star*, February 27, 1872. Edmund Crawford, another suspect who had been in jail since October, eventually announced his intention to demand a trial. *Los Angeles Star*, April 8, 1872. However, he was never tried.

27. Several different law firms represented the various defendants at the time of their arraignment. Minutes, 17th Judicial District Court, February 5, 1872, LAACR. However, it appears that the firm of Kewen & Howard served as counsel for all of them at trial. *Los Angeles News*, February 9, 1872; *Alta California* [San Francisco], February 21, 1872.

28. Minutes, 17th Judicial District Court, March 7, 1872, LAACR; *People v. L. M. Mendel*, Case No. 1084, December 2, 1871, 17th Judicial District Court, Criminal Cases, LAACR.

29. Minutes, March 7, 1872, 17th Judicial District Court, LAACR.

30. *Los Angeles News*, March 14, 1872.

31. *Los Angeles News*, February 22, 1872.

32. *Alta California* [San Francisco], February 27, 1872; *Los Angeles News*, March 13, 1872, and March 17, 1872.

33. *Los Angeles Star*, March 28, 1872; *Los Angeles News*, March 28, 1872.

34. Some modern historians have opined that Los Angeles's authorities reluctantly and halfheartedly took belated action against the suspected mob members only after being prodded by the press. However, the facts indicate otherwise. As discussed in Chapter 9, County Coroner Joseph Kurtz promptly impaneled a jury at ten o'clock on the morning after the massacre, which spent four long days examining 79 witnesses. Once the evidence was gathered, County Judge Ygnacio Sepúlveda convened a grand jury without delay on November 8. The grand jurors spent 23 days examining 111 witnesses before indicting 37 people for crimes committed against the Chinese. Meanwhile, as mentioned at the beginning of this chapter, local law officers had arrested 13 suspects by November 20 and were looking for 14 others. Ten of the indicted men were brought to trial during the district court term that immediately followed the grand jury's report.

35. *Los Angeles News*, March 23, 1872, March 26, 1872, and March 28, 1872.

36. *Los Angeles Star*, March 20, 1872.

37. *People v. L. M. Mendel*, Case No. 1084, December 2, 1871, 17th Judicial District Court, Criminal Cases, LAACR; *Los Angeles News*, March 27, 1872.

38. Minutes, 17th Judicial District Court, March 27, 1872, LAACR.

39. *Los Angeles News*, March 28, 1872; *Alta California* [San Francisco], March 28, 1872.

40. *Cincinnati Gazette*, April 16, 1872.

41. *Los Angeles Star*, March 28, 1872.

42. Minutes, 17th Judicial District Court, March 30, 1872, LAACR; *Alta California* [San Francisco], March 28, 1872, and March 31, 1872.

43. Letter, A. R. Johnston to R. M. Widney, April 1, 1872, in *People v. Mendel*, Case No. 1089, December 2, 1871, 17th Judicial District Court, Criminal Cases, LAACR.

44. *Alta California* [San Francisco], April 3, 1872; *Los Angeles News*, April 7, 1872; *Los Angeles Star*, April 8, 1872; Leonard Pitt, *The Decline of the Californios: A Social History of the Spanish-Speaking Californians, 1846–1890* (Berkeley: University of California Press, 1966), 244.

45. California Penal Code § 193 (1872), codifying Section 26 of the Crimes and Punishment Act of 1850.

46. *Evening Express* [Los Angeles], March 30, 1872; *Los Angeles News*, March 31, 1872.

47. *Los Angeles News*, March 29, 1872, March 30, 1872, March 31, 1872, and April 2, 1872.

48. *Los Angeles News*, March 31, 1872, April 2, 1872, April 3, 1872, and April 7, 1872; *Wing Chung Co. v. Los Angeles City*, Case No. 1941, June 22, 1872, 17th Judicial District Court, Civil Cases, LAACR (testimony of Jesús Bilderrain).

49. Act of March 27, 1868, ch. 344, § 1, [1867–68] California Statutes 418.

50. Minutes, 17th Judicial District Court, June 3, 1872, LAACR.
51. Act of March 27, 1868, ch. 344, § 3, [1867–68] California Statutes 419; *Wing Chung Co. v. Los Angeles City*, Case No. 1941, June 22, 1872, 17th Judicial District Court, Civil Cases, LAACR.
52. *Los Angeles News*, June 6, 1872; *Wing Chung v. Los Angeles*, 47 California Reports 531 (1874).
53. *Wing Chung Co. v. Los Angeles City*, Case No. 1941, June 22, 1872, 17th Judicial District Court, Civil Cases, LAACR.
54. *People v. Sam Yuen*, Case No. 1164, November 19, 1872, 17th Judicial District Court, Criminal Cases, LAACR.
55. *Los Angeles Star*, November 20, 1872.
56. *People v. Crenshaw*, 46 California Reports 65 (1873).
57. *Los Angeles Star*, June 11, 1873.
58. *Los Angeles Star*, May 22, 1873.
59. Bell, *On the Old West Coast*, 175–76.
60. *People v. Swenson*, 49 California Reports 388 (1874). Two cases in which Chinese parties prevailed in appeals to the California Supreme Court are discussed in Chapter 6: Ah Mouie's civil suit against the Los Angeles sheriff and jailor and the criminal prosecution of Sing Ye's torturers.
61. The fact that no "leading citizens" were brought to trial has caused some writers to speculate that the Los Angeles authorities shielded the upper-class perpetrators from prosecution. Horace Bell was an early proponent of that view, complaining that all of the indictments were unjustly brought against "poor Mexicans without influence, and a lone Irishman, a shoemaker." Bell, *On the Old West Coast*, 175. However, this theory finds little support in the surviving eyewitness testimony. As discussed in Chapter 9, prominent Angelenos such as George M. Fall and Henry M. Mitchell were accused by a single witness of having encouraged the lynch mob. In contrast, several people swore that most of the men who were tried had actively participated in breaking through the roof of the Coronel adobe and shooting at its occupants or had openly admitted having killed Chinese victims.
62. *Los Angeles News*, March 28, 1872.
63. *Los Angeles Star*, December 22, 1870.

Chapter 11

1. *Evening Express* [Los Angeles], August 5, 1872, August 7, 1872, and August 8, 1872; *Los Angeles Star*, August 6, 1872, and August 7, 1872; *Los Angeles News*, August 6, 1872, and August 8, 1872; *Alta California* [San Francisco], August 6, 1872, and August 8, 1872.
2. *Los Angeles Star*, October 30, 1871, and February 27, 1872; *Los Angeles News*, April 30, 1872.
3. *People v. Ah Yan and Ah Yu*, Minutes, Justice of the Peace (Gray), April 6, 1872, Los Angeles Area Court Records, Huntington Library (hereafter

"LAACR"); *People v. Tung Cy and Ah Kong*, Case No. 160, September 3, 1873, Los Angeles County Justices Court, LAACR; *Los Angeles Star*, November 16, 1871, February 24, 1872, February 27, 1872, and September 4, 1873; *Los Angeles News*, November 16, 1871, February 23, 1872, February 25, 1872, and April 7, 1872.

4. Remi Nadeau, *City-Makers: The Story of Southern California's First Boom, 1868–76* (Los Angeles: Trans-Anglo Books, 1965), 141; Harris Newmark, *Sixty Years in Southern California, 1853–1913*, 4th ed. (1916; Los Angeles: Dawson's Book Shop, 1984), 504; Ludwig Louis Salvator, *Los Angeles in the Sunny Seventies: A Flower from the Golden Land*, trans. Marguerite Eyer Wilbur (Los Angeles: Bruce McCallister and Jake Zeitlin, 1929), 43; Albert F. Webster, "Los Angeles," *Appleton's Journal: A Monthly Miscellany of Popular Literature* 1 (September 1876): 211; Ira M. Condit, *The Chinaman as We See Him, and Fifty Years of Work for Him* (Chicago: Fleming H. Revell, 1900), 21.

5. William R. Locklear, "The Celestials and the Angels: A Study of the Anti-Chinese Movement in Los Angeles to 1882," *Historical Society of Southern California Quarterly* 42 (March 1960): 245–53; US Senate Resolution 201, 112th Congress (passed October 6, 2011); *San Francisco Chronicle*, October 11, 2011. As of this writing (March 1, 2012), a companion resolution in the House of Representatives had not come to the floor for a vote.

6. *Los Angeles Times*, October 16, 1892; *Worcester Daily Spy*, May 30, 1882; *Evening Bulletin* [San Francisco], December 27, 1888, June 24, 1889, and April 18, 1890; *San Francisco Chronicle*, April 19, 1890.

7. *People v. Wong Chu Shut*, September 27, 1877, 17th Judicial District Court, Richard Courtney Collection, Huntington Library; *Los Angeles Star*, May 15, 1877, May 19, 1877, and May 20, 1877; *Los Angeles Herald*, May 15, 1877; *Evening Republican* [Los Angeles], May 19, 1877; *Evening Express* [Los Angeles], May 19, 1877; *Los Angeles Times*, April 25, 1915; J. A. Graves, *My Seventy Years in California, 1857–1927* (Los Angeles: Times-Mirror Press, 1927), 275–79; Horace Bell, *On the Old West Coast*, ed. Lanier Bartlett (New York: Grosset & Dunlap, 1930), 177.

8. Patrick J. Healy and Ng Poon Chew, *A Statement for Non-Exclusion* (San Francisco: [publisher unknown], 1905), 37; *New York Herald*, May 18, 1877 (describing Dorney as "chief organizer" of the Order of Caucasians); Richard Steven Street, *Beasts of the Field: A Narrative History of California Farmworkers, 1769–1913* (Stanford: Stanford University Press, 2004), 282–83, 307; *Los Angeles Times*, January 5, 1888 (referring to Dorney as a former staff writer); *Seattle Post-Intelligencer*, June 12, 1892 (Dorney's obituary). Patrick Sarsfield Dorney was listed as an author of *Constitution, Rules and By-Laws for Subordinate Camps of California Encampment, Order of Caucasians* (Sacramento: H. A. Weaver, 1876).

9. John Steven McGroarty, ed., *History of Los Angeles County* (Chicago: American Historical Society, 1923), 1:74 (Widney); Henry Thomas Hazard

biographical file, Los Angeles Public Library; J. M. Guinn, *A History of California and an Extended History of Los Angeles and Environs* (Los Angeles: Historic Record, 1915), 2:76–77 (Sepúlveda).

10. James Franklin Burns, "James Franklin Burns, Pioneer," *Historical Society of Southern California Quarterly* 32 (March 1950): 65.

11. *Los Angeles Times*, September 27, 1882 (Botello), and April 20, 1883 (death of Celis).

12. Michael M. Rice, "I Saw the Wild West Tamed!," *Los Angeles Times*, May 13, 1934; [J. Albert Wilson,] *History of Los Angeles County, California* (1880; reprint, Berkeley: Howell-North, 1959), 84; Hubert Howe Bancroft, *The Works of Hubert Howe Bancroft*, vol. 35, *California Inter Pocula* (San Francisco: History Co., 1888), 562–68; *Los Angeles Times*, July 23, 1888; *An Illustrated History of Los Angeles County, California* (Chicago: Lewis Publishing, 1889), 250.

13. *Los Angeles Times*, October 27, 1883, August 18, 1895, and August 20, 1895; Bell, *On the Old West Coast*, 280.

14. *Los Angeles Star*, January 18, 1872 (discussing the Coronel building's proposed demolition); *Los Angeles Times*, October 24, 1886, and July 24, 1887; *Los Angeles Herald*, October 24, 1886.

15. Marco R. Newmark, "Calle de los Negros and the Chinese Massacre of 1871," *Historical Society of Southern California Quarterly* 26 (June–September 1944): 98; *Los Angeles Times*, January 10, 1888, and January 12, 1888; *Los Angeles Herald*, January 11, 1888.

16. *New York Times*, February 15, 2008; *Los Angeles Times*, July 17, 2007; *Chicago Sun-Times*, November 23, 2011; *Washington Post*, February 5, 2009.

17. *New York Times*, August 5, 2008, November 21, 2008, and January 9, 2009.

18. *Los Angeles Times*, November 10, 2010, and November 11, 2010; *New York Times*, November 15, 2010, November 29, 2010, and July 31, 2011; *Wall Street Journal*, February 22, 2011; *Washington Post*, September 21, 2010.

19. *Alta California* [San Francisco], October 26, 1871; Ralph Keyes, *The Quote Verifier: Who Said What, Where, and When* (New York: St. Martin's Griffin, 2006), 22.

A Note on the Sources

1. Letter, Him Mark Lai to Eve Armentrout, November 17, 1975, Him Mark Lai Papers, Ethnic Studies Library, UC Berkeley.

BIBLIOGRAPHY

Books

Abrahams, Ray. *Vigilant Citizens: Vigilantism and the State.* Cambridge: Polity Press, 1998.

Arkush, R. David, and Leo O. Lee, trans. and eds. *Land Without Ghosts: Chinese Impressions of America From the Mid-Nineteenth Century to the Present.* Berkeley: University of California Press, 1989.

Bancroft, Hubert Howe. *The Works of Hubert Howe Bancroft.* Vol. 24, *History of California.* San Francisco: History Co., 1890.

———. *The Works of Hubert Howe Bancroft.* Vol. 35, *California Inter Pocula.* San Francisco: History Co., 1888.

———. *The Works of Hubert Howe Bancroft.* Vol. 37, *Popular Tribunals.* San Francisco: History Co., 1887.

Barth, Gunther. *Bitter Strength: A History of the Chinese in the United States, 1850–1870.* Cambridge: Harvard University Press, 1964.

Bell, Horace. *On the Old West Coast.* Edited by Lanier Bartlett. New York: Grosset & Dunlap, 1930.

———. *Reminiscences of a Ranger; or, Early Times in Southern California.* Los Angeles: Yarnell, Caystile & Mathes, 1881.

Bowles, Samuel. *Our New West: Records of Travel between the Mississippi River and the Pacific Ocean.* Hartford: Hartford Publishing, 1869.

Brace, Charles Loring. *The New West: Or, California in 1867–1868.* New York: G. P. Putnam & Son, 1869.

Brown, Richard Maxwell. *Strain of Violence: Historical Studies of American Violence and Vigilantism.* New York: Oxford University Press, 1975.

Chan, Sucheng. *Asian Americans: An Interpretive History.* Boston: Twayne Publishers, 1991.

Chang, Iris. *The Chinese in America: A Narrative History.* New York: Viking, 2003.

Chen, Yong. *Chinese San Francisco, 1850–1943: A Trans-Pacific Community.* Stanford: Stanford University Press, 2000.

Cheng, Lucie, and Suellen Cheng. "Chinese Women of Los Angeles, A Social Historical Survey." In *Linking Our Lives: Chinese American Women of Los Angeles,* 1–26. Los Angeles: Chinese Historical Society of Southern California, 1984.

Condit, Ira M. *The Chinaman as We See Him, and Fifty Years of Work for Him.* Chicago: Fleming H. Revell, 1900.

Cone, Mary. *Two Years in California.* Chicago: S. C. Griggs, 1876.

Coolidge, Mary Roberts. *Chinese Immigration.* New York: Henry Holt, 1909.

Creason, Glen. *Los Angeles in Maps.* New York: Rizzoli, 2010.

Daniels, Roger. *Asian America: Chinese and Japanese in the United States since 1850.* Seattle: University of Washington Press, 1988.

Deverell, William. *Whitewashed Adobe: The Rise of Los Angeles and the Remaking of Its Mexican Past.* Berkeley: University of California Press, 2004.

Estrada, William David. *The Los Angeles Plaza: Sacred and Contested Space.* Austin: University of Texas Press, 2008.

Evans, Albert S. *À la California: Sketches of Life in the Golden State.* San Francisco: A. L. Bancroft, 1873.

The First Los Angeles City and County Directory. 1872. Reprint, Los Angeles: The Ward Ritchie Press, 1963.

Fogelson, Robert M. *The Fragmented Metropolis: Los Angeles, 1850–1930.* Cambridge: Harvard University Press, 1967.

Gibson, Otis. *The Chinese in America.* Cincinnati: Hitchcock & Walden, 1877.

Gong, Eng Ying, and Bruce Grant. *Tong War!* New York: Nicholas L. Brown, 1930.

Graves, J. A. *My Seventy Years in California, 1857–1927.* Los Angeles: Times-Mirror Press, 1927.

Guinn, J. M. *Historical and Biographical Record of Southern California.* Chicago: Chapman Publishing, 1902.

———. *A History of California and an Extended History of Its Southern Coast Counties.* 2 vols. Los Angeles: Historic Record Co., 1907.

———. *A History of California and an Extended History of Los Angeles and Environs.* 3 vols. Los Angeles: Historic Record Co., 1915.

Healy, Patrick J., and Ng Poon Chew. *A Statement for Non-Exclusion.* San Francisco: [publisher unknown], 1905.

Hirata, Lucie Cheng. "Chinese Immigrant Women in Nineteenth-Century California." In *Women of America: A History,* edited by Carol Ruth Berkin and Mary Beth Norton, 223–44. Boston: Houghton Mifflin, 1979.

Holt, Hamilton, ed. *The Life Stories of Undistinguished Americans as Told by Themselves*. 1906. Reprint, New York: Routledge, 1990.

Hoy, William. *The Chinese Six Companies*. San Francisco: Chinese Consolidated Benevolent Association, 1942.

An Illustrated History of Los Angeles County, California. Chicago: Lewis Publishing, 1889.

Jew, Victor. "The Anti-Chinese Massacre of 1871 and Its Strange Career." In *A Companion to Los Angeles*, edited by William Deverell and Greg Hise, 110–28. Chichester, UK: Wiley Blackwell, 2010.

Kin, Huie. *Reminiscences*. Peiping, China: San Yu Press, 1932.

Kwong, Peter, and Dušanka Miščević. *Chinese America: The Untold Story of America's Oldest New Community*. New York: New Press, 2005.

Lai, Him Mark. *Becoming Chinese American: A History of Communities and Institutions*. Walnut Creek, CA: AltaMira Press, 2004.

Ling, Huping. *Surviving on the Gold Mountain: A History of Chinese American Women and Their Lives*. Albany: State University of New York Press, 1998.

Los Angeles County Pioneer Society. *Historical Record and Souvenir*. Los Angeles: Times Mirror Press, 1923.

Louie, Emma Woo. *Chinese American Names: Tradition and Transition*. Jefferson, NC: McFarland, 1998.

Lyman, Stanford M. *Chinese Americans*. New York: Random House, 1974.

Mayo, Morrow. *Los Angeles*. New York: Knopf, 1933.

McGroarty, John Steven, ed. *History of Los Angeles County*. 3 vols. Chicago: American Historical Society, 1923.

McWilliams, Carey. *Southern California Country: An Island on the Land*. 1946. Reprint, Freeport, NY: Books for Libraries Press, 1970.

Nadeau, Remi. *City-Makers: The Story of Southern California's First Boom, 1868–76*. Los Angeles: Trans-Anglo Books, 1965.

Newmark, Harris. *Sixty Years in Southern California, 1853–1913*. 4th ed. Los Angeles: Dawson's Book Shop, 1984. First published 1916.

Nordhoff, Charles. *Nordhoff's West Coast: California, Oregon and Hawaii*. 1874–1875. Reprint, London: KPI, 1987.

Peffer, George Anthony. *If They Don't Bring Their Women Here: Chinese Female Immigration before Exclusion*. Urbana: University of Illinois Press, 1999.

Pfaelzer, Jean. *Driven Out: The Forgotten War Against Chinese Americans*. New York: Random House, 2007.

Pitt, Leonard. *The Decline of the Californios: A Social History of the Spanish-Speaking Californians, 1846–1890*. Berkeley: University of California Press, 1966.

Qin, Yucheng. *The Diplomacy of Nationalism: The Six Companies and China's Policy toward Exclusion*. Honolulu: University of Hawai'i Press, 2009.

Rose, L.J., Jr. *L. J. Rose of Sunny Slope, 1827–1899: California Pioneer, Fruit Grower, Wine Maker, Horse Breeder*. San Marino, CA: Huntington Library, 1959.

Royce, Josiah. *California: A Study of American Character from the Conquest in 1846 to the Second Vigilance Committee in San Francisco.* 1886. Reprint, Berkeley: Heyday Books, 2002.

Salvator, Ludwig Louis. *Los Angeles in the Sunny Seventies: A Flower from the Golden Land.* Translated by Marguerite Eyer Wilbur. Los Angeles: Bruce McCallister and Jake Zeitlin, 1929.

Sandmeyer, Elmer Clarence. *The Anti-Chinese Movement in California.* 1939. Reprint, Urbana: University of Illinois Press, 1973.

Secrest, William B. *Lawmen and Desperadoes: A Compendium of Noted, Early California Peace Officers, Badmen and Outlaws.* Spokane: Arthur H. Clark, 1994.

Senkewicz, Robert M. *Vigilantes in Gold Rush San Francisco.* Stanford: Stanford University Press, 1985.

Smith, Sarah Bixby. *Adobe Days.* 1931. Reprint, Lincoln: University of Nebraska Press, 1987.

Speer, William. *The Oldest and Newest Empire: China and the United States.* San Francisco: H. H. Bancroft, 1870.

Spitzzeri, Paul R. *The Workman and Temple Families of Southern California, 1830–1930.* Dallas: Seligson, 2008.

Starr, Kevin. *California: A History.* New York: Modern Library, 2005.

Street, Richard Steven. *Beasts of the Field: A Narrative History of California Farmworkers, 1769–1913.* Stanford: Stanford University Press, 2004.

Tong, Benson. *Unsubmissive Women: Chinese Prostitutes in Nineteenth-Century San Francisco.* Norman: University of Oklahoma Press, 1994.

Truman, Ben C. *Semi-Tropical California.* San Francisco: A. L. Bancroft, 1874.

Tsai, Shih-shan Henry. *China and the Overseas Chinese in the United States, 1868–1911.* Fayetteville: University of Arkansas Press, 1983.

———. *The Chinese Experience in America.* Bloomington: Indiana University Press, 1986.

Warner, J. J., Benjamin Hayes, and Joseph P. Widney. *An Historical Sketch of Los Angeles County, California.* 1876. Reprint, Los Angeles: O.W. Smith, 1936.

Willard, Charles Dwight. *The Herald's History of Los Angeles City.* Los Angeles: Kingsley Barnes & Neuner, 1901.

[Wilson, J. Albert]. *History of Los Angeles County, California.* 1880. Reprint, Berkeley: Howell North, 1959.

Workman, Boyle. *The City That Grew.* Los Angeles: Southland Publishing, 1936.

Yun, Gor Leong. *Chinatown Inside Out.* New York: Barrows Mussey, 1936.

Yung, Judy, Gordon H. Chang, and Him Mark Lai, eds. *Chinese American Voices: From the Gold Rush to the Present.* Berkeley: University of California Press, 2006.

Yung, Judy. *Chinese Women of America: A Pictorial History.* Seattle: University of Washington Press, 1986.

———. *Unbound Feet: A Social History of Chinese Women in San Francisco.* Berkeley: University of California Press, 1995.

Articles

Andrews, Sidney. "Wo Lee, and His Kinsfolk." *Atlantic Monthly* 25 (February 1870): 223–34.

Armentrout-Ma, Eve. "Urban Chinese at the Sinitic Frontier: Social Organizations in United States' Chinatowns, 1849–1898." *Modern Asian Studies* 17 (1983): 107–35.

Barth, Gunther. "Chinese Sojourners in the West: The Coming." *Historical Society of Southern California Quarterly* 46 (March 1964): 55–67.

Blew, Robert W. "Vigilantism in Los Angeles, 1835–1874." *Southern California Quarterly* 54 (Spring 1972): 11–30.

Bohme, Frederick G., trans. and ed. "Vigna Dal Ferro's *Un Viaggio Nel Far West Americano*." *California Historical Society Quarterly* 41 (June 1962): 149–61.

Boyle, Frederick. "Chinese Secret Societies." *Harper's New Monthly Magazine* 83 (September 1891): 595–602.

Burns, James Franklin. "James Franklin Burns, Pioneer." *Historical Society of Southern California Quarterly* 32 (March 1950): 61–66.

Chew, Ng Poon. "The Chinaman in America." *Independent* 54 (April 1902): 801–03.

———. "The Chinese in Los Angeles." *Land of Sunshine* 1 (October 1894): 102–03.

———. "The Chinese in California." *Lippincott's Magazine of Literature, Science and Education* 2 (July 1868): 36–41.

Choy, Philip P. "Golden Mountain of Lead: The Chinese Experience in California." *California Historical Quarterly* 50 (September 1971): 267–76.

Cook, Jesse B. "San Francisco's Old Chinatown." *Police and Peace Officers' Journal of the State of California* 9, no. 6 (June 1931): 5–6, 28–33.

Culin, Stewart. "Chinese Secret Societies in the United States." *Journal of American Folk-Lore* 3 (January–March 1890): 39–43.

———. "Customs of the Chinese in America." *Journal of American Folk-Lore* 3 (July–September 1890): 191–200.

———. "The I Hing or 'Patriotic Rising,' a Secret Society Among the Chinese in America." *Proceedings of the Numismatic and Antiquarian Society of Philadelphia* 3 (November 1887): 51–57.

De Falla, Paul M. "Lantern in the Western Sky." Pts. 1 and 2. *Historical Society of Southern California Quarterly* 42 (March 1960): 57–88; 42 (June 1960): 161–85.

Dorland, C. P. "Chinese Massacre at Los Angeles in 1871." *Annual Publication of the Historical Society of Southern California* 3 (1894): 22–26.

Dorney, P. S. "A Prophecy Partly Verified." *Overland Monthly*, 2nd ser., 7 (March 1886): 230–34.

Far, Sui Seen [Edith Maude Eaton]. "The Chinese Woman in America." *Land of Sunshine* 6 (January 1897): 59–64.

Glanz, Rudolf. "Jews and Chinese in America." *Jewish Social Studies* 16 (July 1954): 219–34.

Grant, J. A. C. "Testimonial Exclusion Because of Race: A Chapter in the History of Intolerance in California." *UCLA Law Review* 17 (November 1969): 192–201.

Guillow, Lawrence E. "Pandemonium in the Plaza: The First Los Angeles Riot, July 22, 1856." *Southern California Quarterly* 77 (Fall 1995): 183–97.

Guinn, J. M. "Los Angeles in the Later Sixties and Early Seventies." *Publications of the Historical Society of Southern California* 3 (1893): 63–68.

Hayes, John. "Skilled Farming in Los Angeles." *Overland Monthly* 7 (November 1871): 448–54.

Hirata, Lucie Cheng. "Free, Indentured, Enslaved: Chinese Prostitutes in Nineteenth-Century America." *Signs: Journal of Women in Culture and Society* 5 (Autumn 1979): 3–29.

Lai, Him Mark. "Historical Development of the Chinese Consolidated Benevolent Association/Huiguan System." *Chinese America: History and Perspectives*, 1987, 13–51.

Locklear, William R. "The Celestials and the Angels: A Study of the Anti-Chinese Movement in Los Angeles to 1882." *Historical Society of Southern California Quarterly* 42 (March 1960): 239–56.

Loomis, A. W. "Chinese 'Funeral Baked Meats.'" *Overland Monthly* 3 (July 1869): 21–29.

———. "Chinese Women in California." *Overland Monthly* 2 (April 1869): 344–51.

———. "How Our Chinamen Are Employed." *Overland Monthly* 2 (March 1869): 231–40.

———. "The Six Chinese Companies." *Overland Monthly* 1 (September 1868): 221–27.

Lyman, Stanford M. "Chinese Secret Societies in the Occident: Notes and Suggestions for Research in the Sociology of Secrecy." *Canadian Review of Sociology and Anthropology* 1 (May 1964): 79–102.

———. "Conflict and the Web of Group Affiliation in San Francisco's Chinatown, 1850–1910." *Pacific Historical Review* 43 (November 1974): 473–99.

Mason, William. "The Chinese in Los Angeles." *Museum Alliance Quarterly [Los Angeles County Museum of Natural History]* [6] (Fall 1967): 15–20.

Masters, Frederic J. "Among the Highbinders: An Account of Chinese Secret Societies." *Californian Illustrated Magazine* 1 (January 1892): 62–74.

———. "Highbinders." *Chautauquan* 14 (February 1892): 554–58.

Monkkonen, Eric H. "Homicide in Los Angeles, 1827–2002." *Journal of Interdisciplinary History* 36 (Autumn 2005): 167–83.

———. "Western Homicide: The Case of Los Angeles, 1830–1870." *Pacific Historical Review* 74 (November 2005): 603–17.

Morley, Charles, trans. "The Chinese in California, As Reported by Henryk Sienkiewicz." *California Historical Society Quarterly* 34 (December 1955): 301–16.

Mulford, Prentice. "Glimpses of John Chinaman." *Lippincott's Magazine of Popular Literature and Science* 11 (February 1873): 219–25.

Newmark, Marco R. "Calle de los Negros and the Chinese Massacre of 1871." *Historical Society of Southern California Quarterly* 26 (June–September 1944): 97–98.

———. "Early Los Angeles Bench and Bar." *Historical Society of Southern California Quarterly* 34 (December 1952): 327–46.

———. "Two Community Builders of Los Angeles." *Historical Society of Southern California Quarterly* 33 (June 1951): 135–46.

Ngon, Fong Kum. "The Chinese Six Companies." *Overland Monthly,* 2nd ser., 23 (May 1894): 518–26.

North, Hart H. "Chinese Highbinder Societies in California." *California Historical Society Quarterly* 27 (March 1948): 19–31.

Phillips, George Harwood. "Indians in Los Angeles, 1781–1875: Economic Integration, Social Disintegration." *Pacific Historical Review* 49 (August 1980): 427–51.

Pickering, W. A. "Chinese Secret Societies and Their Origin." Pts. 1 and 2. *Journal of the Straits Branch of the Royal Asiatic Society* 1 (July 1878): 63–84; 3 (July 1879): 1–18.

Pitt, Leonard. "The Midwesternization of a Cowtown." *California History* 60 (Spring 1981): 29–49.

Quelp, trans. "Chinese Letters." *Pioneer; or, California Monthly Magazine* 3 (March 1855): 161–66.

Reynolds, C. N. "The Chinese Tongs." *American Journal of Sociology* 40 (March 1935): 612–23.

Shankman, Arnold. "Black on Yellow: Afro-Americans View Chinese-Americans, 1850–1935." *Phylon: The Atlanta University Review of Race and Culture* 39 (Spring 1978): 1–17.

Spitzzeri, Paul R. "Judge Lynch in Session: Popular Justice in Los Angeles, 1850–1875." *Southern California Quarterly* 87 (Summer 2005): 83–122.

———. "On a Case-by-Case Basis: Ethnicity and Los Angeles Courts, 1850–1875." *California History* 83 (Fall 2005): 26–39.

———. "'Shall Law Stand for Naught?': The Los Angeles Chinese Massacre of 1871 at Trial." *California Legal History* 3 (2008): 185–224.

Splitter, Henry Winfred. "Los Angeles as Described by Contemporaries, 1850–90." *Historical Society of Southern California Quarterly* 37 (June 1955): 125–38.

Stern, Norton B., and William M. Kramer. "Emil Harris: Los Angeles Jewish Police Chief." *Historical Society of Southern California Quarterly* 55 (Summer 1973): 163–92.

Stimson, Marshall. "The Organized Bar in Los Angeles." *Historical Society of Southern California Quarterly* 33 (June 1951): 119–33.

Tisdale, William M. "Chinese Physicians in California." *Lippincott's Monthly Magazine* 63 (March 1899): 411–16.

Webster, Albert F. "Los Angeles." *Appleton's Journal: A Monthly Miscellany of Popular Literature* 1 (September 1876): 210–14.

Wellborn, Mildred. "The Events Leading to the Chinese Exclusion Acts." *Publications of the Historical Society of Southern California* 9 (1912–1913): 49–58.

Widney, R. M. "Chinese Riot and Massacre in Los Angeles." *Grizzly Bear* (January 1921): 3–4, 22.

Williamson, Lillian A. "New Light on J. J. Warner." *Annual Publications of the Historical Society of Southern California* 13 (1924): 5–28.

Woolsey, Ronald C. "Pioneer Views and Frontier Themes: Benjamin Hayes, Horace Bell, and the Southern California Experience." *Southern California Quarterly* 72 (Fall 1990): 255–74.

Zesch, Scott. "Chinese Los Angeles in 1870–1871: The Makings of a Massacre." *Southern California Quarterly* 90 (Summer 2008): 109–58.

Unpublished Sources

Bell, Horace. Papers. Huntington Library.

Bingham, Edwin R. "The Saga of the Los Angeles Chinese." MA diss., Occidental College, 1942.

Burns, James Franklin. "Reminiscences." Huntington Library.

Chinese in California Virtual Collection. Bancroft Library. Accessed March 1, 2012. http://bancroft.berkeley.edu/collections/chineseinca.

Common Council Records. Los Angeles City Archives.

Ellis, Henry Hiram. Papers. California Historical Society.

Lai, Him Mark. Research Files. Ethnic Studies Library, University of California, Berkeley.

Los Angeles Area Court Records. Huntington Library.

Lou, Raymond. "The Chinese American Community of Los Angeles, 1870–1900: A Case of Resistance, Organization, and Participation." PhD diss., University of California, Irvine, 1982.

Marriage Records. Los Angeles County Registrar's Office.

McDannold, Thomas Allen. "Development of the Los Angeles Chinatown: 1850–1970." MA diss., California State University, Northridge, 1973.

Mesmer, Joseph. Papers. Special Collections, University of California, Los Angeles.

Ow, Yuk. Research Files. Ethnic Studies Library, University of California, Berkeley.

Quintana, Isabella Seong-Leong. "National Borders, Neighborhood Boundaries: Gender, Space and Border Formation in Chinese and Mexican Los Angeles, 1871–1938." PhD diss., University of Michigan, 2010.

Thom, Cameron E. Papers. Huntington Library.

Vertical Files. Los Angeles Public Library.

Widney, Robert Maclay. "Scrapbook and Folder of Miscellaneous Items." Huntington Library.

INDEX